Pushing the Digital Frontier

Pushing the Digital Frontier

Insights into the Changing
Landscape of E-Business

Edited by Nirmal Pal & Judith M. Ray
The Penn State eBusiness Research Center

WITHDRAWN

AMACOM

American Management Association
New York • Atlanta • Boston • Chicago • Kansas City • San Francisco • Washington, D.C.
Brussels • Mexico City • Tokyo • Toronto

This publication is designed to provide accurate and authoritative
information in regard to the subject matter covered. It is sold with
the understanding that the publisher is not engaged in rendering
legal, accounting, or other professional service. If legal advice or other
expert assistance is required, the services of a competent professional
person should be sought.

Library of Congress Cataloging-in-Publication Data

Pushing the digital frontier : insights into the changing landscape of e-business /
edited by Nirmal Pal & Judith M. Ray.
    p.   cm.
Includes bibliographical references and index.
ISBN 0-8144-0644-0
    1. Electronic commerce.   2. Electronic commerce—Management.
3. Business enterprises—Computer networks.   I. Pal, Nirmal.   II. Ray,
Judith M.

HF5548.32.P87   2001
658.8'4—dc21   00-068256

Printing number

10   9   8   7   6   5   4   3   2   1

To our eBRC Corporate Sponsors—IBM, Unisys,
Xerox, AT&T Wireless, SAP America,
and Delphi Ventures

—Nirmal Pal and Judith M. Ray

To Mitra, Neela, and Nupur

—Nirmal Pal

To my parents—Tom and Barbara; my
children—Jen, David and Julie, Adam and Vicki,
Lauren, and Katy; and my husband, Bill

—Judith M. Ray

Contents

Foreword

*Judy Olian, The Smeal College of Business Administration,
The Pennsylvania State University*
Stuart I. Feldman, IBM Research, IBM Corporation

Writing a book surveying the landscape of e-business is a little like writing a memoir about a child's life, at the time of birth. We are still at the early stages of the Internet revolution, and it would be folly of us to make lasting pronouncements about the impact this revolution will have on our lives or on the practice of business. Yet, with utmost certainty, we assert that our lives will never be the same—in the way we communicate, collaborate, play, learn, practice religion, conduct politics, change governments, date, socialize, create culture, transact business, travel, entertain, or inform ourselves. Today, almost 60 percent of Americans use the Web on a regular basis, a higher proportion than in any other country. Web access and use across the planet is rapidly becoming pervasive.

This book covers one piece of the web revolution—that which affects the practice of business. The information revolution has spawned numerous changes: in the rules underlying global alliances and hyper-competition, in the regulatory environment affecting financial and accounting standards, in supply chain structures and processes, and in the way organizational resources are configured and deployed.

Looking down from 100,000 feet, what are the key themes that intersect these pervasive changes? These themes do not exhaust the areas in which the Internet affects business practices, so all predictions are unreliable. Yet, in our view, they capture certain essential changes in business models and practices stemming from the Internet revolution. Specifically, we note e-business changes on organizational relationships, leadership forms, and market structures. The overarching principles are openness and acceleration: The tempo is increasing; evolutionary steps eventually lead to revolution.

New Organizational Relationships

Free Agency

E-business enables a range of employment relationships because of the freedom to affiliate in a variety of ways with the mother company, without regard for time and space. These fluid forms of employment relationships take on various shapes, including e-lancing,[1] outsourcing of what would previously be seen as core functions, shorter contractual affiliations with companies, frequent job hopping, and continuous reorganization and reassignments within organizations. Rapid reconfigurations of work processes, the replacement or enhancement of many processes with information technology and digital content, and the ability to perform core functions of a business through digital networks—these are the drivers of expansions of the typical employment relationship. With communication and collaboration enabled without the need for colocation or personal contact, the range of feasible organizational relationships is almost unlimited. Moreover, knowledge workers frequently gravitate to the free agent model because they are in the enviable position to sell their professional and knowledge services to the best and highest bidder. In short, the idea of permanent, single company relationships may become a thing of the past; free agency, multiple employers, and employees operating out of an island home will become more common. The loyalty between firm and employee has already been called into question; in the future, so will the role and longevity of many enterprises.

Compressed Supply Chains

E-business is built on a model that uses information networks to shave time and costs off the collaboration and fulfillment processes across partners in the supply chain, replacing physical goods (i.e., inventory) with virtual ones (i.e., forecasts and logistic information). Digital collaboration across partners in the supply chain enables shortened cycle time and even the removal of layers in the supply chain so that, at the extreme, the end-user (whether a business or a consumer) can deal directly with the source provider. This disintermediation of noncritical providers in the value chain occurs as actors in the supply chain deal directly with one another, with more agile and seamless handoffs among partners. On the other hand, we are seeing the creation of new intermediaries (e.g., brokers or aggregators such as DoubleClick) whose essential value comes from providing access to information or access to an aggregation of partners, and from the deepening of relations to key partners in the chain.

Co-opetition

Co-opetition occurs when industry players alternate between competitor and cooperator roles, often playing these roles concurrently. Digital networks enable the rapid change from one form of relationship (e.g., fierce competitor) to another (i.e., strategic partner or ally), depending on the particular moment of opportunity in the market. The challenge is to reconfigure from one role to another without allowing the intellectual property and unique knowledge advantage to leak through these collaborating, and somewhat open, information networks. There is also the cultural challenge of switching perceptions of the other company, from head-to-head competitor to partner in the battle to win and perhaps back to foe.

Obliteration of Edges

New organizational networks create fuzziness among boundaries, within and across organizations. This fuzziness is a needed feature of the architecture that exploits the efficiencies and innovation opportunities enabled through information technologies. Silos and boxes around units and functions miss the point of digitized collaboration. Collaboration calls for ease in operating across unstructured routines or traditional boundaries rather than fierce protection of turf and functions, which has been more of the tradition within and across organizations.

New Leadership

E-Leadership

New models of leadership require additional and perhaps different skills within organizations reliant on e-business and digitized networks. The e-leader must be comfortable with, and a driver of, agitation and change—changing alliances, competitors, business opportunities, financial outlooks, organizational structures, and configurations, all of which transpire in Internet time. The e-leader must tolerate the paradox of information openness and intellectual asset protection. This leader must be comfortable in relinquishing control over information and the power that comes with it, by enabling information access. At the same time, this leader must fiercely protect precious intellectual assets—people and ideas—and inspire these knowledge workers to remain with the company. In terms of traditional leadership models, this is a role for the "transformational leader" rather than power-based leadership or charismatic leadership. There are fewer trappings of power in open information networks, and the power of personalities is often eroded in virtual (i.e., non-face-to-face) environments. These are leaders who "are felt without being seen," stirring up the case for change, fostering innovation, creating trust, inspiring excitement about the company's future. They must be comfortable with persistent ambiguity and destructured environments within and across organizations and industry boundaries.

Un-hierarchy

Leaders used to sit at the top of a pyramid. The notion of hierarchy loses much of its meaning in open information environments with fuzzy boundaries between organizations. The hunger for mergers and acquisitions among senior executives and the frequent restructurings of firms mean that the trappings of hierarchy are often fleeting and temporary. Hierarchies are inconsistent with organizations structured on decision making that resides with knowledge workers, on information that is pushed to the lowest level, on the need for rapid response, and on teams and alliances that function through multiple decision makers. Instead, there will arise dynamic webs of relationships, personal and corporate.

New Marketplaces

The Bazaar

E-business has spawned the emergence of highly interactive, rapid-fire electronic marketplaces or "bazaars." The face-to-face bazaar, with open storefronts and bartering among players selling goods or services, has expanded to include electronic bidders from anywhere, in spot markets. In these electronic bazaars bidding time may be condensed to seconds. These bazaars no longer depend on long-term contracts laboriously negotiated, but can use new mechanisms for establishing relationships and measuring reputations. They can be used not only for spot purchases of goods or services, but also to help negotiate longer-term deals. E-marketplaces exist among consumers (e.g., eBay) or between businesses and consumers (e.g., Priceline). The biggest new bazaars reflect electronic markets trading business-to-business, such as Enron's utility exchange, or the Big Three automakers' procurement market for all of their supply needs, Covisint. These bazaars enable dynamic pricing, intricate auctioning and negotiation strategies, and multiple partners. Their reach is unlimited, bounded only by the technical capacity of the supporting software and systems and the rules of engagement, not by the traditional limits of time and space.

Club Membership

Participation in these marketplaces is not always free and open, despite the accessibility of the technology. There are, on occasion, club or initiation fees, or some form of access restriction to participate in these new marketplaces. Examples include industry consortia such as the Automotive Network Exchange (ANE), which is open only to preferred members, or restricted access to electronic auction markets (e.g., the Hyatt-Marriott Electronic Procurement Market). These "clubs" can offer competitive advantages through cost savings and volume discounts, access to preferred sources and know-how, and even revenue streams generated by the clubs themselves, assuming antitrust rules are not invoked. In a networked environment, access to these preferred trading clubs offers advantages of speed and scale not present in traditional clubs. In fact, access to a digital club may be a firm's primary source of strategic advantage, given the cost advantages that may not be available to competitors and the scale of the network connected to the club.

Trust Brokers

It is critical to execute reliably in a digital marketplace of a global scope. In the absence of known relationships, and in markets that are spontaneous and opportunistic, trust in the capacity to fulfill an order is often the basis for the transaction. This offers a role to trust brokers. Quality "seals of approval" in a digital marketplace are becoming more important given the criticality to screen for execution capabilities. These trust brokers become an incentive and penalty mechanism to uphold the "digital order" in global, real-time electronic markets. They may also bear risk and act as a new form of high-speed, high-value insurance covering operational and other risks in the e-world.

■　■　■

Making our observations in the midst of this e-revolution, these are some of the themes we see defining the new rules of business. Undoubtedly, we may be proved wrong in certain of these, and many will evolve further than we can imagine at this point. Many of the tendencies are contradictory, and reading a crystal ball inside the whirlwind is difficult.

This book elaborates on these themes. Read on, and brace for the next round. . . .

Endnote

1 T. W. Malone and R. J. Laubacher, "The Dawn of the E-Lance Economy," *Harvard Business Review* (September–October 1998), pp.144–153.

Acknowledgments

We gratefully acknowledge the contributions of our chapter authors, all of whom are well known in their respective fields of work and research. All of them are very busy individuals, yet they all responded to the cause of writing this book collectively, and found time to work on the chapters in order to share their insights and expertise with others. For many of the chapters, we teamed a well-known academic and an industry leader from different geographic locations. For other chapters, we brought together academics from different universities or industry leaders from different organizations. Anyone who has attempted or completed such a collaborative book writing venture will appreciate what it took for our blue-ribbon panel of authors to deliver their chapters on time and with new and deep insights. Most important, we were able to complete this project in Internet speed—a critical accomplishment in addressing a subject that itself moves at web speed.

We also thank Professor Bill Ray of Penn State for sharing with us his years of book writing experience in the early stages of this project.

Finally, we thank the team at AMACOM for patiently and expertly guiding us in our first foray into the publishing frontier.

Nirmal Pal and Judith M. Ray

Editors' Note

Businesses across the globe are exploring the opportunities and challenges of transforming themselves through the emerging Internet and related technologies. In response, Penn State's Smeal College of Business Administration and the new School of Information Sciences and Technology have jointly established the Penn State eBusiness Research Center (eBRC). This center will build new knowledge, tools, insights, and approaches for students, researchers, and practitioners in e-business. With initial sponsorship from IBM, Unisys, Xerox, AT&T Wireless, Delphi Ventures, and SAP America and growing relationships with a few other select firms, eBRC will focus on understanding the implications of e-business.

The center conducts research on how businesses strategize, operate, market, and manage in the realm of electronic commerce and business. It will grow as a source of knowledge, provide a suite of educational courses, and build networking and interchange opportunities for researchers and practitioners of e-business.

From our center at Penn State's University Park campus, we are building a network with researchers at universities around the world, as well as with researchers in consultancies, hardware and software suppliers, and other enablers of e-business. We're developing a "virtual global network" of e-business scholars and developing close links with industry partners with whom we can share, learn, and enable new developments in e-business. For more information on eBRC, please visit our website at *www.ebrc.psu.edu.*

In June 2000, eBRC conducted a workshop in Washington, D.C., to drive our research agenda, provide insights to our corporate sponsors, and build a community of practice among academic and industrial thought leaders in e-business nationwide.

This workshop, the second in our series, focused on developing an overarching framework for conceptualizing research into, and the development of, e-business. More than thirty thought leaders from academia and industry participated in this workshop and its serious discussions concerning e-business principles of valuation, governance, and execution. It was in this session that we first brought up the idea of collaborating on writing a book on e-business that would represent our collective wisdom in this fast-changing landscape.

Because it is difficult for one person to build expertise in all areas of e-business and its implications, we gathered together a blue-ribbon panel to write various chapters of this book, with individual authors drawing from their personal experiences and expertise in their areas of focus. Consequently, there are occasional overlaps in thoughts and insights in various chapters that we, the editors of this book, did not try to rationalize. We believe the strength of this book is the variety of in-depth knowledge and personal perspectives that the chapter authors bring with them. These authors include academics who are well known and highly regarded for their in-depth research and publication in various areas of e-business and e-commerce. Their perspectives are complemented by a set of business and government leaders who have contributed case studies describing what their e-business approach or solution has been in certain situations. The end result is a book that combines the emerging best practices and thought leadership within industry and government with those from academia.

Nirmal Pal and Judith M. Ray
The Penn State eBusiness Research Center

Pushing the Digital Frontier

Introduction

E-business is changing everything, from the way we work, play, and learn to the way governments and businesses conduct their operations. The impact of e-business is felt in every industry—from process to petrochemicals, from automobiles to airplanes, from computers to telecommunications, from books to broadcast media, from banking to other financial services, from retail to wholesale, and so on.

The Fast-Changing Landscape of E-Business

Internet trade is highest for the computers and electronics industry, where the growth rate has been reported at 40-percent-plus per year. For motor vehicles, paper and office products, and shipping and warehousing, the growth rate per year is as much as or greater than 20 percent. There are only a few industries where the growth of e-commerce is less than 10 percent. Years 2000 and 2001 are at the inflection point in the growth curve of e-commerce.

E-business is very egalitarian. It affects both rich and poor nations. Developed, developing, and underdeveloped countries are beginning to leverage emerging e-business processes to their advantage. In fact, it seems that developing and underdeveloped countries may have an advantage in the sense that they can leap over a whole generation of copper-based telecommunications systems to optical fiber-based and wireless technology.

Velocity

Bill Gates has talked about the velocity of change brought about by the phenomenon we call e-business. He has said that the 1980s were all about computing, the 1990s were all about bandwidth, and from here on it's all about velocity. The Industrial Revolution brought with it a rate of change that was unforeseen in earlier periods. The speed of change after World War II has accelerated faster and faster in every decade, reaching its peak in the last few years. As we stand at the threshold of a new decade, a new century, and a new millennium, we see this momentum gathering even more steam, and our strategic planning visibility and window are shrinking, constantly driven by the increasing velocity of change.

Value Drivers

It is important to understand the value drivers of this change from both a personal perspective and a business perspective. At an individual level, e-business brings many more options to choose from in terms of what products and services meet our needs, which in turn gives more power to us as consumers than we have seen at any time in the past. This is just one perspective of value to an individual. E-business brings other values as well, such as the ability to balance home and work by working from home when physical presence is not needed. It also helps by bringing to us continuous and lifelong learning opportunities.

Value should also be seen in terms of how e-business can be leveraged by businesses to improve the efficiencies and effectiveness of their operations. Figure I-1 groups these e-business value drivers into four distinct areas.

The first and foremost value to businesses comes from improving *operational excellence*. This is achieved by systematic manipulation of the three key resources of process, technology, and human capital by using e-business. This is also called optimization, and as business managers, we understand this concept very well. As such, American businesses have demonstrated an unprecedented level of productivity gains in the last several years that have resulted in faster time and a lower cost to market. Most, if not all, of this productivity came from leveraging information technology within the overall context of e-business.

The next value driver is *excellence in relationship management* with all stakeholders by use of e-business. A firm's stakeholders include customers, suppliers, distributors, business partners, employees, stockholders, and a general category called "influencers." E-business allows inclusion of stakeholders within the relevant key business processes. In many industries, the leaders have implemented exchanges or trading networks bringing all tiers of suppliers closer to the manufacturers and buyers. Enron Corp.'s energy exchange or Ford/General Motors/

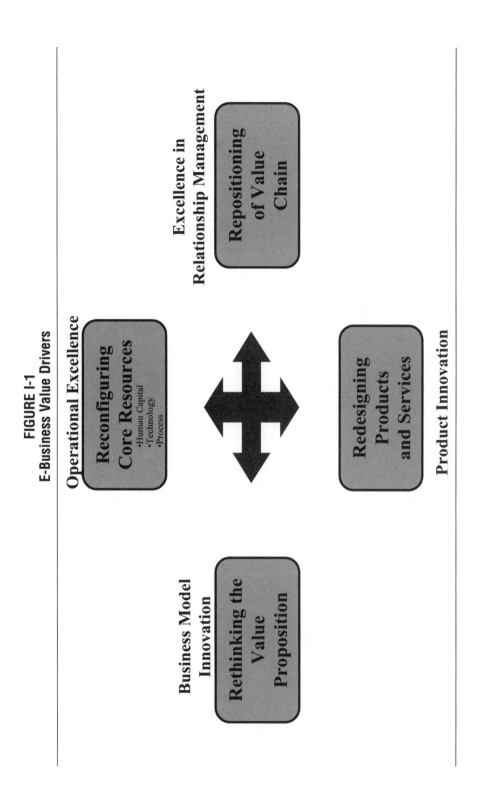

FIGURE I-1
E-Business Value Drivers

DaimlerChrysler's exchange, called Covisint, are good examples of this value driver. In addition, e-business provides great leverage to build strategic alliances, thus bringing competencies together to deliver value and allowing for noncore functions to be sourced from these alliances.

The third area of value is derived from *product and service innovations* driven by e-business. Package delivery companies are a good example. They were first to give their customers package delivery data access so that customers could easily track the status of their packages at any time of day or night. Then they allowed their customers the capability to print labels on their packages, and so on. Customers happily took on these activities previously performed by the delivery companies because these services delivered a high value to them and their operations. Organizations such as IBM Corp., Dell Computer, and Cisco Systems created extranet sites for each of their key corporate customers, thus allowing them to place orders for equipment and services directly—and to track the status of these orders—which are then integrated directly with the vendor's order fulfillment systems. These actions greatly improved efficiency of the vendor companies' order fulfillment processes and customer satisfaction.

The fourth area of value drivers encompasses *new business models* derived from brand-new ways of creating and delivering value to the constituents. These new business models are changing the very foundation of many well-established industries and businesses and thus are altering the competitive landscape. Take Amazon.com, for example. Whether or not Amazon is making money is one question that we can deliberate on for a long time, but what is crystal clear is that this company has changed the book selling and buying business forever. It is relatively easy for a born-on-the-Web company to introduce new business models—after all, they don't have the baggage of legacy processes and systems. Companies such as Enron are also moving fast and have created new ways of dealing within the energy sector; General Electric, IBM, and the like are similarly trying to reinvent better and novel ways of doing business.

Valuations
The NASDAQ performance in the third and fourth quarters of 2000 brought down the market valuations of the technology sector. But even at this low level of performance, the market valuation of Cisco or Dell far exceeds those of traditional giants such as GM or Ford. Stock performance on Wall Street is a high priority on the minds of all corporate executives. How tangible and intangible assets are evaluated and then reflected in the stock price is an area of continuing research.

Vulnerability
If all is so rosy, why is it that we see so many dot-com failures and so many redos and reworks in e-business adoption patterns? Investors are

getting disillusioned with the dot-com world because making money in the online world is proving to be trickier than anyone suspected. On September 29, 2000, Priceline.com's share price dropped 46 percent after it warned that revenue would not meet expectations. On October 4, 2000, Amazon's share price dropped 23 percent, followed one week later by Yahoo's drop of 21 percent on October 11. Walmart.com closed down its website for a few weeks presumably to work on revamping its front-end and back-end systems. This astounded many, because most other dot-coms are able to maintain their operations while reworking or enhancing their online presence. Wal-Mart's traditional business is growing by leaps and bounds, but its online operations are lagging behind. If anything at all, this situation demonstrates how complex and vulnerable the situation has become.

It is becoming a "live or die" situation for many pure play online operations, and at the same time many of the traditional companies with deep pockets are able to emulate their dot-com counterparts. We are beginning to see the emergence of a converged and hybrid model of the physical and online world. The alliance between Amazon.com and Toysrus.com is the biggest mix of bricks-and-clicks to date and is a great illustration of the hybrid model.

As we can see from these few examples, the frontier of the digital world is changing constantly. Executives are faced with building the foundation and then growing their business operations in what seems like shifting sand. There is no best practices database to refer to, because best practices are just emerging. There is no history to base our hypotheses on, because history is being carved out as we speak: inch-by-inch, with each failure and success. Sitting on the fence and waiting to see what happens is no longer a good tactical option, because the bar is raised every 90 to 120 days, and you have to be in the game to win.

As the underlying e-business technologies themselves evolve constantly and rapidly, management faces a constant challenge to be proactive in initiating and managing change to remain competitive in the marketplace, and not to be changed by default.

Time is of the essence. The meek shall not inherit the earth in this game. The foolhardy will perish. Relentlessly "pushing the digital frontier" to attain and sustain leadership is how this game will be played out. Are you ready for this game?

Our premise in this book is not to be prescriptive, as prescription varies case by case. This book is descriptive—using anecdotes to make a point, case studies to deliberate key issues, and personal experiences and insights to provide the reader multiple lenses to choose from for examining the subject.

The intended audience of this book is the business executive who is managing a traditional business that's converging with the new online world, as well as the executive who is managing a pure play, born-on-the-Web business and perhaps moving the other way.

Formulating and then executing a competitive business strategy is more important today than ever before. CEOs stay awake at night worrying about a multitude of rapidly changing forces in the environment that affects their businesses (see Figure I-2). Each one of these factors by itself is significant. But when you look at all of these factors together and consider the speed with which they are changing, you realize how the executive decision-making process has become significantly more complex in the new world.

We have organized the book chapters in an order that makes the best sense to us, so that if the chapters are read sequentially, the topics will unfold in a logical and orderly progression. But this book can be read from back to front as well as from front to back because the chapters are relatively independent in content. It is the overall theme of the ever-changing digital frontier that provides linkages and synergy.

We present excerpts of each of the chapters here so that you, the reader, can choose to read them in an order that best suits your situation at the moment. It is important to note that the views and insights expressed in the chapters are those of the authors themselves and do not necessarily reflect the view of the organization to which they belong.

Organization of the Book

Chapter 1: The Digital Economy and "Black Diamond Management"

Fariborz Ghadar and John Leonard deliberate on how the digital economy is forcing a fundamental and permanent shift in the way enterprise strategies are developed, and in the process raise significant new challenges for managers. To the inexperienced skier, a black diamond slope means trouble; to the expert, however, it means exhilaration and reward. Managers need to see the digital economy as an unprecedented opportunity for reward and understand its meaning to excel. The chapter uses anecdotes of successful organizations to discuss best practices and to make a key point that sheer size is not always a prerequisite for success. It is all about new perspectives for business; new approaches to competition, customer respect, and intimacy; new business processes; and a need to involve employees and line managers and help them transition to the new world.

Chapter 2: Leveraging E-Business in a Networked Economy

Liam Fahey and Rajendra Srivastava discuss the concept of market-based assets of networked organizations and how management of the

FIGURE I-2
Issues Keeping CEOs Awake at Night

- Shareholders' Impatience
- Hiring and Retention of Key Skills
- Globalization Issues
- Management Gridlock
- Market Valuation Concerns
- Competition from Dot-coms
- Personalization Demands
- Industry Reconfigurations
- Worldwide Oversupply
- Organizational Inertia
- Value Chain Disaggregation
- Regulatory Issues

new relationships will lead to the development of net assets, thereby creating value over and above that created by the organizations individually. They provide insights about the investments in, and valuation of, e-business opportunities by analyzing market capitalization and book value differentials. They conclude that the majority of the uncaptured market value tends to emanate from intangible assets, particularly knowledge, relationships, and brand loyalty. These intangible assets drive future expectations of financial performance and can be used as a rationale for explaining the high market capitalization of the new economy companies.

Chapter 3: Leveraging Old Economy Fundamentals for the New World

Rocki-Lee DeWitt and Kathryn Rudie Harrigan talk about the challenges that old economy companies face in repositioning themselves to capture value from core resources by tapping the innate flexibility that a well-considered strategy for the new economy provides. In addition to increasing the potential range of transaction partners and exploiting the strategic flexibility in value chain relationships, Internet economics offers the potential to improve operational efficiency dramatically. Three interrelated elements must be mastered in developing a successful Internet strategy. A business must 1) have a deep and thorough understanding of success requirements, 2) find a way to extend its identity and reputation to dominate virtual real estate, and 3) explicitly consider what it takes to keep its vertical strategy flexible.

Chapter 4: Regulatory Issues in E-Commerce

Richard Taylor and Elliot Maxwell capture the essence of the regulatory environment and the key global issues shaping electronic commerce. E-business is by definition a global phenomenon; therefore it is important to understand how various agencies around the world are positioning themselves around e-business and e-commerce. The authors describe in detail the global implications of the key issues involved: jurisdiction, privacy, taxation, consumer protection, intellectual property, and content regulation. In the end, the lesson for executives in the regulatory environment for electronic commerce is this: What government does, matters. The regulatory environment can deeply affect what you can do and the success of your enterprise, so you need to engage in the process of shaping it.

Chapter 5: Rebalancing Management in the Emerging E-Marketspace: From Control to Leadership

David Partridge and Nirmal Pal deal with the challenges of business leadership in the new online world. As market forces transform from a "make and sell" world to a "sense and respond" world, leaders have to understand the changes required within their organizations and their leadership. The dimensions of these changes are from competent to responsive employees, transaction-driven to lifetime loyal customers, independent to interdependent suppliers, and control-oriented management to leadership. As traditional companies compete with born-on-the-Web companies and try to leap across their own digital divide, understanding the challenges to this migration, and how to overcome them, becomes a major leadership issue. The key is to achieve a strategic balance between a company's vision, governance framework, and execution structure.

Chapter 6: Growing Pains: The Precarious Relationship between Offline Parents and Online Offspring

Michael Brown, Kevin Corley, and Dennis Gioia offer a discourse on offline parent companies creating online children and then nurturing them in a collaborative and harmonious relationship, or raising their offspring as cannibals, capable of devouring the competition and potentially the parent that helped it grow in the first place. On the basis of their investigation and analysis, they offer a set of recommendations for managing the identity tensions and learning issues that are inherent in a hybrid endeavor. These suggestions are directed to both offline parents and their online offspring, which will better enable both organizations to meet the challenges of a complicated and ever-dynamic e-business environment. Accounting for these important issues can help avoid some dysfunctional, internal turmoil and strife in an e-business atmosphere that is already hypercompetitive and inhospitable enough without the added difficulties that come with precarious relationships between "bricks" and "clicks."

Chapter 7: Managing the Emerging Technology

Hemant Bhargava and Jun Lee provide valuable insights about emerging technologies and practices that will help organizations remain open and flexible in response to the changing technological environment so that past information technology investments remain useful and valuable in the future. Developing an open, flexible, and scalable e-business information system solution is no easy task. An effective, long-term, outward-looking solution places many demands on business executives. They must carefully study and choose technological, architectural, and companywide solutions; compose from building block components rather than start from scratch; design according to industrywide standards rather than ad hoc formats; and create platform-neutral applications rather than those wedded to particular underlying technologies and platforms.

Chapter 8: Evaluations and Metrics for the E-World

Charles Rieger, Douglas Boothe, and Mary Donato offer a prism for business executives to view the value of their efforts in e-business and to help them in managing these strategic efforts. They suggest a framework within which e-business value can be understood, and then provide examples of how e-business value can be measured and managed. As the examples highlight, e-business measurements and metrics are a vital element in the achievement of corporate strategies. The authors help quantify and qualify the alignment of e-business initiatives to business objectives. Failure to identify measurements and success metrics before implementation eliminates the alignment or tight connection you want between the business objective and the tracking and diagnostic metrics in order to correct course and refine objectives and ultimately identify the return on e-business investment (ROeI) for the initiative.

Chapter 9: Competencies and Capabilities: Staffing the E-Business

Thomas Summerlin and Albert Vicere talk about the velocity of change brought about by e-business. Throughout history, and even during the Industrial Revolution, there existed a far wider time frame between massive waves of change. But today is different. We are challenged with a workforce that must decide on careers that may not exist in a few months or, even more significantly, have yet to be defined and come to fruition. The rules for success in business are changing, as are the characteristics and capabilities of effective leaders, practitioners, and workers. By thinking about these changes, and by measuring yourself and your organization against emerging models of effectiveness, you will be off and running to the exciting world of "e."

Chapter 10: Linking Business Imperatives to Human Capital Strategies: The Case of Encyclopedia Britannica

John Boudreau, Benjamin Dunford, and Peter Ramstad discuss the emergence of alternate forms of employment in the new economy in the shape of self-managed work teams, virtual teams, and free-lance workers, where individuals function primarily as independent consultants, leveraging information technology to complete specific tasks. In this kind of environment, managers are not needed for daily tasks, but become increasingly important in terms of determining a strategy and a supportive management system and culture. The authors use the Encyclopedia Britannica story to demonstrate that disruptive technologies such as the Internet can change not only individual businesses, but also entire industries. Thus, talent pools that involve strategic leadership will be important across all industries. Developmental experiences that take technical experts and develop their ability to lead and facilitate teams are likely to be valuable across a wide variety of future strategic possibilities.

Chapter 11: Personalization in the New Digital Environment

Venkatesh Shankar welcomes you to the world of web-based personalization. Personalization in the online context can be defined as the set of actions that tailors a company's website to a particular user or group of users. The goal of personalization is to create customized value, not customer value. Customer value is about delivering value to a general customer. Customized value is about creating and delivering value solutions for each customer or customer group. Amid the fast-changing scenarios of e-business, successful companies should see the forest ahead of the trees with respect to personalization. They need to realize that the Web is not just a new medium or channel, but a transformation vehicle that can create personalization around customers' multiple touchpoints and continuously grow customized value.

Chapter 12: Collaborative Commerce: The Agile Virtual Enterprise Model

William Adams, Raymond Wallace, and Arpan Sengupta provide a lens for examining collaborative commerce through a business model for the Agile Virtual Enterprise (AVE). The authors build the business case for application of the business model based on experience that spans a decade of operating virtual companies as well as related business theory. They provide a framework for organizations to simultaneously work collaboratively and independently with new customers and emerging markets. Their premise is that the AVE model and theory of collaborative commerce is a proven method of economic growth through collaboration in the new economy. The Agile Virtual Enterprise began as a vision of futurists, became a possibility for business theorists, and is now an economic necessity for corporate executives.

Chapter 13: E-Learning Solutions: Aligning Critical Development Factors

Shawn Clark, Cole Camplese, Kristin Camplese, and James Thomas describe a model for e-learning solutions development. They contend that aligning structure, strategy, and development factors is necessary not only for the successful design of online course delivery, but also for the effective e-learning experience needed for a twenty-first-century education. They offer an alignment model to leverage and integrate five key domains for planning and executing the e-learning development process. These domains are strategy, information technology, organization, process, and content. Organizations and managers must therefore recognize the need to adapt their planning approaches to achieve strategic alignment.

Chapter 14: E-Government: An Executive Road Map to the Digital Frontier

Frederick Loomis and Charles Gerhards identify several strategic issues facing executives who must lead or interact within the e-government environment. Governments function much the same as commercial enterprises—from ordering supplies and paying bills to providing products and services and charging customers fees for specific services. Federal, state, and local governments are reinventing themselves—empowered by web technologies to transform how they work and collaborate and comply with their citizens' growing expectations. The chapter provides an executive road map for navigating and leading e-government initiatives, presented along with other resources and best practice models. Finally, the current state of practice of e-government is explored with an in-depth analysis of the Commonwealth of Pennsylvania case study.

CHAPTER 1

The Digital Economy and "Black Diamond Management"

Fariborz Ghadar, The Smeal College of Business Administration, The Pennsylvania State University

John K. Leonard, CIGNA Corporation (Retired)

Those familiar with downhill skiing will recognize the term *black diamond*. This is the designation given to the more challenging trails likely to be encountered at typical ski slopes. It contrasts with the so-called green (or easy) and blue (or intermediate) trails. The black diamond symbol is intended to put the skier on notice that the trail ahead is demanding and requires special skills. To accomplished skiers, it also means they'll have the thrill and satisfaction of using their capabilities to the fullest. Following this pattern, it can be said that the digital economy has put all managers on the black diamond trail whether they chose it or not. To stretch the analogy, it is as if the manager/skier embarked on a trail labeled blue or green, only to find out that it changes to black diamond without notice partway down the hill. For those who master it, the rewards are great; for those who think they are on "blue" or "green" trails, there is significant danger ahead.

The digital economy is forcing a fundamental and permanent shift in the way enterprise strategies are developed and, in the process, raising significant new challenges for managers. Managers with responsibility for developing strategy are finding a paradox: Whereas strategic plans were once considered the enduring guideposts by which corporations determined annual operating plans and budgets, the e-business world now requires that strategies be considerably more fluid, innovative, and broader in perspective. Furthermore, they must be developed with shorter time horizons to recognize dramatically shortened product life cycles. What was once long-term and relatively static is now continuously up for grabs. The role of the corporate strategic planner in the era of e-business is, as a result, more challenging and more rewarding.

While any manager can today see the effects of a web-enabled world, the sentiment can be best expressed by the comments of Gary Hamel, the highly respected strategic consultant and author, who says:

> We are rushing toward a world in which everyone and everything will be connected to everything and everyone else. . . . The pace of economic evolution has always been a function of the number and quality of interconnections between individuals and the ideas they hold. . . . The Internet promises to create a dervish-like dance of intellect, imagination, and capital that is entirely free from the . . . constraints of the past.[1]

And this already-frenetic pace is likely to accelerate. The arrival of wireless and broadband technology is just around the next corner and figures to be among the most profound changes yet. Despite indications in the second half of 2000 that the rate of technology spending by corporations is moderating, *The Wall Street Journal* reported high confidence by corporate management that digital networking and customer communication would drive the future of virtually all businesses. Examples of old economy firms investing in new technology are easy to find, but are no less compelling for their frequency. Clorox Corporation, the bleach and household products maker and about as old economy as you can get, anticipates an 85 percent reduction in order processing costs through a new digital network that will take three years to install. If there is any doubt that we are only at the beginning, management guru Peter Drucker has opined that the winners in the new economy will not emerge for ten years![2]

To some senior managers, it probably seems that the rules changed just as they were becoming good at the game. Throughout their careers, they were taught that vision and strategy development were the chief responsibilities of the organization's leaders. They routinely accepted the dictum that size—mostly achieved through megamergers—was a panacea for increased usage of technology and the resultant shorter product life cycles. They had the expertise to assess the many factors that drive strategy; they had the scars from the failed ideas; they had the deep understanding of business fundamentals that drove time-tested business models; and they had the discipline to properly analyze strategies and make quantitatively-based choices. Now these principles have all changed.

The material that follows is intended to provide guidance to help those responsible for setting and implementing strategic directions in established firms. It assumes that the factors that have always been critical to setting directions for successful enterprises—objectivity, customer focus, insights about the business environment, and disciplined resource commitment—are well understood and already incorporated in strategic thinking. It goes beyond these givens, however, to assist those enterprises that have mastered the strategic planning for the so-called old economy and now must make the shift to a new era—and do so urgently and practically. It focuses on the two most vital considerations for e-business strategy:

1. *Pace of Technology Change.* First, we discuss how technology has accelerated product development and obsolescence. This is the equivalent of how steep the ski slope has become—with unfamiliar terrain, managers find themselves propelled faster than ever before in strategies to "sense and deliver." Most important, we explain why sheer enterprise size is not the only answer to this challenge.

2. *Style of Management.* Second, we turn from the steepness of the slope to the skier. The new environment requires new perspectives. This, in turn, has created the emergence of a new style for those responsible for setting strategic directions, which we call black diamond management.

Global Business Strategy in an E-Business World

In the postwar era, when the United States dominated the world economy and produced more than half of the world's output, American businesses segmented foreign markets primarily by economic size and chose strategies based on product technology—approaches still widely followed today. Yet in an e-business world the demands of global markets have changed radically. Many marketers no longer have the luxury of earning adequate profit at each stage of a product's life cycle. They must apply globally the rules they learned selling around the corner: "Get to the marketplace quickly, at a reasonable price, and you might even have to look at profitability from a total life cycle viewpoint."

Most successful global companies achieve a reputation for providing value throughout the "international product life cycle." Shorter product life cycles and more expensive research and development have resulted in global firms seeking strategic partners with emerging technology companies very early in the product development cycle. AT&T Ventures, like others in many industries, attempts to identify these rising stars of technology to invest in early and incorporate in the AT&T alliance framework. Others companies, such as Cisco Systems, buy varying technology upstarts in an attempt to refresh and maintain their technological edge. Thus the value leaders with marketing clout need to ally themselves with new technology firms to avoid an otherwise inevitable slide into mature, commoditized markets with cutthroat competition and slim profit margins.

The accelerated product life cycle and rising costs of product development and global distribution brought about a strategic reassessment. This reassessment argued for global strategic alliances and the need to be number one or number two to be considered successful in the new environment. The Internet, while further shortening the product life cycle, has also in many industries, notably financial services, reduced the cost of global distribution. In essence this lower-cost phenomenon accompanied by extensive, detailed, and timely customer information will bring about another paradigm shift in global strategy. This portion of Chapter 1 examines this paradigm shift and recommends alternative paths in this rapidly evolving business environment.

A world map reflecting relative purchasing power would emphasize the biggest national markets. The "triad" of the largest economies—North America, Japan, and Western Europe—accounts for 70 percent of world production and consumption. The map would not indicate the areas of fastest growth, however: That is, the 5–15 percent annual rates of growth in developing regions such as Southeast Asia and Latin America. Nor would the map indicate the critical differentiating role played by technology in determining global market strategies.

From 1963 through 1986, a massive study of global business—the Harvard Multinational Enterprise Project, which encompassed hundreds of U.S., European, Japanese, and emerging-nation corporations—found that companies' strategies are influenced heavily by their product technologies. High-technology producers behave differently from firms with less advanced wares. Although this study covered a period predating the emergence of Internet technologies, we believe that its conceptual framework and empirical findings nonetheless can guide managers today in understanding the issues that arise as they develop their companies' e-business strategies. For example, the study revealed a three-stage international product life cycle guiding strategic behavior:

> *Phase 1: High Tech.* At this stage, products have unique "leading edge" technologies; high engineering content; few manufacturers and competitors; high gross profit margins; manufacturing capabilities within the triad; high R&D-to-sales ratios (10 percent or more); technically oriented advertising support; and relatively small, predominately domestic markets.
>
> *Phase 2: Growth and Internationalization.* Products at this stage have some standardization with established technologies; greater emphasis on process engineering; more competitors; declining gross

profit margins; international manufacturing; less emphasis on R&D; more mass marketing and advertising; and growing domestic and export markets.

Phase 3: Maturity. In this stage, products have thorough standardization; little emphasis on engineering; intense competition; thin profit margins (a price-to-cost ratio approaching 1.0); manufacturing where factors of production are least expensive; reduced R&D and advertising expenses; and saturated markets worldwide.

This study argued that over time, a specific product moves along the life cycle, from phase 1 to phase 2 to phase 3. But companies invest in more R&D to improve their products, refresh their technologies, and push them back toward phase 1. Marketing can serve the same objective by convincing customers, through advertising and promotion, that the product is better.

Companies in the 1963–1986 study positioned themselves at various points along the international product life cycle. We identified common patterns of external and internal behavior for each group. There were some prominent features of the different positioning types.

A-companies—positioned solidly in phase 1—call themselves leading-edge technologists. An example is supercomputer leader Cray Inc. Such companies concentrate their operations in triad nations. These firms nurture a "nerd" culture where "weird is in" and innovation is worshiped. They hire a diverse set of managers, including women and minorities, because a knowledge base is the critical factor in employment. A-companies reward technical employees well, often with stock options. Their attitude toward the marketplace is that "we know better than the customers do," so the customer has to adapt to the company.

B-companies—based in phase 2 with forays into phase 1—portray themselves as leaders in reliable, "proven" technologies distinct from the risky "bleeding edge" of A-companies. A prime example is IBM Corp. Executives in B-companies speak the language of business and hew to a businesslike culture. During their earlier period they look alike and talk alike, because company culture is very important to provide a globally consistent product and/or service. B-companies have an arrogance that trades on the power of their brand names. B-companies typically have strong sales forces.

C-companies—positioned across phases 2 and 3—promote their mix of performance and price in a "value" positioning. These firms are the gods of marketing; they've won global markets by moving into markets with quality products at reasonable prices. The company culture emphasizes being sensitive to host cultures in foreign markets, acting accordingly, and segmenting markets conscientiously. Salaries and benefits tend to be lower for employees compared to A- and B-companies.

D-companies—positioned firmly in phase 3—compete on the basis of price with standard products and position themselves as inexpensive—an example is Hyundai Corporation's original positioning of its automobiles in North America. The approach to customers is price-driven. Often employee benefits are slim. Companies move production offshore in search of lower-cost alternatives.

This established international product life cycle positioning has lost its effectiveness in most industries, however. Dramatically shorter product life cycles, more expensive R&D, and pressure to outrun changing market tastes forced global business and consumer product manufacturers to adopt a new framework. The product life cycle positioning framework worked well when product life cycles were long, but with shorter life cycle products, the newer framework is more appropriate.

According to the once-established product life cycle positioning, if a firm had a mix of products at different international life cycle stages, it tended to have a single dominant product set with clear global competitive position. A firm positioning itself as a B-company, for example, does not appear "weird" enough to sell A-products, nor is it "sensitive" enough to sell C-products or "cheap" enough to sell D-products.

To respond to this strategic dilemma, companies often created separate business units to market their varied product scopes. To correct for the possibility that multiple units would call on the same customers, corporations appointed global account managers to coordinate all of the activity relating to major customers. A complex set of dotted-line relationships attempted to coordinate the activities of functional, regional, business unit, and global account managers.

Yet the speed of technology forced strategic realignment to accelerate. On average, product life cycles have shrunk from fifteen to twenty years in the postwar era to about three years today. Meanwhile the cost of product development has skyrocketed. Companies must invest in R&D lest they slide toward market maturity, but short life cycles do not permit them to recoup R&D investments unless they have a global position in the marketplace. Thus, a typical refrain heard from CEOs in the 1980s and early 1990s was: "We needed to expand our products globally and quickly, gain market share, and make our product or service the standard of the industry. This way we can recoup the rising cost of product development in shorter and shorter life cycles."

In response, A-companies pursue alliances with C-companies, which have deeper pockets and more marketing muscle. And C-companies seek the technical expertise of the A-firms, which can keep C-products from sinking to D-status. Companies in the chemical, computer, telecommunications, and automotive industries, for instance, have developed such partnerships. Automobili Lamborghini needed to develop a new state-of-the-art engine, but didn't have the volume to afford its development costs, so it allied with Chrysler, which supplied the requisite marketing muscle and production volume and wanted new engine technology.

Historically, companies with technical strengths often faced political risks in foreign countries, and instances of this can be found where nations invited foreign companies to manufacture locally. Once the government partner learned the technology, it nationalized the factory. This threat has become less critical as the expropriated technology life cycle has shortened. Contrast Compaq Computer's willingness to share short-lived personal computer technology with emerging nations such as China, versus chemical companies' reluctance to share advanced cigarette filter manufacturing in that market.

The pressure of short product life cycles and reduced political risk forces firms to move quickly into global markets, selling products at reasonable prices, in order to rapidly gain a large market share. Historically, it has been thought that in order to win, companies must be first or second in market share, and if you're number four, you must find a niche where you'll be number one or number two. Companies therefore formed alliances to acquire the market presence and investment resources demanded by that strategy.

Global marketing success required an integrated organization that moved into markets with speed and flexibility. If you couldn't do it alone, you might need partnerships to do it well and with best-in-class processes. Focus operations on core competencies, and benchmark to be certain about your position. Partner with others if you lack the superior core capability.

In this era of global strategic alliances, the linchpin of the alliance was the customer-focused partner. C-companies were winning out by mass-customizing their products. The platform can be standardized, but in the marketplace you must meet the customer's needs. The customer wants reasonably priced new technology around the globe. The keywords are *new, quick, global,* and *affordable.* This need to be bigger and more global appears to be what drove megamergers.

Is Bigger Necessarily Better?

Just as the experienced skier knows that the height of a ski slope may or may not indicate its difficulty, we need to reassess the popular thinking that it's good to be big in a globalizing economy. After all, megadeals seem to be occurring everywhere we turn and on an impressively global scale. In the oil sector, there's Exxon and Mobil, not to mention

BP's mergers with Amoco and Atlantic Richfield. In the automobile industry, Daimler-Benz and Chrysler have joined forces; Ford has taken over the automobile operations of Volvo; and Renault has acquired a significant stake in Nissan. Similar merger examples can be found in industries as diverse as telecommunications, entertainment, financial services, soft drinks, and even cement. Fueling these global megamergers is the accepted belief that industries inevitably become more concentrated as the world's markets become more globalized.

Companies are told that in order to create economies of scale in marketing, manufacturing, and research and development—as well as to scare off potential competitors—they have to be one of the biggest players in their industry. Thus they view mergers as a do-or-die proposition.

The conventional view that only the biggest companies survive in a globalizing economy was formulated in the 1970s by the Boston Consulting Group. It is referred to often as the "rule of three," and it states that a stable competitive market never has more than three significant competitors. Jack Welch's widely quoted dictum that General Electric must be either number one or two in its various businesses is consistent with this thinking. In the 1990s Mercer Management Consulting popularized the plight of the silver medalist: Companies are either number one, Mercer argued, or they are nobody.

Actually, globalization does not require a few megafirms to swallow up an entire industry. This assumption that the global economy is a winner-take-all economy has become common wisdom—but there's no evidence to support this premise. The theoretical links between the globalization of an industry and the concentration of that industry are weak. Empirical research indicates that global—or globalizing—industries have actually been marked by steady decreases in concentration in the post–World War II period.[3] All twenty industries studied showed this same result.

The automobile industry, for instance, has become a more global business since World War II, but it hasn't become more concentrated. General Motors's worldwide market share is at its lowest point in more than five decades. Some recent mergers, such as the DaimlerChrysler deal, have slightly increased concentration, but only to a modest degree compared with the past half-century. Even high-technology industries, such as computer hardware, computer software, and long-distance telephony, have seen market-share erosion. The share of worldwide sales for the top five companies in each of these industries declined from 1988 to 1998, according to Standard & Poor's Compustat data.

The dominant strategic option in the era of shorter product life cycles and increasing cost of product development and marketing appeared to argue for global megamergers. In fact, recent research conducted by Fariborz Ghadar of Penn State University and Pankaj

Ghemawat of Harvard Business School argued about the dubious logic of these global megamergers.[4] The rapid rise of the Internet will further bring into focus the fact that bigger may not be better.

Being the buyer in a big deal doesn't guarantee that you are the winner as the "conqueror" and the company being acquired automatically becomes the loser. Even in cases where the big deal makes sense, it may be better for your company's shareholders if you're the seller rather than the buyer. America Online's proposed acquisition of Time Warner is a case in point. Time Warner's shareholders did well in the immediate aftermath of the announcement—many of them rushed to cash out. AOL's shareholders, by contrast, did not do as well.

However, in an era that is witnessing technological discontinuities, managers must not focus so much on size as a goal but rather on the development of new business models that help them compete. In fact, there has been significant erosion of industry concentration over the past twenty years. What has happened is that the big guns are being attacked in all different areas by smaller players who seem to appear out of thin air. These small entities are either coming up with a new technology platform or a nonlinear business model, or they are just marketing to different niches. An example is Schwab.com (see sidebar). These niches—a subset of the market—have unique characteristics, and companies that concentrate on such niches have experienced rapid growth rates.

SMALL PLAYER ADVANTAGE: SCHWAB.COM

The success of Schwab is reflected by the speed by which it penetrated the market.

After just one year of web-based trading starting in January 1998, 60 percent of all Schwab's trades were being completed over the Internet.

Schwab gained nearly 1 million new customers (almost all of them online) in that same year; while commissions increased 60 percent, online assets doubled, and total assets were up 33 percent.

This shows that if a well-conceived Internet interface is designed, the results can be mind-boggling.

Source: Gary Hamel, *Leading the Revolution* (Boston: Harvard Business School Press, 2000), pp. 223–225.

In fact, the global market can be shared among a number of competitors, with niche players representing a significant part of the success. The strategic role that niche players possess is critical to explore because not every company can (or should want to) be the largest in its industry.

While we still see the old "build and sell" paradigm in some industries, the new market realities of the Internet argue for a new paradigm, namely, "sense and deliver." Because of the increasingly shortened international product life cycle, organizations have to do business according to this new framework. This has led to the rise of various niche players, which have in turn been fueled by, and benefited from, e-business.

THE SENSE-AND-DELIVER FRAMEWORK: CISCO SYSTEMS

Cisco's support center received 3,000 calls per month in 1991, and it was anticipating 12,000 calls per month in 1992. The call center did not have the resources for such a level of telephone calls at that time and thus set up Cisco Connection Online.

In 1992 Cisco Connection Online received 700,000 hits per month, clearly indicating that there were many questions that were not previously being answered. These hits may have been due to difficulty getting through on the phone lines, calls taking too much time, or possibly customers feeling uncomfortable asking what they perceived as stupid questions. The success of Cisco Connection Online prompted Cisco to attempt to sell products online using CCO.

By March 1997, Cisco was booking $10 million per month on the Web by selling routers. This was a good start, and it set a target to surpass $150 million per month, with Internet sales equaling 30 percent of total sales.

By March 1998, Cisco had exceeded this goal and was bringing in $10 million every five hours. Fifty percent of those sales, or $4 billion, came from the Internet. The average order size was $25,000. Cisco's web-based sales channel has annualized savings of $270 million, 3.5 million hits per day, and 80,000 registered users.

By 1999, Cisco was bringing in $10 million every three hours, with 75 percent of sales, or a run rate of 6.5 billion, on the Internet.

In March 2000, 82 percent of Cisco's sales were done via the Web.

Source: Speech by Michael Edholm of Ericson.

Companies could take advantage of the Internet and other technology to deliver services better and cheaper. Or they could focus on only a slice of the market and work on achieving unassailable customer loyalty.

The Significance of Brand

In an era of rapid change, accelerated and shorter product life cycles, and reduced delivery costs such as we see in the e-business environment, what you stand for is crucial. Your brand's primary function is to articulate this important message. Your brand must clearly communicate what you represent in a consistent, believable manner. After all, if product life cycles are short and cost is not the driver, the customer ultimately does business with you because of what you stand for, believing that you will provide a unique set of value drivers. Customers won't necessarily buy the cheapest PC—they'll buy the one they believe will work properly, will run their other software packages in a reliable manner, and will be maintained and serviced. In short, they'll choose the one that they believe in—a brand they trust. When many knock on the door to do business, customers will only talk to a limited number of entities they trust—whose brand they believe in. Brand management in the era of e-business is even more critical than ever before. Develop, nurture, and enhance that brand or you will not survive in an e-business world.

Cultivating an Internet Presence

A Forrester Research survey projects that the volume of e-business should rise five times every two to three years, and by 2004 it will reach $6.8 trillion worldwide.

Whether the Internet exceeds $6.8 trillion of business by the year 2004 or not, we can be sure that the impact on the global firms and their strategic paradigm will be enormous. Ken Olsen of Digital Equipment Corp. (DEC) said in 1977 that there was no reason for anybody to want a computer in the home. DEC was later bought out by Compaq—which just confirms again what Yogi Berra, the great sage of the New York Yankees, once said: "It's tough to make predictions, especially about the future."

Getting in Shape for the Black Diamond Trail

If the changing role of product life cycles and the common response of megamergers represent the equivalent of the ski slope, the manager is the equivalent of the experienced skier trying to master new terrain. It is axiomatic that those responsible for strategic planning are sufficiently experienced to have learned strategic precepts in the 1970s and 1980s—well before the impact of e-business was conceivable. The planning approach they were taught was linear, incremental, and quantifiable, or, as Hamel says, "ritualistic, reductionist, extrapolative, positioning, elitist, a feasibility sieve."[5] Changing these concepts is never easy. Peter Drucker is fond of noting the reluctance of large organizations to respond productively to disruptive changes that come with new technology, whether it be the Brownie camera, the PC, or online retailing.

The manager's job in adopting new approaches is made more difficult because so many of the concepts previously held in deep respect—

like the importance of being number one or two in market share—are in conflict with a web-driven world. Managers are victims of their "learning horizons"—they simply never experienced anything like the digital business model when they were advancing through the ranks. For example, organizational structures have been based on the premise that strategic business units (SBUs) allow for focus, competitive measurement, and management accountability. While all this can be true, SBUs now have the effect of constraining management decision making to a fragmented, historical view of the business and one that is ill-equipped to harness the power of electronic networks and other boundary-less technology.

At the same time, previously reliable weather vanes are misleading. Managers were trained to take comfort (or shelter) in clearly defined customer needs. As long as the customer indicated an interest, a manager was fully justified in pursuing a relevant course of action. But what happens when customers' needs change so quickly and radically that they can't even articulate them? What happens when new solutions, unfamiliar brands, and unheard-of flexibility constantly flood the market with choices, opening possibilities that customers never dreamed would exist? All this is happening now. Even a keen sense of competitive benchmarking can be detrimental when the real threat is from previously unidentified competitors who have been made possible only because technology enabled them. Could Barnes and Noble really have predicted and prepared for the arrival of Amazon.com?

Finally, shareholder expectations have changed dramatically, putting further pressure on management. Geoffrey Moore, in his book *Living on the Fault Line*, demonstrates that investors are drawn to new enterprises because they can be assured that their capital will go toward innovation and not merely be used to fix historical problems.[6]

It may be clearer that a different approach is needed than it is what that approach should be. And, of course, each firm's circumstances are sufficiently different that generalized prescriptions are unlikely to apply. There are, however, six themes that should guide a manager to not only cope with the new conditions, but provide the means by which an organization can thrive. As with the black diamond skier, they emphasize speed, knowledge of the terrain, anticipation of the unanticipatable, fast reactions, and just plain guts. The good news is that for each there is evidence that at least one far-seeing management team has been able to successfully adapt.

A New Perspective

A manager's perspective for strategic planning can no longer be based on static business conditions or even proven business models. Now technology changes rapidly, new competitors emerge through e-business capabilities, and customer demands constantly escalate. As Drucker has said, the challenge is that "reality has changed but the theory of the business has not."[7] Managers who were taught to develop plans based on long-term assumptions about their business must get used to the fact that the long-term simply doesn't exist in an e-world and that the only thing they can count on is disruption. One test to employ is this:

> Any strategic plan that doesn't make explicit allowances for unanticipated change, and provide for a contingency plan to address it, is incomplete.

Decisions made to face radically changed conditions are bold and risky ones, especially for established, successful firms where incrementalism and the security of (apparently) precise financial scenarios are the norm. It serves well to know that at least some companies such as Corning and Marriott have made the change from old to bold successfully.

THE OLD BECOME BOLD

Marriott International has largely left the business of hotel ownership (it owns only 1 percent of the hotels it manages). In the view of Marriott management, a strategic change was necessary in an era of electronic pricing since it made margins more appealing in managing the facilities, not in owning them. Now, Marriott concentrates on marketing its many brands and using the data gathered through hotel management for building additional occupancy for hotel owners and selling additional services to guests. In a different way, Corning Inc. saw an opportunity in building the infrastructure for the world of e-business. It left the business of cookware manufacturing and medical testing to concentrate on fiber optics. In the two years ending December 15, 2000, Marriott's stock is up about 50 percent and Corning's is up about 460 percent (adjusted for splits) compared to the S&P 500 increase of 14 percent.

A New Way to Compete

Managers must view the competitive climate differently, both in identifying threats and in developing their own approaches. It could be said that the New World Order has come to the business arena with many of the same unsettling opportunities and problems as faced by nations. The focus has shifted from the Cold War–like era of huge corporations struggling for incremental market share against each other, to one where new and smaller enterprises—again, enabled by technology—are proving the most disruptive. E-business shatters the cherished competitive analysis articulated by Michael Porter and on which many of today's managers were taught to rely. Virtually all of Porter's "barriers to entry"—economies of scale, capital requirements, entrenched cost advantages, protected distribution channels, and favorable government policy—are eliminated or significantly diluted.[8] Only brand survives as a defense. Relatively abundant capital (more than $60 billion from venture capital sources in 2000 alone) encouraged the formation of new entrants and sustained them even if their business model created red ink, dragging down the whole category with them.

The impact of new competitors cannot be avoided. Many established firms see the effects too late; others make tentative steps toward "e-commerce" and consider the problem under control. However, the response of some insightful firms has been to join in unprecedented approaches to guarding their position. In some ways, peace has broken out among the major players as they partner in market systems, courtesy of revolutionary technology (see sidebar on "Co-opetition"). While these alliances are unproved and have significant challenges, the level of cooperation among historically bitter rivals is unprecedented and provides compelling testimony to how much the competitive climate has changed.

CO-OPETITION

In a process known as "co-opetition," firms such as Merrill Lynch, Goldman Sachs Group Inc., Morgan Stanley Dean Witter, and other investment bankers are cooperating to build an information portal for investors. Auto companies Ford, GM, and DaimlerChrysler are linking buying practices through an online exchange called Covisint. Managed-care providers such as CIGNA, Aetna, and United Health have allied to fight WebMD/Healtheon's attempt to capture the data flowing among healthcare providers and patients. Even Coca-Cola and Pepsi are working together.

The Customer Still Rules

Good strategic plans have always put the customer at the forefront, but the e-savvy manager recognizes that never in the history of business strategy development has the customer ruled with such authority. In the 1980s and 1990s, marketplace power shifted from manufacturers to distributors because it was the distributors who controlled the customer. Wal-Mart is probably the best example. Now, however, technology is fostering a shift of marketplace power to the ultimate buyer. Opportunities to exploit the new circumstances abound, whether the manager uses better customer buying data, microsegmentation, and cross-marketing, or improved customer relationship management

(CRM) for improved service and cross-selling. The key, however, is to ensure that the new technology improves the *solutions*—and not just the products—that are offered (see "Service from Solutions" sidebar). New approaches are particularly evident in the financial services business, where change has been spurred on by reduced regulation.

SERVICE FROM SOLUTIONS

Fidelity Investment Management, long known for its creative use of technology to become the world's largest family of mutual funds, is seizing this opportunity. Its publicly stated strategy is to provide a full range of services that enable consumers to plan and purchase virtually all types of financial services. Underlying the strategy is management's full appreciation for the importance of a company's brand in the new economy. In fact, as product life cycles shorten, options for customers proliferate, and many new entrants make their presence known, the role of reliable brands is more vital than ever before. Trading on its strong brand name and reputation for customer service and choice, Fidelity has branched into selling insurance products, including life, auto, and homeowners. The use of technology plays three special roles:

1. It enables Fidelity to use its vast store of customer information for marketing purposes, thereby improving targeting, penetration, and customer satisfaction.

2. Just as importantly, selling over the Web helps Fidelity overcome a traditional competitive barrier that has protected insurance companies for years: control over distribution channels. Fidelity simply replaces sales representatives with websites.

3. It has also allowed Fidelity to avoid heavy development costs. By establishing electronic networks to insurance companies that efficiently "manufacture" auto and homeowners' coverage for Fidelity's clients, Fidelity provides a meaningful service while retaining control over the customer.

Making the Old New

Even when the strategic priority is improving existing processes, the e-business manager must see the opportunity in a different light. Increased information, faster communications, and shortened supply lines all become possible with e-business. Hamel breaks companies into three categories: rule takers (i.e., the perpetual followers), rule makers (i.e., the traditional leaders), and rule breakers (i.e., those who are reinventing businesses). His view is that the third category—the rule breaker—is the place to be in the e-business world.[9]

RULE MAKER?

A cautionary tale on the other side of the ledger is Wal-Mart Stores, Inc. Having succeeded fabulously at beating its original archcompetitor Kmart Corp. by managing traditional business processes better, it has stumbled badly in selling through the Web. Several false starts and failed partnerships have left it a laggard in electronic retailing, behind J.C. Penney; Sears, Roebuck and Co.; and others. Even as sales through traditional channels increase in accord with management's projections, its stock in December 2000 was languishing at 30 percent below its historical, January 2000 peak. Investors want innovation and proof that Wal-Mart can make the leap to the digital economy. More of the same is simply not enough.

RULE BREAKER!

An example of an established firm seizing new opportunities by breaking rules is the paper-goods manufacturer Kimberly-Clark Corp. Kimberly-Clark (maker and marketer of Kleenex facial tissues, Huggies disposable diapers, and other well-known consumer paper products) has an innovative arrangement with Costco Wholesale Corp. (operator of warehouse discount stores). Kimberly-Clark, using electronic networks that provide real-time information, is responsible for monitoring inventory at local Costco stores and for scheduling replacement delivery. Impractical without the networks, the new approach benefits both parties. First, it shifts the cost of warehousing goods from the store to the supplier. Second, it gives the supplier better data on customer-buying habits and more precise allocation of goods, virtually ensuring that they are never out of stock. While not the primary focus, to the consumer, lower prices reflect greater efficiency. Costco management says this is why Kimberly-Clark's Huggies, and not Procter & Gamble's Pampers, is the leading diaper brand in Costco stores.

Change on the Home Front

The world of e-business creates changes inside the firm as well as outside. In prior eras, technology was seen as a means of achieving greater productivity, usually by reducing labor and associated costs. Now, however, a far more sophisticated view has emerged. It holds that the digital era puts even greater emphasis on the quality of human capabilities, if for no other reason than to keep up with the rapid pace of change and technology design. Frontline employees are both the foot soldiers and the generals for the new approach to strategy.

This new view, however enlightened, creates its own challenges. It has never been easy to communicate senior management's business ambitions down to the rank and file. When change has been implemented rapidly and successfully, it was usually because of a "burning platform" signaling impending doom if an enterprise did not change its ways. For the rank and file, the impact of e-business creates great uncertainty and mistrust, coming, as it does, during a time of great economic growth and low unemployment.

Referring to the midwestern regional industries that were so damaged by the economic restructuring of the 1970s and 1980s, Charles Babcock forecasts that the "Internet rust belt" will have a similar impact on travel agents, bank tellers, real estate sales staff, stockbrokers, and bookstore clerks—"anyone who enjoys a middleman position by virtue of the information he or she controls."[10] Rather than making their task easier, technology has caused a sense of dread.

This problem becomes even more difficult since the disruptive and fluid nature of e-business is difficult even for senior managers to grasp. In his book *Simplicity: The New Competitive Advantage in a World of Better, Faster, More,* Bill Jensen describes a typical workday in the digital economy:

> Off to work you go. You make choices. . . . Some are according to the plan, the process, the strategy, the budget. Some are not. That's human nature. . . . The "New Economy"—which changed work from making things to making choices—also changed the impact of each choice. Not only do you have to make more decisions, faster, but also every decision is interconnected to the next one. The universal problem seems to be how hard people have to work just to figure out what to do. Task work has been streamlined, but knowledge work has become more cluttered and confusing.[11]

Once again, however, there is evidence that not only can the problem be overcome, but that the new e-business world offers opportunities to do things better. In this case, the example is Intel Corp.'s program of giving frontline employees a larger role in strategy development and implementation (see sidebar on Intel's "Fingertip Strategy").

FINGERTIP STRATEGY

Intel's chairman and former CEO Andy Grove blames management's uncritical belief in its own strategic rhetoric for the company being slow to exit memory chips in favor of microprocessors, and credits frontline employees for a better approach. As reported by Christopher A. Bartlett in the *Harvard Business Review* (November–December, 1994), he said:

"Our most significant strategic decision was made not in response to some clear-sighted corporate vision but by the marketing and investment decisions of frontline managers who really knew what was going on."

He calls this formulating strategy "with your fingertips." Any firm can follow this lead. While companies have tried everything from stock options to casual dress codes to ensure the loyalty and commitment of employees, the real test is whether rank-and-file employees feel they are a part of the company's strategy. Managers can make their own test of employee involvement. Simply ask employees to answer the following six simple questions:

1. What is the organization trying to accomplish—in summary?
2. What am I supposed to do to contribute—in detail?
3. What help will I get?
4. How will I be evaluated?
5. How will I be rewarded?
6. What will success look like?

The Black Diamond Manager

And what of our erstwhile black diamond manager? In the e-business era we must look to the role of management itself. Drucker puts to rest any impression that management will remain unscathed in the changing environment when he notes:

> Today's corporation is structured around layers of management. Most of these layers are information relays, and like any relays, they are very poor. Every transfer of information cuts the message in half. There needs to be very few layers of management in the future and those who relay the information must be very smart.[12]

But it's not easy being smart. Steve Drotter, a human resources consultant to leading U.S. corporations and coauthor of *The Leadership Pipeline,* a forthcoming book on management development, says that the half-life of some management skills in companies he works with is as short as three years, compared to seven just a few years ago.[13] How many firms plan to refresh their management's knowledge and skills at this frequency?

What's more, the quality of management in a firm will be a visible factor in how outsiders view its future. This trend has been apparent for some time as investors became comfortable with shedding physical assets as a value determiner in favor of intellectual property: Just compare the market values assigned to bricks-and-mortar companies like GM and Ford to those of Intel, Cisco, and Microsoft.

A new approach developed by Cap Gemini Ernst & Young puts further perspective on this issue. The Value Creation Index (VCI) measures the correlation between a company's stock price and how it stacks up on nine factors that evaluate so-called qualitative characteristics. The highest-rated category was a firm's commitment to consistent innovation. The quality of management and employees in general were either second or third (depending on the type of firm under review). Technology did not fare well on its own: It ranked eighth. According to the VCI, management factors account for 50 percent of the value assigned to the firm. As usual, Hamel sums it up well: "In the Internet age it is not technology that creates new wealth, but radical new business concepts."[14] And those business concepts, of course, are what black diamond management is all about.

What's clear from these leaders in management development is that e-business is viewed as critical to the continued success of their firms and that they will invest appropriate resources to pursue it. The enduring quality of the management teams at General Electric Company and Johnson & Johnson is a pretty good indicator that they are on the right track.

LEARNING AT GE

Looking for examples of firms who understand this changed role of management takes one in a familiar direction: GE. Peter Drucker states unequivocally that Jack Welch's legacy is the people pipeline he developed, and the work continues. To ensure that its managers can exploit the digital age, GE uses its well-known executive training programs, but goes a step further. At GE Power Energy Services, all managers have a personal coach with tutoring tailored to their particular needs, whether it be internal development or just using e-mail. There's even a corporate framework that sets standards for e-business learning.

THE J & J REMEDY

Another household name that takes management development seriously in the e-business era is Johnson & Johnson. J & J's CEO and chairman Ralph Larsen set the tone when he included in his four priorities for 2000 innovation and use of the Internet to serve J & J customers. And, like GE, J & J headquarters takes a strong interest in ensuring that J & J managers are developing with e-business foremost in their minds. In fact, J & J has harnessed the power of the Web to install its "I-lead" self-training process in all 190 business units. Alan Anderson, vice president of education and development on the J & J corporate staff, says that all J & J executives will be trained and measured through this system by 2002.

Conclusion

To the inexperienced skier, black diamond means trouble; to the expert, however, it means exhilaration and reward for optimized skills. Managers need to see the digital economy as an unprecedented opportunity. When great change occurs, it opens possibilities for those who grasp its meaning to excel. What's more, it should be evident from the examples offered throughout this chapter that some enterprises are showing the way, in effect smoothing the trail, and that sheer size is not a prerequisite for success. New perspectives, new approaches to competition, respect for the customer, radical improvements in conventional processes through the use of new technology, involvement of frontline employees, and efforts by managers to make the transition to the new world are the keys.

Endnotes

1 Gary Hamel, "Revamping the Corporation from the Inside Out," *Business2. com* (September 2000), p.136.

2 James Daly, "Sage Advice," *Business2.com* (August 2000), p. 134.

3 Ghemawat and Ghadar, *Harvard Business Review* (July–August 2000).

4 *Ibid.*

5 Gary Hamel, "Strategy as Revolution," *Harvard Business Review* (July–August 1996), p. 69.

6 Geoffrey A. Moore, *Living on the Fault Line* (New York: HarperCollins, 2000), p. 50.

7 Peter Drucker, "Theory of the Business," *Harvard Business Review* (September–October 1994), p. 98.

8 Michael Porter, "How Competitive Forces Shape Strategy," *Harvard Business Review* (July–August 1979), pp. 138–9.

9 Hamel, "Strategy as Revolution," p. 69.

10 Charles Babcock, "Do You Live in the Internet Rust Belt?" *Interactive Week* (September 2000), p. 1.

11 Bill Jensen, *Simplicity: The New Competitive Advantage in a World of Better, Faster, More* (San Francisco: Perseus Press, February 2000), pp. 10, 20.

12 Daly, "Sage Advice," p. 139.

13 Ram Charan, Steve Drotter, and Jim L. Noel, *The Leadership Pipeline: How to Build the Leadership Powered Company* (San Francisco: Jossey-Bass, 2000), p. 3.

14 Gary Hamel, "Revamping the Corporation from the Inside Out," *Business2. com* (September 2000), p. 136.

2

Leveraging E-Business in a Networked Economy

Liam Fahey, Babson College and Cranfield School of Management (U.K.)

Rajendra Srivastava, Goizueta Business School, Emory University

This chapter examines the emerging role of e-business and how it is changing competitive landscapes, business processes, and marketing practices. We argue that the Internet creates an environment where businesses thrive on specialization and collaboration with producers of complementary products and services. Thus, customers and co-aligned partners "reside on the Net" to form market-based assets or value networks. It is the management of these relationships that leads to development of net assets that add to the value of businesses. We also show that "driving the future" involves proactive market management. It will not be enough to be market-driven.

Introduction

Much has been said about the new economy. The promise is still there, but our faith has been bruised since the March 2000 NASDAQ debacle. Still, the financial performance of most Old World firms continues to pale relative to that of the more successful New World upstarts. Consider merely one comparison of highly visible firms in both worlds. General Motors with 1999 sales of $175 billion and earnings of more than $5 billion had a market capitalization of $37 billion. Dell Computer, with 1999 sales of $26 billion and earnings under $5 billion, had a market cap of $131 billion. Detroit and many of the Old World companies attribute part of the disparity in financial performance to the investing public's fascination with growth in the go-go world of e-business.

But it has become apparent in the past year or so that most Old World firms no longer wish to stand idly by and be overrun by the onslaught of the e-business world. The pages of the weekly and biweekly business magazines report the actions and commitments of firms as diverse as ABB, P&G, Boeing, Bechtel, Chevron, Enron, and Home Depot to integrate e-business into every facet of their business operations and interactions with external entities (including suppliers, channels, end-customers, and technology partners). Indeed, some of most respected Old World behemoths such as GE and IBM have publicly proclaimed with great fanfare that they wish to incorporate e-business into every business process, function, and activity.

Even Detroit, in spite of considerable early reluctance, has begun to adopt e-business as one means to reconfigure its traditional ways of doing business (and in so doing to embrace e-business as one weapon in its artillery to battle low market-to-book and price-earnings valuations). Detroit has enthusiastically announced e-procurement-focused business exchanges that are targeted toward squeezing out excess inventory costs and spurring more competitive practices among their component and assembly vendors. Briefly, these approaches are about cost minimization and not value maximization. In a sense, e-business today is where Henry Ford was in the early 1900s when, in the interest of assembly-line efficiency, he remarked that the customer could have any color car as long as it was black (which was the cheapest and fastest-drying color). Consider the following case of the marketplace opportunity provided by the AutoFlex option.

The Shape of Things to Come—The AutoFlex Option

Currently, customers purchase or lease a single automobile that remains in their possession until they sell it or return it after the lease period expires. They have access only to the auto they purchase or lease. The bad news, as almost every automobile purchaser knows, is that the experience of searching for the "right" automobile, haggling with dealers, and closing on the sale leaves it less than exhilarating. Yet it need not be that way.

E-business enables a potential new form of customer experience. Let us call it AutoFlex. Under the AutoFlex option, the firm proposes that customers sign a "relationship agreement" in which they will pay a negotiated amount of money to receive the rights to use a range of vehicles under specified conditions. It may involve either a one-time lump sum or an annual or monthly payment. Under the agreement, the customers will not "own" any individual automobile. Rather, they will obtain one "everyday" vehicle. This will be the customers' dominant or most widely used auto. They will also receive the right to obtain other vehicles. For example, they might choose to use a four-by-four for a certain number of weekends for skiing, camping in the mountains, or simply family uses. They may choose a luxury automobile for certain family "entertainment" occasions. For transporting the soccer or little league team during a weekend tournament, they could choose a mini-van. In summary, the agreement can be structured in many ways; it can be changed at any time, subject to the approval of both the firm and the customer. Pricing would reflect a cost structure associated with a weighted average rate for a portfolio of vehicles used. In addition, the AutoFlex agreement could, at the customers' option, roll in insurance, service and maintenance, financing, and both local and global availability.

Is this solution likely to be of interest to customers? Yes. It conveys considerable customer value in comparison to what all customers currently encounter or experience in owning and using automobiles. It provides greater flexibility in automobile availability. It allows frequent change in the terms of the "agreement." It can be adapted to meet changing customer circumstances.

But what will the firm have to do to realize this marketplace opportunity? In particular, what business assets, processes, and skills are needed to implement this innovative "customer solution"? The AutoFlex option constitutes a new business model for the firm: It involves a whole new way of thinking about, organizing for, and doing business in the auto industry. It requires a new perspective on customers' needs and on how to create and serve these needs. As a consequence, designing, executing, and enhancing the AutoFlex option illustrates the role, importance, and contribution of business processes to the new business model.

Implementing this "customer solution" necessitates not only change within key business processes but also integration across them. Development of the new solution (i.e., the new product development process) requires extensive (and electronic) interaction with customers: testing the new solution concept and identifying possible solution configurations. Manufacturing, logistics, and distribution (i.e., the supply chain management process) must adapt purchase and delivery of supplies, components, and materials to new and rapidly changing projections of the portfolio of vehicles required to meet customer needs. Interaction with customers before, during, and after each "relationship agreement" (i.e., the customer relationship management process) allows the electronic collection of extensive customer data. Such data can be assessed to determine different customer segment needs, and responses to, and adaptation of, the agreement contract. In short, e-business enables swift and incisive collection and assessment of massive amounts of data and information between the firm and its suppliers, alliance partners, channels or dealership outlets, and individual end-customers.

In summary, the AutoFlex option fundamentally changes the way business is conducted. The option is premised on the merits of *solution customization*. Design and execution of the option would not be possible without extensive relationship-based intimacy involving multiple forms of interaction with, and feedback from, customers. The ability to sustain the desired customer functionality is greatly facilitated through networked partnerships (e.g., a network of company- and independently-owned dealerships that allow customers to take advantage of the new option irrespective of their geographic location). Its evolution is heavily influenced by close interaction with multiple types of customers. It requires fundamental new thinking in the way dealerships would have to interact with each other, with the manufacturer, and with customers and providers of complementary services (e.g., financing, insurance, logistics).

And what will its impact be relative to previously noted e-procurement-focused practices that are emerging from Detroit? Rather than simply focus on efficiency and cost reduction (the primary driving goals of e-procurement), the AutoFlex option integrates products and services required by customers into a single effective customer solution. Relative to price-focused marketing practices that can end up destroying customer loyalty and brand equity, integrated solutions, exemplified in AutoFlex, create new customer functionality making a product/service package more useful for a customer, give rise to new and rewarding customer purchasing and product use experiences, and as a consequence, increase customer switching costs. Thus, integrated solutions, enabled by advances in e-business, build customer loyalty, not destroy it. Brands are not dead. As they evolve to include more service and relationship dimensions, they simply become more valuable.

Impact of E-Business Practices on Corporate Performance

While measurement difficulties abound, the principles of driving corporate performance, or creating shareholder value, are simple. Because of the time value of money (discounting for risk), earlier cash flows are more highly valued, and certainly higher levels are preferred to lower ones. Reduced risk is valued as well. The shareholder value-based planning approach proposed by Alfred Rappaport is based on three "value drivers":

1. Acceleration of cash flows, with earlier cash flows being preferred because risk and time adjustments reduce the value of later cash flows

2. Enhancement of cash flows by increasing revenues and reducing costs, working capital, and fixed investments

3. Reduction in the risk associated with cash flows by decreasing both their volatility and vulnerability and hence, indirectly, the firm's cost of capital[1]

The question, then, is: What is the impact of e-business on acceleration, growth, and vulnerability and volatility of cash flows? One proposed framework links core business processes (e.g., new product development, supply chain management, and customer relationship management) that enhance customer value to drivers of shareholder value (e.g., cash flow enhancement and acceleration and reduction of vulnerability and volatility of cash flows).[2] We adapt this framework (see Figure 2-1) to assess the impact of e-business on financial performance along two dimensions:

- Its impact on the efficiency and effectiveness of these processes
- The evolution of new practices and processes

Improving Efficiency and Effectiveness of Existing Business Models

At one end, e-business enhances the efficiency of business processes. For example, when Dell Computer Corp. shifted from a call center–based sales model to Dell Online, it resulted in faster communications throughout the value chain from its vendors to its customers. This increase in the speed and accuracy of information resulted in both faster order-delivery cycle times and reduced working capital requirements (in part due to lower inventory). It also led to outsourcing of subassemblies and therefore reduced investments in fixed costs. The result has been sustained improvement in financial performance (see Figure 2-2).

One large national trucking firm has used the electronic connections afforded by e-business developments to reconfigure each sub-process in its overall supply chain management process. For example, it now connects directly with all of its pickup sites to more finely schedule pickup times, amount of trucking capacity at each site, and allocation across trucks depending on the geographic distribution of delivery sites. Customers can now connect directly with the firm to immediately determine the location of each "load" and its approximate arrival time.

In the previous two examples, e-business largely improved existing processes. However, as illustrated by the AutoFlex example, the most significant impact of e-business clearly involves integration across core business processes (see Figure 2-3). In fact, improvements in core processes are often due to their integration with other processes. Dell's supply chain management (SCM) process becomes more efficient be-

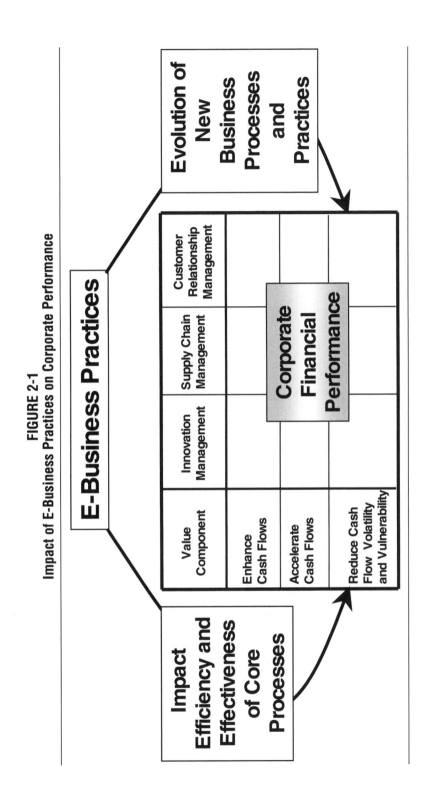

FIGURE 2-1
Impact of E-Business Practices on Corporate Performance

FIGURE 2-2
The Dell Business Model

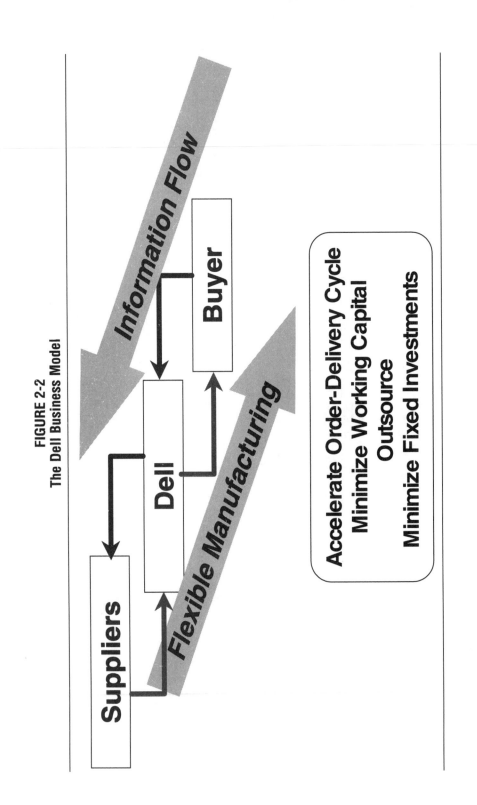

FIGURE 2-3
Integrating Business Processes That Drive Customer Value

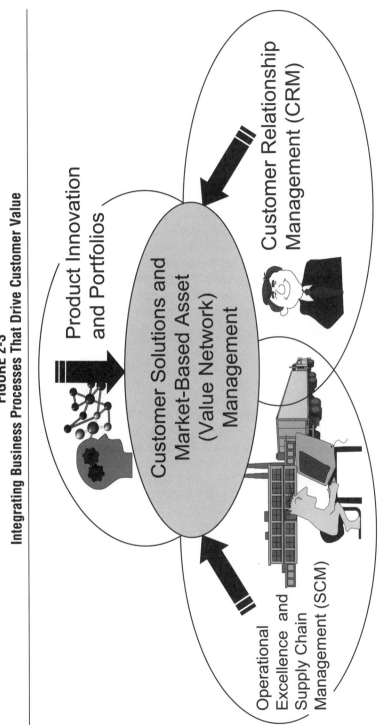

Product Innovation
and Portfolios

Customer Relationship
Management (CRM)

Customer Solutions and
Market-Based Asset
(Value Network)
Management

Operational
Excellence and
Supply Chain
Management (SCM)

cause it is enabled by data and information generated through its customer relationship management (CRM) process. Thus Dell has integrated SCM and CRM processes to develop a more defensible competitive position. Similarly, Intel Corp. has benefited from the integration of new product development (NPD) and SCM processes. Design engineers at customers such as Dell and Hewlett-Packard (HP) cannot only obtain information on specific components, but they can also get insights into Intel's technology road map to help visualize their own future products. This NPD-SCM process integration requires that Intel share knowledge hitherto held close to the chest. Finally, Cisco Systems has managed to successfully integrate all three processes (SCM-NPD-CRM) to become the ultimate virtual company. Managing networks of relationships in the World Wide Web in Internet time—a fundamental prerequisite to establishing and fostering the virtual underpinnings of its organizational form—constitutes Cisco's most basic and perhaps most readily leveraged core competence. These market-based asset management skills have allowed Cisco to outperform Microsoft, an icon of brand and market-based asset management.

Evolution of New Business Processes and Practices

And yet the real impact of e-business is only now becoming apparent: the emergence of truly new business processes giving rise to new business models with the potential to affect several traditional industries. Consider the business model for Travelocity.com Inc. Travelocity interconnects a range of "sellers" including airlines, car rental agencies, hotels, vacation providers, insurance firms, and other information providers with a host of "buyers" including corporations, consumers, and a variety of agents and affiliates. The value to customers depends on the size and variety of the vendor or seller network. Thus Travelocity. com is more attractive than, say, Delta.com because it offers the potential for lower fares and more convenient arrival and departure times. In addition, the customer has access to hotels, car rental agencies, and information on vacation packages and tourist attractions.

At the same time, the value of Travelocity to vendors is based on the size and quality of the buyer network. Since Travelocity makes money on the degree of interaction between buyers and vendors, its own financial value is based on network interactivity. While it is commonly accepted that providers of complementary services (e.g., hotels and airlines) enhance the value of a network, this example demonstrates that even competitive providers help each other in a collaborative network such as Travelocity's. Thus Travelocity's market-based assets include customers, vendors, content providers (e.g., sites that provide local weather, business, and tourist information on destinations), and other network affiliates (e.g., search engines and portals with hotlinks to Travelocity). While Delta is focused on one-to-one business transactions, Travelocity can arrange many-to-many relationships.

The leverage inherent in such new business processes, and in particular, the capacity to continually evolve new core competencies and distinctive value for customers, resides in part in their effective linkage to knowledge management. This is so because e-business, as noted previously, brings to the fore the role and importance of another largely intangible asset—data and information. The networked interrelationships with a wide range of marketplace players, as evidenced in the Travelocity example, afford the collection of types of data heretofore not possible, as well the mining and assessment of such data to generate categories of information that were hardly imaginable a few years ago.

However, such knowledge is not generated for its own sake. Thus, the question must be asked: How can it contribute to superior financial performance? Consider the following analysis sequence: The cancellation of a convention in Acapulco two weeks from now leads to an inventory of 1,500 unsold rooms at a particular Hilton hotel. How can Travelocity help? By trawling through its constantly updated database, it can identify individuals who visited the resort about the same time last year. It finds that these were snowbirds from Minnesota—employees of 3M and St. Paul Insurance. Travelocity can quickly put together a discount vacation package for 3M and St. Paul employees sponsored by their companies, Travelocity, Northwest Airlines, and Hilton. In short, leveraging knowledge resides at the heart of Travelocity's market-making activity and thus underpins its capacity to create both customer value and financial returns.

Figure 2-4 summarizes salient characteristics of e-business processes and their impact on marketplace and financial performance. First, networked market-based assets reside on the Internet. Value is created, indeed accelerated, by managing these "network externalities." Winners learn to aggregate supply and demand. Existing evidence suggests that the networked economies nurture instant relationships and that success is predicated on management's ability to manage alliances and co-branding opportunities.

Second, while business may be conducted in "Internet time" and the WWW is almost frictionless (i.e., marginal costs of transactions are near zero), the e-business infrastructure is expensive. Along with the benefits of aggregation and network externalities in the winner-takes-all economy, chances are that the big—especially the Net-savvy big—will keep getting bigger.

Third, e-business is a knowledge-driven activity. Information is freely available and is resident on the Internet—the business intelligence professionals' dream environment! But its value lies in proactive use in creating and driving business solutions. Its value is time-sensitive—it refreshes and decays quickly. It's a latent asset until leveraged

FIGURE 2-4
Market-Based Assets in E-Business Networks

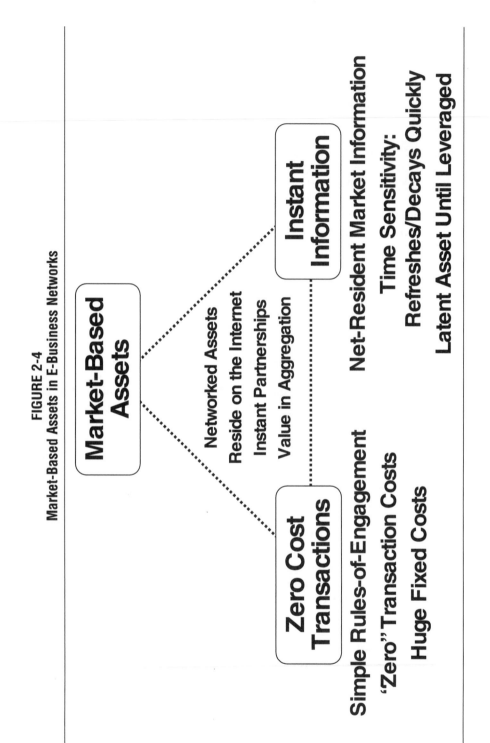

for competitive advantage. Sadly, while much data is generated, many organizations have yet to manage it productively. Additionally, since e-business solutions can open and shut doors to opportunity rather quickly, organization agility is at a premium. This requires sharing of knowledge, development of "rules of engagement," and network governance structures to take full advantage of network opportunities.

Investment in and Valuation of E-Business Opportunities

A quick survey of financial markets reveals that even for Old World economy companies, the ratio of market capitalization to book value is running at over 5:1 (the ratio is often over 10:1 for companies with a heavy emphasis on e-business and the networked economy). Where, then, is the 80 percent of market value that is not measured by accountants? The answer is fairly obvious, but its implications are anything but straightforward. The majority of the uncaptured market value tends to emanate from intangible assets—knowledge (e.g., of emerging technologies), relationships (e.g., with customers or vendors), and perceptions held by external parties (e.g., brand loyalty). These intangible assets can be both internal (e.g., process capabilities and intellectual property embedded in the organization) and external (e.g., networked relationships and a broad range of market-based assets and capabilities). These types of intangible assets drive future expectations of financial performance.

Market-Based Assets and Value Networks

Networked market-based assets help a firm create value over and above that created by market-based assets individually. For example, the Intel Pentium microprocessor's successful defense against both DEC's Alpha and the IBM/Motorola/Apple PowerPC chips is in part related to its network of end-users, original equipment manufacturers (OEMs), and software vendors. The "best" products in terms of functionality (e.g., performance, reliability, and durability) do not necessarily win. The best-networked ones usually do. Success is then based on greater collaboration, information sharing, and trust across value chains. Market values of dot-com start-ups can in part be attributed to the size and growth rate of interconnected networks. The larger the size and growth rate of installed bases of subscribers or users, the greater the value of Travelocity as both a media and transaction channel to the vendor network (i.e., the airlines, hotels chains, car rental agencies, travel package providers, global financial services, facilitators, and the like), and vice versa.

Investing in Market-Based Assets to Create Value

Naturally, such market-based assets do not come free. An organization such as Travelocity must invest in developing and nurturing this multiplicity of networks and grow its capabilities for both transaction and service management (via website and call center management). Recognition of customers, distributors, and value networks as market-based assets raises the question as to whether strategic expenditures such as acquisition of customers and establishing network relationships should be treated as operating expenses or capital investments.[3]

For management purposes, treatment of marketing expenditures as capital investments could provide brands with a defensible claim when competing for resources with other capital expenditures—especially in industries where off–balance sheet assets are a large proportion of the market value of firms.[4] For example, E*TRADE's investment of $400 million in marketing has come under fire since the fast-start dot-com financial institution has diluted current earnings and cash flow in the process. Yet, in light of customer acquisition costs between $200 to $400 per customer, the company should acquire at least 1.5 million new customers (it has already acquired about 2 million customers and is the most frequently visited discount brokerage site).

How much does it need to break even? Assuming a ten-year amortization and a 10 percent cost of capital, it needs a first-year cash flow of $80 million from customers. That's about $40 per customer, or about 2.5 $16 trades. That should be easy. Everything else such as income from cross-selling activities (e.g., credit cards, loans, insurance, bonds, mutual funds) should be pure gravy. Or let's look at the value of these customers. A customer with $50,000 in various accounts with a 2 percent earnings spread should net a $1,000 annuity (assuming customer retention) for E*TRADE. This annuity can be valued at $10,000 at a 10 percent cost of capital to E*TRADE. The value of a million such customers would be $10 billion. This value (not a bad payoff for a $400 million investment) is, of course, contingent on customer retention. While dot-coms have shown a great interest in acquiring "eyeballs" (i.e., the most customers based on website hits) and measuring "stickiness" (i.e., the ability to keep customers at your website), attention must shift to closing the loop with transactions and repeat sales (i.e., loyalty).

E-Business Initiatives as Strategic (Real) Options

E-business investments are typically required to build customer bases, distribution, and partner networks. These relationships can be tapped to provide significant cash flows in later stages of the product life cycle. These investments are "strategic options" that can pay off in later stages of the product life cycle in terms of increased cash flows (due to a combination of higher revenues and lower costs). They give the firm the right, but not the obligation, to participate in the market. Early-mover advantages and switching costs can preclude later entries (or at least make them more expensive and risky) and can enhance future performance. The value of these options has been shown to increase with uncertainty because potentially negative outcomes can be eliminated with improved information and contingent managerial actions over time.[5]

Conclusion

E-business is still in its early phase of development. As illustrated in Figure 2-5, e-business practices will transition from e-commerce (with emphasis on cost/price reductions and speed) to e-marketing (where attention shifts to customer acquisition and retention, and value enhancement through customization and support services) to true e-business. In a true e-business, e-everything is absorbed into integrated core business processes that stretch globally across multiple markets and drive performance across value networks. This transition requires that assessment of e-business performance shift from eyeballs and stickiness to shareholder value creation (i.e., to enhancing, accelerating, and protecting cash flows). As we have discussed in this chapter, market-based assets such as networked relationships and market data itself created by e-business may reside largely outside the enterprise. And, finally, managing knowledge-driven networked enterprises will require investments in human capital and intellectual property.[6]

Endnotes

1 Rajendra Srivastava, Tasadduq Shervani, and Liam Fahey, "Market-Based Assets and Shareholder Value: A Framework for Analysis," *Journal of Marketing* Vol. 62, No. 1 (January 1998), pp. 2–18; Alfred Rappaport, *Creating Shareholder Value* (New York: The Free Press, 1986).

2 Rajendra Srivastava, Tasadduq Shervani, and Liam Fahey, "Marketing, Business Processes and Shareholder Value: An Organizationally Embedded View of Marketing Activities and the Discipline of Marketing," *Journal of Marketing* Vol. 63, No. 4 (October 1999 Special Issue), pp. 168–179.

3 Srivastava, Shervani, and Fahey (1998), "Market-Based Assets and Shareholder Value," *Journal of Marketing* Vol. 62, No. 1 (January), pp. 2–18; and "Marketing, Business Processes and Shareholder Value." *Journal of Marketing* vol. 63, No. 4 (October 1999 Special Issue), pp. 168–179.

4 Stern Stewart Europe Limited, "Internet Valuation: Why Are the Values So High?" *EVAluation* Vol. 2, No. 1 (February 2000), pp. 1–21.

5 Stern Stewart Europe Limited, loc. cit.

6 James Brian Quinn, *The Intelligent Enterprise* (New York: The Free Press, 1992).

FIGURE 2-5
Evolution of E-Business Practices

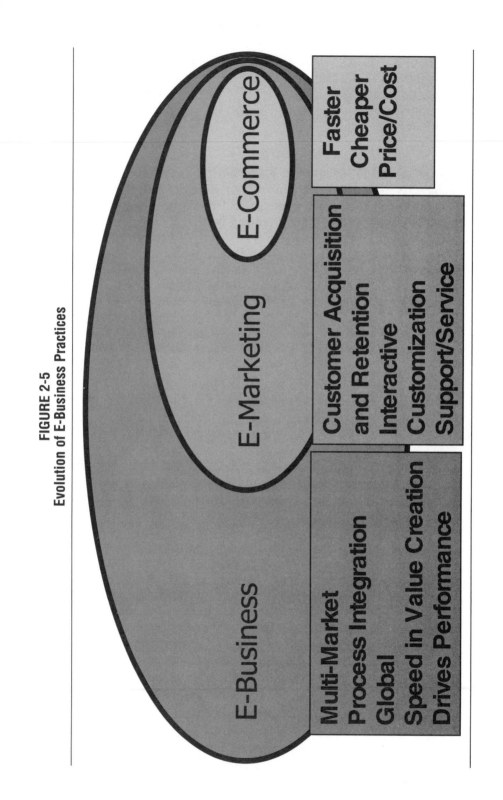

3

Leveraging Old Economy Fundamentals for the New World

Rocki-Lee DeWitt, The Smeal College of Business Administration, The Pennsylvania State University

Kathryn Rudie Harrigan, Graduate School of Business, Columbia University

Everyone needs an Internet strategy, even if that strategy is to do nothing for now. The time has never been better to develop an Internet strategy that may involve acquisition of extant dot-com firms. Consumer and business awareness of the Internet continues to grow while the market valuation roller coaster has humbled many dot-com wannabes. Established firms enjoy a hiatus during this market downturn, albeit brief, to take measured consideration of the risks and returns of the virtual market and decide what to do about it.

Every firm is part of a vertical chain. The number of links in the chain that a firm participates in will vary according to a number of factors. All you need to do is one transaction well enough to become a member of other firms' value chains. Internet economics encourages firms to participate in virtual firm arrangements to harvest returns from their investments before it is too late. Consequently, in the business-to-business (B-to-B) arena, everybody is becoming a buyer from, or supplier to, everybody else.

The Internet and its related technologies make four things possible. First, it provides access to a wider set of input and customer markets, which extends its reach worldwide. Second, it increases the transparency of flows and prices of goods and services to eliminate bargaining disadvantage arising from information asymmetries. Third, it negates most barriers to entry and changes the nature of vertical relationships. Fourth, it eases the coupling and decoupling of vertical (or value) chains. The Internet and its related technologies inform new competitive considerations when linking into the vertical chain, and Internet strategies focus on how established firms (and de novo firms) can pursue the business opportunities present in these vertical chains.

The Internet is an embryonic technology where the final rules are yet to be determined. For entrenched firms, the challenge is to reposition themselves to capture value from resources by tapping the innate flexibility that a well-considered strategy provides. Ultimately, any firm must deliver something that is unique and valuable to be viable in this context. As in the past, sound strategic reasoning should underlie a firm's choices of the number and relatedness of stages in the vertical chain that a firm participates in. For de novo firms, the Internet provides a wedge for entering well-established competitive arenas— perhaps even a means of knocking incumbent firms off balance.

Old Economy Rules of Competition

Strategies for old economy industries emphasize issues of physical assets. Old economy industries are characterized by capital intensity, oligopolistic industry structures, and market imperfections (largely due to regulatory and trade barriers). Over the past decade, firms in these industries have pursued increased size and efficiency through mergers, restructuring, and outsourcing of noncore processes. Forays into information technology emphasized enterprise systems designed to enhance internal control and coordination. Newly acquired firms were standardized on a single technology platform. Internet strategies took a backseat to the search for Y2K bugs. While some moved to electronic data interchange (EDI) systems and used the Internet as one more tool in their multimedia reporting and publications kit, most firms failed to ask radical questions about their vertical chains and the need for an enduring physical presence supported by ownership of tangible assets. They did not update their competitive strategies.

Organizational Changes in the Automotive Industry

In the global automotive industry, an early bastion of B-to-B activities, the early potential and possible limits of the Internet are evident. While earlier restructuring moves featured the separation of tangentially related businesses from the parent company, today's coupling and decoupling initiatives work to keep core businesses related, but separate. The creation of Visteon (first as a separate entity within Ford Motor Company and subsequently as a wholly owned subsidiary) both preserved Ford's access to components and freed the division to develop and sell products to other automotive and powered-equipment providers. This effort created an almost $20 billion company and moved eighty-three plants and forty-nine sales, engineering, and technical centers into the Visteon organization, separating the physical assets and business decisions away from Ford automotive. The potential for growth in sales to the remaining three-quarters of the domestic auto industry was too attractive an opportunity to limit Ford's total business to a dedicated in-house component and systems provider. (Ford accounted for 24.1 percent of the U.S. combined car and truck market shares in 1999; 88 percent of Visteon Corp.'s initial business came from Ford.)

DaimlerChrysler has established a full-range e-business solution, DCX NET. This unit consolidates all of DaimlerChrysler's existing and future e-business investments and holdings. Like Visteon, DCX NET has been created with an independent governance and capital structure. In contrast to Ford, this solution appears to create a parallel structure to the existing physical and analog structure. Given the relative newness of the DaimlerChrysler merger, this approach represents a platform for digitally integrating the operations and cultures of the two entities. Adjustments of physical property are likely to follow.

Each of the automotive manufacturers has used the Internet to reinforce its global customer reach. The DaimlerChrysler web page is constructed in two languages at the home page level, befitting the company's dual country heritage. The Ford web presence has a venue for creating a purchasing link between the web surfer and Ford's dealer network. Relationships that broaden input access are less transparent. Extranets—dedicated web connections between individual suppliers and automotive manufacturers—remain relatively opaque to residential consumers.

Structural Changes in the Automotive Industry
The most interesting Internet-generated changes have been wrought on relationships among the automotive firms themselves, as well as among the vertical relationships between firms, their suppliers, and their distributors. Covisint is purported to be the largest Internet marketplace in the world; it was designed as *the* universal network of suppliers to the automotive industry. Each of the automotive firms has launched its own website for selling cars to consumers (through participating dealers that collect local taxes). More recently, DaimlerChrysler, General Motors, and the United Auto Workers (UAW) union have joined with America Online to provide access to Workscape, a central, secure source of human resources self-service solutions. In each case along the value chain, there has been an opportunity to aggregate common functions across firms to improve efficiency and drive competition toward features and functionality of products and services.

Substantive change has yet to occur in the areas that require regulatory change, as contrasted to regulatory approval. Consequently, downstream relationships continue to be vulnerable to new competitor inroads. Ford Motor has taken a lead in reaching out directly to its Ford customers, establishing portals that will keep Ford customers connected to Ford, independent of where they might locate or shop. The national dealers association provides support services to help dealers build a web presence that gets them closer to their customers. Autoby tel.com, Cars.com, Autoweb.com, and other merchandisers have worked with dealers to provide consumers with alternative channels for purchasing, financing, insuring, and servicing their new and used vehicles.

The increased transparency of flows, stocks, and prices of goods and services created by online auctions has been both a blessing and a curse for automotive firms. The emergence of online auctions for used vehicles has the potential to clear the market and allow manufacturers to do a better job of balancing new vehicle production with aftermarket sales and services. The publication of MSRP (manufacturers suggested retail price) and invoice price helps narrow the range of haggling that frequently leads to consumer dissatisfaction with the entire vehicle purchasing process. Astute automotive firms are intervening in the used-car auctioning process to retain customer loyalty to their brands.

As evidenced through these examples, rivalry today occurs at multiple levels in the value chain with Internet-enabled battles and collaborations making the competitive landscape malleable. Firms find themselves fighting with enlightened old economy firms as well as a host of new competitors and a growing range of options for doing business. As the old economy firms are forced to migrate into new economy settings by developing Internet strategies, they need to ask themselves what to keep, what to jettison, and what to add.

In addition to increasing the potential range of transaction partners and increasing strategic flexibility in value chain relationships, Internet economics offer the potential to reduce operating costs dramatically. Firms seeking guidance about what capabilities to build into their Internet strategies need answers to the following key questions:

1. What is valued in the new economy?
2. Where will the definitive battles be fought between incumbents and innovative start-ups?
3. What are the critical elements for success in the new economy?

What Is Valued in the New Economy?

Uniqueness and value still matter. Innovation, customization, availability, speed, and integrity are the key dimensions for differentiation. The germane entry barriers have been reduced to intellectual property, resource scarcity (especially scarce knowledge workers), and brand equity. Relationships with exchange partners (i.e., customers and suppliers) are paramount, but sole ownership of physical assets is less important (unless scarce or inimitable).

A new hierarchy of scarce Internet real estate approximates the power of first-mover advantages. Maslow's hierarchy of needs is still applicable, but switching costs (going from one portal to another) are nil as all Internet firms begin to look the same to customers. The greatest opportunities for mindshare exist when an enterprise gets there first and gets there often. Ubiquitous products and services with the greatest digital content—be they frequent in purchase or use—command the highest rent (hence the high potential of Bertelsmann and Napster). If the firm's growth path to ubiquity involves greater investments in handling physical content, firms like Amazon.com must access a portfolio of virtual and physical inventory-handling and delivery capabilities. Alternatively, if omnipresence is built around the creation of physical content, firms must access a portfolio of virtual and physical input sourcing and product creation capabilities.

In the new economy, customer expectations of flawless experiences have significantly escalated, while the rising number of virtual intermediaries engaged in fulfilling demands increases the risk of errors that can expand geometrically. The instantaneous nature of the Internet creates a mind-set that seeks immediate gratification in fast deliveries that are available anytime, anywhere, and in any form that a customer wishes. The consumer's highly jaded outlook desires frequent novelty, powered by speedy innovations and a fast impatience with firms that cannot conform. For now, residential customers have forgotten the meaning of vendor integrity since they perceive all vendors as being the same—an equally risky experience.

The Internet channel is merely another channel for reaching alien consumers. Vendors must be able to identify and understand customer needs, recognize whether their own goods and services can fit the bill, and subcontract tasks to reliable partners if another's goods and services are more suitable. Relationships must span widely to procure what is needed and deliver it where it is wanted. Managers must continually monitor the performance of the network of relationships and adjust the network's membership, lest the negative experience of one customer snowball into an Internet-wide bandwagon of negativity.

Battlegrounds

Now that you know what is valued, it should be easier to identify the definitive battlegrounds. Four will be key:

- Knowledge workers
- Value-chain relationships
- Brand equity
- Reputation

Competitive bidding for scarce resources, such as knowledge workers, tests the nerves and pocketbooks of the most experienced business leaders. Knowledge workers best understand how to leverage the previous experience and relationships of the firm to get the job done right. Competitors—incumbent and new alike—need to extend their presence by trying to recruit critical boundary-spanning knowledge workers such as purchasing managers and sales managers. Preventative measures to retain knowledge workers must be launched now.

The Internet reduces information asymmetries by making value-chain markups transparent. Distributors and intermediaries will be dislocated when web-revealed markups are deemed unjustified by those paying for such margins. Severe channel dislocations will occur where no legal protection exists for bypassing dealer networks and small retailers that add no value to online transactions.

A brand is powerful, simplifying shorthand for features, functionality, and reliability offered to customers, especially in the B-to-B space. Since dot-com firms have behaved as though they believed that first-mover advantages existed when advertising more aggressively than their cash flows could support, any valuation of businesses now contemplated in acquisition strategies should explicitly include the value of the efficacy of brands developed in this new market arena.

Reputation is the fourth field of rivalry. Working with outsourcing partners extends the reach of the firm but entails risks to reputation as well as brand equity. Firms must become adroit at risk management to screen out partners that endanger in-house capabilities while defending the firm's established market positions and good name. Expect protracted publicized legal battles over rights to domain names. For example, Nissan Motors—originally selling in the U.S. under the Datsun brand name—appears to own every possible domain name that includes "Nissan," but has yet to secure rights to using "Nissan.com." The Internet is a public venue for the anonymous expression of displeasure—by customers, employees, suppliers, investors, competitors, and others who merely make mischief. No firm wants to discover that a website such as [your brand name here]sucks.com has become a haven for airing grievances in public. Evaluate the risks and rewards of permitting your distributors to use your brand names and trademarks to legitimize and validate their web presence, and grant such rights cautiously.

Critical Elements for Success in the New Economy

Three interrelated elements must be mastered in developing a successful Internet strategy. First, management should have a deep and thorough understanding of the success requirements for each stage of their value chain and recognize the economics associated with each stage. Understanding where rents can be collected for value created suggests where in the value chain a firm might locate its web presence, as well as how that firm is vulnerable to competitors that it might not otherwise recognize as rivals. Second, management should consider how the firm's current identity and reputation (as established by brand identity, corporate identity, and network of preexisting relationships) can be extended to dominate virtual real estate. This consideration informs the extent to which the firm needs to invest in new identity-building outlays, opportunities for reallocating assets to the new initiatives, and the risks of the Internet initiatives to the established firm. Finally, management should explicitly consider how to keep its vertical strategy flexible.

Locating the Firm's Web Presence

Every firm should strive to become an "exchange"; this means being a value-added provider to suppliers and customers alike. Only those entities that are at the first step in the value chain—raw material extraction—or those who are at the last step in consumables—need to do one transaction. Else, there would be no need for intermediate stages in a value chain. For example, in consumer durables, an ongoing relationship with a consumer can alter a customer-facing organization into opportunities to sell new and trade used.

To develop a "source and apply" bargaining chip, management must understand what the firm is best at doing and make it readily available to others. A firm should also use this time to review and to remediate unfair bargaining positions that are likely to be revealed as prices at each successive stage of the value chain become transparent. Be sure to accommodate considerations of product, service, and market breadth at each stage.

As a portal to suppliers, you are their vendor. Their input has value in use that comes from your unique ability to transform their inputs into more appealing offerings. Your value may come from bundling with other suppliers' inputs, providing immediate availability in critical "in use" settings (such as parts provided by Caterpillar's network of dealers), or providing installation and aftermarket service.

As a portal to customers, you are their supplier. You are the first stop that loyal customers make when seeking anything online. Your role is to make critical assessments of input providers and assure the customers the best possible experience to ensure their frequent return. Here sustainable advantages may arise from breadth or depth of offering, apprising customers of new features and functionality, or monitoring performance and wear of an intermediate good in use.

If your firm becomes a successful marketplace exchange, its management must prioritize which transaction perspective will be favored and recognize that misrepresentation of exchange partners' positions will be an incentive for trading partners to trade through other exchanges or go direct. Established firms are very leery of the value offered by exchanges. For example, General Electric does not let another business come between GE and a GE customer. Instead GE forces itself to transform faster and more dramatically than would be necessary in an uncontested arena. GE recognizes the magnitude of the prize that victors can claim in the coming battle and fights aggressively to preserve its relationship capital.

Being or Becoming Known

Uniqueness and value reside in the mind of the exchange partner. For established firms, it is critical to understand the value of one's own business identity. A reputation is a very fragile asset to entrust to the care of partners. To the extent that partners represent the firm, they create (or destroy) its reputation by their actions (or lack thereof).

For a new firm, the goal is getting your name in front of the public. Burn rates have largely been reflected in advertising expenditures and delivery platforms to buy market share. New firms must put their products or services into use. Good customer experiences will be the basis for subsequent transactions. Customer disappointment and negative feedback require immediate attention. Positive online feedback offers opportunities to reinforce your brand positively at the speed of light.

Building and Extending What You Are Known and Respected For

Once a firm has established the strength of its bargaining chip, it must consider how to leverage that chip into a portfolio of related competencies. Once an exchange partner is able to locate you, you have an opportunity to continue and build a relationship according to your partners' transaction preferences. Do not presume that because they found you online that they are disinterested in other forms of interaction. The Internet is merely one of several distribution channels for reaching customers. While the Web extends the firm's reach, the jury is still out on how the Web accommodates the richness of a relationship. Therefore, be sure to reinforce a virtual presence with a host of relationship options, especially where product complexity and customization are considerations. Web inquiries about highly engineered products are commonly supplemented by telephone call responses.

A reputation for innovation may be parlayed into capabilities for applying knowledge to facilitate customization. A reputation for customization may be extended back into capabilities for assessing and accessing innovation. Internal streamlining may be parlayed into capabilities for finding ways to anticipate customer needs, obtain what they desire, and deliver it quickly. A reputation for knowing and understanding customers' needs may be extended back into the creation of product platforms to foster creation of a family of products ready to meet evolving customer needs. (This is how Sony Corp. manages its family of consumer electronics products.) Strong internal systems may be parlayed into the yet-untapped benefit of trust and vendor integrity—by demonstrating the importance of delivering private transactions as promised.

Words of Wisdom for Balancing the Old and the New

Use your bargaining chip to gain entrance to the best vertical chains. As a customer-oriented partner, your role is to find solutions for the customer. As a supplier-oriented partner, your role is to find applications for the supplier. Understand whose interests you are representing and manage your network accordingly. Do not take extant value-chain relationships for granted. In particular, do not assume that existing customers or suppliers are automatically interested in replicating their relationship with your firm when they transact online. Although you may offer partners the convenience of anytime, anywhere availability of online transactions offered twenty-four hours a day, seven days a week, fifty-two weeks a year, the global scope of the Internet may introduce partners to new trading alternatives. Above all, be sensitive to new customer impatience associated with the terms "stockouts" and "backorders."

Continuously upgrade your bargaining chip to keep the attraction alive. Follow the product or service into use and learn. Do not rush to jettison the old business infrastructures and practices until all laggard customers have been migrated to the new ones. Markets can and should be segmented by the risk aversion of the customer; laggards need love, too. Highly depreciated production assets may find economic utilization in other applications.

Be focused, but don't get "set in your network." Recognize that the Web automatically extends geographic reach. A failure to provide language alternatives may increase the nationalistic identity of a company and hamper its global initiatives. Hear the voice of the customer.

Unmet expectations should be accommodated. Build a measure of customer delight as an insurance policy into every transaction to manage risk. Discourage switching by building a bank account of customer guilt. Run rich and lean at the same time.

Avoid becoming "set in your network" by evaluating your partners continually as they evaluate you. The grass may well be greener on the other side of e-space. Continuously strive to improve and do better. A limiting factor is the number of conversations you can sustain, especially where features and functionality cannot be adequately represented in physical specifications and brochureware. This requires that all firms have backroom strength to support transactions. A cadre of skilled customer service representatives will be required to explain the range of options and serve customer needs in ever-shortening windows of buying interest.

Finally, recognize that although brokerage may be a first step in bringing suppliers and buyers together, as a business model, even infomediation is likely to be unsustainable. If the only value added is in introducing a supplier to a customer, trading partners have little need to trade through your exchange during their ongoing relationship. The information you provide to foster trade between them must offer unique insights not found in other infomediaries, and there must be reasons to return to your exchange for future trading.

CHAPTER 4

Regulatory Issues in E-Commerce

Richard Taylor, Institute for Information Policy, College of Communications,
The Pennsylvania State University
Elliot Maxwell, U.S. Department of Commerce

More than ever, corporate management needs to understand the global issues shaping electronic commerce and participate in the global public discourse around them. The success or failure of particular industries or companies will be critically affected by choices in the area of policy, law, and regulation—the policy environment that provides the overall context in which e-commerce operates. While some may favor a hands-off policy, having no "rules of the road" could result in market disruptions, loss of consumer confidence, and technical chaos. On the other hand, having rules that are too onerous could impose restrictions, administrative burdens, and costs that would make e-commerce unfeasible without accomplishing the desired policy goals. This chapter focuses on selected issues that have been at the core of many policy discussions: jurisdiction, privacy, consumer protection, taxation, intellectual property, content regulation, and the global digital divide.

E-commerce has emerged at a time when the regulatory environment is historically congenial, following the end of the bipolar (U.S.–U.S.S.R.) geopolitical system and riding the crest of longer-term trends

Note: The views expressed in this chapter are those of the authors and do not necessarily reflect the view of any other employee or entity of the U.S. government or The Pennsylvania State University.

toward expanded global trade, open markets, privatization, and deregulation—all founded in a belief that free markets are the best way to allocate scarce resources, drive national growth, and produce the greatest economic benefits for the greatest number. At the same time, there is recognition that the working of markets does not always produce desired social policy outcomes; thus, for example, the concern about a global digital divide (GDD). The phrase *global digital divide* is commonly used to convey the belief that, unless positive action is taken to help less developed countries, billions of people may not benefit from the revolution in information technologies, widening the gaps between the haves and the have-nots, to everyone's long-term detriment. And some issues, such as privacy and consumer protection, cannot be addressed without an understanding of local values.

The rapid spread of e-commerce has been facilitated by developments in telecommunications infrastructure and information technology that permit an unimpeded global flow of communications, information, and financial resources. These factors have also contributed to the globalization of the corporate enterprise through vertical and horizontal expansion, mergers and acquisitions, partnerships, and alliances.

It has been widely remarked that the Internet, by the nature of its technology, is inherently global, does not recognize national borders, and is equally accessible to any person who can get a network connection. At its best, it can connect any person to any other person, or give any person access to any content. At some future date, technological means may make it possible to identify particular users and to treat them uniquely. Given the rapid rate of technology change, it is almost certain that we will see new capabilities used both for business and regulation become part of the fabric of the Internet.[1]

Another overarching concept related to e-commerce is globalization, which for many people captures the idea of global economic growth and increased prosperity for all. However, for some it is imagined in a darker way, as an idea that suggests a surrender of national sovereignty to global multilateral and corporate forces, accompanied by growing inequality, reduced social welfare, abuse of workers and children, and environmental and cultural spoliation.[2] Since e-commerce is seen as a main driver of globalization, it can potentially be the target of concerns raised in Seattle and Davos, Switzerland and Washington, D.C. The expression of these critical views has already had some impact on policymakers and may, in the future, bring these concerns before global policymaking bodies.

Although electronic commerce has in just a few years become a leading global topic, discussed and debated in high places, the initial terms of the policy discourse were set by the United States. The U.S. was, of course, the leader in the development of the Internet; is the home of the largest number of Internet users, websites, and electronic businesses; and arguably has the most to gain or lose from the success of global electronic commerce. The response of other nations, individually or collectively, can be seen as reactive to this backdrop, either pro or con. Thus, before discussing events in international forums, a brief description of U.S. policy is appropriate.

U.S. Policy

On July 1, 1997, the Clinton administration released its proposal, "A Framework for Global Electronic Commerce."[3] In general, it recommended that the nations of the world refrain from regulation and taxation of electronic commerce. It set out five principles, which are still the core of U.S. electronic commerce policy:

1. The private sector should lead.
2. Governments should avoid undue restrictions on electronic commerce.
3. Where governmental involvement is needed, its aim should be to support and enforce a predictable, minimalist, consistent, and simple legal environment for electronic commerce.
4. Governments should recognize the unique qualities of the Internet.
5. Electronic commerce over the Internet should be facilitated on a global basis.

The first three principles are fairly self-explanatory. The fourth principle relates to the concept that, due to the Internet's unique capabilities, e-commerce functions in the virtual world may find different forms of implementation than in the physical world, and policymakers should recognize the difference. However, the challenge is to give life to the spirit of traditional rules in a constantly mutating environment. The fifth principle—a global approach—has been the foundation of U.S. policy from the beginning, driving others to think, not locally or regionally, but globally.

The framework identified potential problem areas, including taxes and duties, restrictions on the type of information transmitted, control over standards development, and the possible imposition of public-utility forms of regulation on services offered. Its goal was to deter prescriptive regulation until the nature of e-commerce was better understood and problems identified. To implement this, it suggested that it was critical for governments to adopt a nonregulatory, market-oriented approach to electronic commerce and provide a transparent and enabling legal environment that would foster e-commerce and growth. The framework was followed by a second issuance, "The Emerging Digital Economy Report,"[4] in April 1998, which offered a detailed understanding of what the United States saw to be the promise of electronic commerce—a future of opportunity and prosperity.

The 1998 report noted that businesses had raised three potential inhibitors to the widespread adoption of Internet commerce:

- The lack of a predictable legal environment
- Concerns that governments will overtax the Internet
- Uncertainty about the Internet's reliability and security

These issues continue to be areas of deliberation and concern.

This, then, has been the U.S. position: The role of government is to promote and support electronic commerce; regulations should enable such commerce, particularly on a global basis; there should be no undue burdens on such commerce; private industry should take the lead in the development of policy and should embrace self-regulation in its own long-term enlightened self-interest; and industry and governmental action should be consistent with the fundamental values of society, such as the protection of privacy and protection of consumers.

While much of the tone of the U.S. position has been internationally accepted, there are a number of ongoing differences over important policy issues. These debates are occurring in a number of international institutions. (Subsequent sections within this chapter describe the global organizations that are playing a role and the most salient issues whose resolution could have a major impact on the overall environment for electronic commerce.)

Electronic commerce and the use—and potential abuse—of the Internet generally raise numerous policy, legal, and regulatory issues, not all of which can be addressed here. It is the authors' intention to describe the framework of the discourse, to place the issues in context, to underscore their significance, to describe the process leading to a global e-commerce regime, and to point to the need for business engagement.

E-Commerce on the Global Agenda

It would be relatively unusual for a book about business strategic issues to include discussion of the deliberations of multiple international bodies. However, in the case of electronic commerce, where the ground rules are still being fashioned, the decisions of such groups can have a profound effect on fundamental business operations. Thus, it is more than useful—it is necessary—for executives to be cognizant of the role of international organizations in making the rules of the game. These proceedings take place in a wide range of multilateral organizations.

The major entities and their roles—first global, then regional—are described in the following sections.

Global Forums

The World Trade Organization (WTO)

The WTO, composed of 139 member countries and dedicated to promoting free trade and open markets, has asserted that electronic commerce falls under its jurisdiction. It has been considering the issue for several years. In 1998, it issued a document, "Special Studies: Electronic Commerce and the Role of the WTO."[5] In that year, WTO members agreed to a moratorium on imposing customs duties on electronic commerce (continuing the existing practice of not tariffing e-mails or faxes). The growing importance of electronic commerce in global trade led the WTO's members to adopt a declaration on global electronic commerce in May 1998. The declaration directed the WTO General Council to examine all trade-related issues arising from electronic commerce and to report on its progress at the next conference in Seattle in December 1999. This project was referred to several bodies: the Council for Trade in Services, the Council for Trade in Goods, the Council for Trade Related Intellectual Property Services, and the Committee on Trade and Development. Each of these bodies produced a report by the end of July 1999. These reports addressed a number of issues, including the classification of transactions on the Internet as either "goods" or "services." These classifications led to different regulatory treatment, and the topic continues to be discussed in the WTO.

The Organization for Economic Cooperation and Development (OECD)

The OECD is an international organization of the industrialized, market-economy countries, with twenty-nine members. It has historically been involved in related policy concerns such as privacy and transborder data flows and tax security policies. In 1997, the OECD released a report on the "Emergence of Electronic Commerce"[6] and sponsored a conference on "Dismantling the Barriers to Global Electronic Commerce." These events laid the foundation for the OECD Ministerial Conference in 1998 with the theme "A Borderless World—Realizing the Potential of Global Electronic Commerce." This conference addressed numerous aspects of electronic commerce, and in a later section within this chapter on "The Emerging World Perspective on Electronic Commerce Policy," we further cover specific policies and actions of the OECD. What is most important to point out, however, is that the decisions of the OECD have great influence because its members represent the bulk of the world's trade, and nonmember countries sometimes are motivated to conform to OECD policies to fully participate in the global trading system.

The G-8

The leading Group of Eight (G-8) nations—the United States, Russia, France, United Kingdom, Italy, Germany, Canada, and Japan—have collectively taken up issues of electronic commerce. At its meeting in July 2000, the G-8 approved the "Okinawa Charter on Global Information Society,"[7] which offered a vision of social welfare and democracy driven by information technology and electronic commerce. It approved a set of principles that stated, among other things, that the G-8 members and others should:

- Facilitate cross-border e-commerce by promoting further liberalization and improvement in networks and related services and procedures in the context of a strong World Trade Organization framework; continued work on e-commerce in the WTO and other international forums; and application of existing WTO trade disciplines to e-commerce.
- Take consistent approaches to taxation of e-commerce based on the conventional principles of neutrality, equity, and simplicity, and other key elements agreed to in the work of the OECD.
- Continue the practice of not imposing customs duties on electronic transmissions, pending the review at the next WTO Ministerial Conference.

The G-8 also adopted principles regarding interoperability, self-regulatory initiatives, privacy protection and electronic authentication, and bridging the global digital divide.

The International Telecommunications Union (ITU)

The ITU, with 189 member countries, is the specialized agency of the United Nations charged with coordinating issues in international telecommunications. In recent years, it has also interpreted its mandate to include assisting less developed countries in expanding their telecommunications infrastructures and in developing the telecommunications foundations of electronic commerce.

The ITU has been supporting the WTO's move toward open and competitive markets, with a primary emphasis on the development of infrastructure. Its World Telecommunications Policy Forum in 1998 addressed opening telecommunications markets in developing countries. This was followed by the second World Telecommunications Development Conference in 1999, at which delegates adopted the "Valetta Declaration and Action Plan"[8] covering many issues of electronic commerce.

The ITU also adopted the "Electronic Commerce for Developing Countries" (EC-DC) initiative, which crosses a number of ITU programs aimed at bridging the digital divide. With seed funds from revenues generated by ITU TELECOM events and project implementation funded mostly by public and private sector organizations, EC-DC has the following objectives:

- Infrastructure Development
- Human Resources Development
- Policies and Strategies for E-business
- Partnership with Industry[9]

E-business infrastructure is currently being deployed in more than eighty countries under the EC-DC project. Because of the ITU's historical roots in the world of telephony and a membership that includes many countries that have not yet liberalized their telecommunications sectors, many e-commerce advocates have been wary of this group's involvement in Internet issues for fear of the imposition of telecom regulation or telecom-charging arrangements. There is widespread support, however, for its efforts to stimulate the development of the underlying telecommunications infrastructure.

The United Nations (U.N.)

Various bodies of the United Nations are addressing issues of electronic commerce. The United Nations Commission on International Trade Law (UNCITRAL) adopted a "Model Law on Electronic Commerce"[10] as early as 1996. In 1997, UNCITRAL charged its Electronic Commerce Working Group with harmonizing the law on electronic signatures and certification authorities in order to increase the use of electronic signatures in international commerce. The working group met in 1998, 1999, and 2000 to consider a set of general principles based on the 1996 model law[11] and has issued a draft model law on electronic signatures, which will be considered by the commission at its June 2001 meeting. In 1997, the United Nations Educational, Scientific, and Cultural Organization (UNESCO) held a conference addressing the "Ethical, Legal, and Social Aspects of Digital Information," and in 1998 the U.N. Commission on Trade and Development (UNCTAD) sponsored a conference on electronic commerce. (The role of UNCTAD with respect to the global digital divide is mentioned further in the section on "The Emerging World Perspective on Electronic Commerce Policy.")

The World Intellectual Property Organization (WIPO)

WIPO is a specialized agency of the United Nations whose mandate is to promote the protection of intellectual property worldwide. WIPO administers some twenty-one treaties in the field of intellectual property.[12] Action may be taken under the WIPO treaties with respect to issues regarding copyright and trademark online. These include the WIPO Performances and Phonograms Treaty of 1996, the WIPO Copyright Treaty of 1996 (both of which have been ratified by the United States and set out rules for the treatment of intellectual property in the digital environment), the Trademark Law Treaty of 1994, and the Berne Convention for the Protection of Literary and Artistic Works.[13] WIPO also offers an online "Primer on Electronic Commerce and Intellectual Property."[14]

Specifically in the digital online domain, WIPO offers alternative dispute resolution services with respect to Internet domain name disputes, and WIPO panels have already heard and resolved hundreds of such complaints.

Regional Organizations

The trend toward globalization of major policy and regulatory concerns has been accompanied by a trend toward regionalization—regional organizations sharing and coordinating their views and either bringing them to the global organizations or deciding to address issues within the region in their own particular fashion. In this respect, the world is being roughly divided into Europe, Asia-Pacific, and the Americas, a tripolar world of trade to replace the old bipolar world of geopolitics. The roles of these regional groups in setting policy should not be underestimated, as they are often the leaders in bringing issues before global institutions. Even if the global organizations do not resolve issues, the regional organizations may still choose to deal with them on a regional basis, but with potentially significant impact on the Internet globally. Regional rules may, for example, go beyond the existing WTO regime in terms of even further broadening of trade commitments. Alternatively, in some cases, regional decisions could create constraints on electronic commerce development.

The European Union (E.U.)

The E.U. has been the most active of all of the regional organizations in developing directives and policies regarding electronic commerce. There was a joint U.S.–E.U. Statement on Electronic Commerce in 1997,[15] but disagreement remained at that time on issues of privacy, encryption, content regulation, and technical management of the Internet. Most of these concerns have subsequently been addressed. The underlying tension is, in significant part, an artifact of different historical and legal approaches to regulation—a European "civil law" (i.e., rules-oriented) approach clashing with an American "common law" (i.e., exceptions-oriented) tradition. In the civil law approach, the creation of rules is necessary to permit action (such as e-commerce), whereas in the common law approach, any action may be taken that is in compliance with existing laws, such as those for consumer protection, but without a need for specific authorization. Thus, the European tradition virtually compels a set of detailed rules, while the American tradition prefers to deal with problems as they emerge.

By 2001, the European Union plans to have in place a broad set of guidelines for conducting business over the Internet. The regulatory efforts focus on four aspects of online business:

- Copyright
- Electronic signatures
- Electronic commerce
- Electronic money

The four directives will join a separate directive covering data protection approved in October 1998. The directives covering e-commerce address issues of jurisdiction, in some cases suggesting that the law of the merchant's country should prevail, but this is in conflict with other exceptions carved out for consumers to sue in the courts of their own countries.

Asia Pacific Economic Cooperation (APEC)

APEC is the primary vehicle for promoting open trade and economic cooperation in the Asia-Pacific region, and its twenty-one members include all of the major economies of the region. In 1997, the APEC leadership directed the development of a program on electronic commerce in the region. In 1998, senior APEC officials met in Penang, Malaysia and established a task force to work on an electronic commerce program. In 1999, APEC and the Pacific Economic Cooperation Council (PECC) jointly sponsored a meeting on electronic commerce in Brunei Darussalam where the recommendations of the task force were presented. They provided common principles for promoting the use of electronic commerce in the APEC region and identified ways that APEC could effectively contribute to the wider development of global electronic commerce. APEC, in cooperation with other regional and industry groups, has an ongoing program to study and develop regional electronic commerce. On July 28, 2000, recognizing the enormous potential of electronic commerce to expand business opportunities, reduce costs, increase efficiency, improve the quality of life, and facilitate the greater participation of small business in global commerce, APEC released its "Blueprint for Action on Electronic Commerce."[16] The blueprint sets forth a number of steps for the enhancement of electronic commerce in the region.

NAFTA, Mercosur, and the Free Trade Area of the Americas (FTAA)

Regional trade in the Western Hemisphere is primarily represented through two groups: the North American Free Trade Agreement (North America) and Mercosur (South America, formed by an agreement between Argentina, Brazil, Paraguay, and Uruguay). However, movement is under way to create a comprehensive regional Free Trade Area of the Americas, which includes consideration of electronic commerce. At the Second Summit of the Americas in 1998, thirty-four Western Hemisphere leaders initiated negotiations to create the FTAA no later than the year 2005. They formed a joint committee of e-commerce experts and mandated it, among other things, to make recommendations on how to increase and broaden the benefits of electronic commerce. The report was released to the public in November 1999. Its recommendations on increasing and broadening the benefits of electronic commerce were drafted with the participation of government and private experts from all over the hemisphere.[17] The second report of the joint committee is due to be delivered to the ministers in April 2001.

Other Organizations

Other multilateral, nongovernmental, and business organizations are engaged both in policy discussions and in action in the area of electronic commerce. These include, but are not limited to, the World Bank and International Monetary Fund (IMF), the International Chambers of Commerce, the Global Business Dialogue on Electronic Commerce,[18] the Trans Atlantic Business Dialog, and the Global Information Infrastructure Commission.

The Emerging World Perspective on Electronic Commerce Policy

The Process: The Challenge of "Policy Interoperability"

It is possible that all of this discussion in international bodies will eventually result in the emergence of a consensus, at least among most developed nations, on an international law of electronic commerce, perhaps not embodied in a single code or adopted fully by all countries, but one to which businesses could look for guidance to avoid running afoul of criminal prosecutions, civil lawsuits, or regulatory roadblocks when dealing with residents of other countries. On the other hand, given the divergence of legal, cultural, and historical legacies, it is also possible—perhaps likely—that such a unified field theory of electronic commerce will not emerge, at least not anytime soon. In that case, the best one can work for, to use a computer network metaphor, is "interoperability" of national laws and policies so as to minimize disputes and allow e-commerce to grow globally. The "safe harbor" agreement that bridged disparate E.U. and U.S. rules on privacy was such an interoperability mechanism that allowed the continuation of e-commerce transactions but accommodated two different legal regimes.

Some of the critical policy issues that have acquired international saliency include jurisdiction, privacy, consumer protection, taxation, intellectual property, content regulation, and the global digital divide.

The Issues

Jurisdiction

Where can your company be sued for its online behavior? Where can it sue, if it needs to enforce contracts or collect debts? And what law will apply in those cases? These can be extremely important questions—executives may even risk jail terms—depending on the answer. Anyone doing business in cyberspace needs to know what laws to obey, what taxes to pay, and what consumer protections must be applied to the sale of products and services. In the physical world, the answer is often straightforward and occasionally complex, but finding the rule is facilitated by the existence of a large number of precedents. Not so in cyberspace.

One of the most vexing legal issues raised by use of the Internet is that of "jurisdiction" in cyberspace—that is, deciding which courts have the power to take control of, preside over, and pass enforceable judgments with respect to a given case involving online behavior. In the United States and several other countries, jurisdiction is usually based on physical presence within a territory or some kind of minimum contacts ("nexus") with a territory, over which a court has authority (and, in the United States at least, also on whether the assertion of such jurisdiction is "fair"). In traditional bricks-and-mortar commerce, the physical location of the parties and the place of the transaction can usually be clearly identified, even if there is a dispute as to whether a particular court's power may reach them. In some countries, jurisdiction may be available based on the citizenship of the plaintiff without any analysis of a company's contacts with that jurisdiction.

Online, it is much more difficult to say where a transaction takes place, and perhaps even where a participant is located or whether a particular party was involved in the transaction. Does it take place at the location of the buyer (which could be any country) or of the seller (likewise)? Does it take place at the location of the Internet service provider (ISP) or the server where the website is located, or at a legal address, or where an order is placed or a product made, stored, or shipped, or in locations through which the message passes? Or does the transaction take place at all of these locations? It is easy to multiply examples of mind-boggling complexity. Courts increasingly must ask to what extent electronic contacts with their state provide a basis for jurisdiction.

Put bluntly, is a business, just because it has a corporate website, which by definition is available globally, subject to the jurisdiction of every country (and subunit) in the world?[19] Can a company be called to account for its website content, its marketing, its consumer relations, and its products, anywhere, anytime? At present, the answer seems to be an unequivocal "maybe." A definitive answer has yet to emerge,[20] and it appears that even the final answer may be "it depends," with respect to particular applications.

Cyberspace has been considered a virtual place, and many people have thought that the Internet was beyond the reach of government control. But a case in a court in France is questioning that assumption—with possible widespread repercussions for online businesses everywhere.

The case that moved the court to act is a sensitive one: Two French antiracist organizations brought civil and criminal charges against Yahoo! and its French subsidiary, which was established to serve French citizens and to comply with French law, for hosting a U.S. auction site that contains Nazi paraphernalia. Yahoo! argued that its business activities in France were directed through its French subsidiary's French language site, which obeyed French law, but the court found that French citizens could still access the U.S. site. Such an activity is legal in the United States, where the site is located, but illegal in France, where web surfers can access both of Yahoo!'s sites (not only Yahoo.fr, but Yahoo.com). A Paris judge commissioned a panel of experts—one French, one European, and one American—to determine whether it is feasible to block online content based on the location of users. The panel determined that no remedy could screen all French users, but that it would be possible to detect 70 percent of them, a figure that Yahoo! disputes. Based on this, the judge ordered Yahoo! to block French users from accessing Nazi memorabilia on its U.S.-based website, with a potential fine of about $13,000 U.S. dollars per day for failure to do so.[21]

As of January 10, 2001, Yahoo! banned all Nazi-related material from its commercial sites. At the same time, it has appealed to a U.S. Federal Court in San Jose, California, to block the French court from enforcing its order.[22]

The large U.S. web auction site eBay removed Nazi memorabilia from its site last year after German groups threatened legal action; like France, Germany bans trade in Nazi wares. The fear among Internet firms is that the French case will be used as a precedent elsewhere, forcing websites to self-police all online content and activities and making them comply with any number of laws from any country or community. The site would then be liable for damages or criminal penalties wherever the Web is accessible. In the current case, Yahoo! has argued before the court that it is technically unfeasible to block access to users based on geography, placing a huge cost burden on online businesses.

To address the issue of jurisdiction, the American Bar Association Section of Business Law in July 2000 released a report, "Achieving Legal and Business Order in Cyberspace: A Report on Global Jurisdiction Issues Created by the Internet."[23] Regarding data protection, for example, the study states, "The proliferation of privacy laws with different specific requirements threatens confusion and jurisdictional conflict, especially since the most recent laws tend to assert a far-reaching jurisdiction to control activities involving data about local consumers." The report encourages the establishment of a "Global Online Standards Commission" to develop uniform principles and global protocol standards, as well as new online forms of dispute resolution.

Issues of jurisdiction become particularly salient in the area of consumer law. Many nations feel strongly that if their citizens are "wronged" in a consumer transaction, they should be able to seek relief in local courts in that country. Thus, one possible rule in this area would simply be that the jurisdiction of the consumer applies in all consumer transactions (i.e., the "law of the consumer," often referred to as "country of destination" jurisdiction). However, it is argued that, for a business, analysis of the laws of all possible jurisdictions, and of every possible transaction, would be very costly and could result in increasing the price to the consumer or limiting the merchant's offerings altogether.[24]

Thus, some businesses are suggesting that the consumer protection law of the jurisdiction of the merchant apply to all transactions (i.e., the "law of the merchant," also referred to as "country of origin" jurisdiction). This is the approach currently being advocated by the Global Business Dialogue on Electronic Commerce, among other industry groups. This approach is strongly resisted by consumer groups and the European Union. They express concern about merchants "shopping" to find the jurisdictions with the legal frameworks most favorable to their business (i.e., engaging in a "race to the bottom" on consumer protection). Another approach (discussed in greater detail in this chapter's section on consumer protection) is to develop a uniform global set of consumer protection guidelines for all transactions on the Internet. This would likely be an extraordinarily difficult and time-consuming path, given the breadth and array of different consumer protection laws in the more than 200 countries around the world and their subnational divisions. This effort could conceivably be sought through an international organization such as the OECD or through one or more treaties. A much more practical and realistic approach is reflected in the efforts to develop simple, cost-effective online alternative dispute resolution systems to reduce the number of disputes that would trigger jurisdictional conflicts.

At present, jurisdiction over Internet transactions is being worked out on a case-by-case basis with no universal rule, but the mainstream of the results seems to be that it depends on the extent and type of contacts with the state in question.[25]

Privacy

Across national and regional boundaries there are differing concepts of privacy and its appropriate enforcement mechanisms—public or private. Privacy is at once a consumer, a policy, and a business issue. To the extent that consumers are concerned about the security of their personal information or financial transactions over the Internet, the growth of business-to-consumer (B-to-C) electronic commerce will be deterred. Different national and regional standards regarding the protection of privacy may impair the ability of companies to offer products or services or transfer information or do business across borders. There has been a strong interest among global, regional, and U.S. national organizations with respect to the protection of online privacy.

The OECD Privacy Principles—In 1980 the OECD was the first international organization to issue a policy for the protection of privacy in computerized data processing. The OECD principles identified in its 1980 guidelines[26] outlined the rights and obligations of individuals in the context of automated processing of personal data and the rights and obligations of those who engage in such processing. The guidelines apply to personal data, whether in the public or private sectors, that poses a danger to privacy and individual liberties because of the manner in which it is processed, or because of its nature or the context in which it is used. These technologically neutral principles are still being used—both in the public and private sectors—and are included in a large number of national and international instruments.

In 1998 the OECD group of experts on information security and privacy decided a current statement for the OECD ministers should be drafted. The statement would express the view that privacy concerns require greater attention in view of recent developments in network technologies. The 1998 Ministerial Declaration on Privacy reaffirmed that the principles outlined in the 1980 guidelines are still valid throughout the world.

E.U. Privacy Protections—In 1998, the European Union Data Protection Directive[27] threatened to disrupt the export of personal data covered by the E.U. directive from Europe to companies in countries whose privacy laws were not deemed "adequate" by the European Union. Taken literally, this could have had a substantial impact on U.S. businesses. For example, multinational businesses that transmitted credit card billing information, human resources data, or other personal information from Europe to the United States could be ordered to suspend such operations. This led to extensive negotiations between the E.U. and the U.S., which did not want to impose a national legislative privacy regime but preferred codes of conduct and industry self-regulation in conjunction with sector-specific legislation regarding sensitive information. This was another classic example of the clash of different conceptualizations of legal structures—but one that, so far, has had a positive outcome that may serve as a model for bridging conflicting legal regimes.

The United States and the European Union have taken steps to conclude a safe harbor Data Privacy Accord that will protect consumers' privacy, maintain data flows, and create the right environment for e-commerce. The accord will help U.S. organizations comply with the European privacy law and prevent the potential disruption of approximately $120 billion in U.S.–E.U. trade.

Safe harbor is a mechanism that, through an exchange of documents, enables the E.U. to certify that participating U.S. companies meet the E.U. requirement for adequate privacy protection. Participation in the safe harbor is entirely voluntary. Companies need to agree to adhere to the privacy requirements laid out in the safe harbor documents for all data received from the European Union and are subject to penalties for a failure to live up to their undertakings.

U.S. Privacy Principles—In the U.S., the Clinton administration's Information Infrastructure Task Force Privacy Working Group issued a document entitled "Privacy and National Information Infrastructure: Principles for Providing and Using Personal Information." More recently, the government lead on privacy issues has been taken by the Federal Trade Commission (FTC).[28] In 1998, it provided a report to Congress setting forth five basic principles:

1. Notice/Awareness
2. Choice/Consent
3. Access/Participation
4. Integrity/Security
5. Enforcement/Redress[29]

Several industry groups have been active in support of self-regulation. Among the leaders has been the Online Privacy Alliance, which has called for:[30]

- Adoption and Implementation of a Privacy Policy by Participating Companies
- Notice and Disclosure of Information Collected and Possible Uses

■ Choice/Consent by the Subject of the Data
■ Data Security
■ Data Quality and Access

The FTC recently released a report painting a not very encouraging picture of the industry's efforts to police itself.[31] The FTC supported legislation, finding that self-regulation had not yet provided sufficient privacy protection for U.S. consumers. Data collection by third parties such as DoubleClick Inc., with whom consumers had no direct relationship, and the sale of Social Security numbers and data beyond Social Security numbers are among the practices that have focused consumer attention on privacy.

Another reason privacy is becoming an ever-more-pressing e-business concern is the mounting laws and regulations that are following close behind expressions of consumer concern. This includes the newly passed Health Insurance Portability and Accountability Act (HIPAA), which gives healthcare providers and insurers two years from October 16, 2000 to put tighter locks on patient information. And there's the Children's Online Privacy Protection Act, passed in April 2000, which led to a set of restrictions on how private information from children can be gathered and used. Some youth-oriented sites, such as Zeeks.com, have argued that the procedures called for to implement the Act are unduly expensive and burdensome and will lead to a reduction in websites with content for children. With numerous Internet privacy bills under consideration in Congress, one thing's for sure: Given the unusually broad base of support for privacy legislation in Congress, if industry does not show it is serious about adopting meaningful privacy policies, Congress will act more aggressively in the area.[32]

While substantial progress has been made in the last several years—the percentage of sites with posted privacy policies has increased dramatically—only 20 percent of the e-commerce sites surveyed by the FTC in the spring of 2000 had posted privacy policies that complied with the OECD guidelines.

The Clinton administration's position was to acknowledge the problems, encourage further action by companies to post strong privacy policies, and proceed cautiously with legislation targeting sensitive information, such as medical, genetic, and financial records and information regarding children. It also advocated the adoption of privacy practices consistent with the OECO guidelines. The adoption of good privacy practices by companies would be strengthened by the use of "seal" programs such as TRUSTe and BBBOnLine (a subsidary of the Council of Better Business Bureaus), which help consumers identify companies that follow the guidelines, provide technology-based solutions (such as the P3P privacy protection software platform), and increase consumer education about privacy choices.

Taxation

A major emphasis of U.S. policymakers has been to keep the Internet free from discriminatory taxes and tariffs (arguably, existing taxes and tariffs could apply, if it were possible to collect them). However, taxing the growth of electronic commerce would seem to present a tempting new revenue opportunity for countries that are still developing strong modern economies.

At the same time, different locations use different kinds of taxes, presenting potentially significant problems for e-commerce. For example, European countries rely heavily on value-added taxes, while the United States employs sales and use taxes. And, of course, these taxes vary from country to country, state to state, and city to city. National and state governments are concerned about the possible loss of revenue to their communities from tax-avoidance by cyberspace firms, and about alleged unfair competition between these firms and local bricks-and-mortar businesses. While taxations of Internet sales is no different in principle from the rules currently governing "remote" sales by phone and mail-order catalog, the existing projections of business to consumer e-commerce have made the potential loss of revenue appear much more threatening to state and local authorities that rely on sales and use taxes for up to 50 percent of their revenues. The tax issue is a complicated one, and any individual company should rely on specific advice from its tax counsel as to how to proceed. In 1996, the U.S. Department of the Treasury issued a paper entitled "Selected Tax Policy Implications of Global Electronic Commerce."[33] Other major countries have also issued discussion papers on this topic. The biggest potential downside for businesses is not that electronic commerce may be subjected to the same taxation as nonelectronic commerce, but that it may be taxed more, by virtue of being subject to additional taxing jurisdictions through which all or parts of a transaction may pass. As in many other areas, existing players may attempt to use tax policy to disadvantage new entrants, particularly those that are strategically threatening.

It is theoretically possible to set up a computer system that would, in fact, keep track of all of the taxes of all of the world's major (and most minor) taxing jurisdictions. Companies may support the development of such systems. Alternatively, a special global taxing regime for electronic commerce, in which countries agree to a standardized tax regime, could arise.

The European Union is the most activist with respect to taxation. The European Commission as well as European tax administrations are very concerned about the challenges presented to taxation systems by globalization and the growth of electronic commerce. They fear that the Internet has the potential to increase tax competition by making it much easier for multinationals to shift their activities to low-tax countries.

International principles for taxing e-commerce were discussed at the OECD Ministerial Conference in Ottawa in 1998. It was agreed that, for consumption taxes, the rules should result in taxation in the jurisdiction where consumption takes place. However, the European Union's current value-added tax (VAT) rules arguably do not meet this requirement. This is because services delivered online by digital means were simply not envisaged at the time the current VAT legislation was established. Thus, when these services originate within the E.U., they are always subject to VAT irrespective of the place of consumption. On the other hand, those services originating outside the European Union are not subject to VAT even when consumed or used inside the E.U.

The current E.U. proposals are to remove the competitive handicap currently affecting E.U. providers of digitally delivered material on both the domestic and world markets by removing the obligation on E.U. suppliers to levy VAT on digital products sold to customers outside the union. At the same time, non-E.U. operators will be required to face the same tax obligations as domestic operators when they sell to consumers within the European Union.

The proposed plan is intended to be simple. For business-to-business transactions, which account for the greater part of online transactions, there is no change. Tax will continue to be accounted for in the E.U. under the reverse-charge system—in other words, traders will assess their own VAT liability.

For businesses outside the European Union, it will only be in the case of sales to consumers that they will be required to register for VAT purposes and charge VAT. Even then, the proposal applies only to the bigger players whose sales in the European Union are in excess of a certain amount—a limit that existing E.U. firms have sought to lower. The proposal was that non-E.U. firms would have the option of registering in a single member state. However, objections have been raised within Europe to the "single point of registration" plan because, it is said, it would lead companies to register only in the lowest tax jurisdiction.

European regulators point out that it is in the interests of legitimate operators to be in compliance with their legal obligations arising from Internet trading. After all, it is argued, they themselves want to ensure that others respect their rights—for example, their intellectual property rights. The incentive for voluntary compliance should not be underestimated.

Any solution requiring a non-E.U. operator to register in all member states where it may make sales would constitute a considerably heavier burden than that faced today by E.U. businesses. Moreover, the existing tax proposal would treat certain digitally delivered goods from outside the European Union in a manner different from their physical manifestations in violation of the principle of neutrality of taxation. Depending on the details of implementation and how the transactions were characterized, the European Union could be accused in the WTO of discriminating against non-E.U. businesses.

Through the OECD, the E.U. nations committed themselves to the principle that no new or special taxes should be considered for e-commerce. However, they believe that the corollary is that existing taxes can, and must, be made to work. The U.S. position is that, while discussions on taxation principles continue at the OECD, no country or region should move forward unilaterally to disturb the status quo.

It is possible to see these developments not as a problem that threatens the fundamental integrity of the tax system, but as an opportunity to modernize existing taxes and make them more efficient. E-commerce in particular has highlighted deficiencies in existing tax systems worldwide, forcing administrations to consider long-overdue reform and simplification—a process now going on at the state level in the United States.

Consumer Protection

Different countries and regions also have different concepts of consumer protection. European countries in particular tend to have very strong consumer protection rules, which have now been extended to the Internet.

OECD General Principles—The OECD has shown steady interest in developing a code of principles for consumer protection. Most recently, in 1999, member countries agreed on Recommendations of the OECD Council Concerning Guidelines for Consumer Protection in the Context of Electronic Commerce.[34] The guidelines touch on:

- Transparent and Effective Protection
- Fair Business, Advertising, and Marketing Practices
- Online Disclosures about the Business, Goods or Services, and Transaction
- Confirmation Process
- Payment
- Dispute Resolution (Legal and Alternative)
- Privacy
- Education and Awareness

Other consumer rules relate to companies contracting with consumers. In 1997, the Council and Parliament of the European Union adopted the Directive on the Protection of Consumers in Respect of Distance Contracts.[35] Under the directive, before the contract's conclusion the consumer is entitled to be informed of:

- The identity of the supplier
- Whether advance payment is required
- The address of the supplier
- The main characteristics of the goods or services
- The price of the goods or services, including all taxes
- Delivery costs
- The arrangements for payment
- Delivery of performance
- The existence of a right of withdrawal

The consumer is also entitled to receive written confirmation of the contract or confirmation in another durable medium.

Article 6 of this directive gives a right of withdrawal to the consumer. In any distance contract, the consumer has a period of at least seven working days in which to withdraw from the contract without penalty and without giving any reason. The period of seven days runs, in the case of goods, from the day of receipt by the consumer, and in the case of services, from the day of conclusion of the contract. Unless otherwise agreed, the supplier must execute the order within a maximum of thirty days from the day following that on which the consumer forwarded his order to the supplier. Failure to do so entitles the consumer to a full refund of any sums paid as soon as possible and in any case within thirty days. Article 9 of this consumer protection directive prohibits "inertia selling"—that is, the supply of goods without an order coupled with a demand for payment, or an unsolicited supply where the absence of response constitutes consent. The rights conferred by the directive are binding in nature and may not be waived by consumers or avoided by choice of jurisdiction or law provisions. An updated version of this consumer protection directive with respect to electronic commerce is currently under consideration.

The draft regulation on jurisdiction was presented by the European Parliament and Council in July 1999 with the aim of harmonizing E.U. member states' international private law on jurisdiction. The wording of the clauses on agreements signed by consumers raised concern among businesses hoping to cash in on electronic commerce. The council's proposal (Article 16) stipulates that in the event of a dispute with a supplier, consumers may bring a case before the courts in their own country on condition that the supplier "aimed its activities" at the consumer's country. Since Internet sites are in theory aimed at consumers in general, irrespective of country, e-commerce merchants feel this proposal may expose them to lawsuits in all member states. They argue that this approach discourages enterprises from launching new sites, as they would open themselves up to the possibility of court action in all of the states where these sites are capable of being received.

While it has made a great deal of progress, the European Union has not completed its e-commerce regime. When in place, it will have a profound effect on the e-commerce environment. It will deal with electronic signatures, copyright protection, advertising, and the liabilities of various players in the e-commerce value chain, among other issues.

The E.U. Directive on Electronic Signatures was adopted in December 1999 and requires all E.U. member countries to implement its terms no later than the middle of 2001. Among other things, the directive allows E.U. member states to provide for the voluntary accreditation of authentication service providers, and prohibits them from requiring prior authorization before a service provider can conduct its operations. The directive also provides that electronic signatures—regardless of the technology or method used to create them—shall not be denied legal effect solely because they are in electronic form. In addition, it expressly provides that electronic signatures that meet certain specifications shall be accorded the same legal effect as handwritten signatures, although to date the European Union has experienced substantial difficulties in identifying flexible and appropriate specifications that are necessary to implement those provisions.

The United States has a well-developed set of consumer protection rules. U.S. policy is based on the applicability of these rules in cyberspace, with the caveat that adjustments may, in the future, need to be made to take into account the unique attributes of the Internet. The U.S. government has endorsed industry efforts to develop codes of conduct and, in particular, develop easy-to-use, efficient, and cost-effective online mechanisms for the resolution of consumer disputes.

The Internet may even make it possible to use new techniques and technologies to offer consumer-oriented services that are actually better than those currently offered in the physical world—for example, those involving comparative shopping, barter, and customized offerings.

Industry Response—Self-Regulation Principles—As in the area of privacy, industry groups have been active in developing self-regulation models. Several of the world's leading Internet and e-commerce companies, assembled as a working group—AOL-Time Warner, AT&T, Dell Computer, IBM Corp., Microsoft Corp., and Network Solutions—have proposed guidelines to protect consumers online and inspire global discussion of legal issues related to consumer transactions in the borderless Internet.

The Electronic Commerce and Consumer Protection Group proposed the new "Guidelines for Merchant-to-Consumer Transactions" and a companion "Statement on Global Jurisdiction Framework for Electronic Commerce." The guidelines are a statement about best practices for web merchants. The companion statement describes how the guidelines were developed and how they may lead, after further experience, to a permanent framework that both protects consumers and enhances the growth of e-commerce.

The guidelines contain a broad range of provisions concerning marketing practices; information about goods and services; information about transactions, cancellation, return and refund policies, packaging, security, customer service, and/or support; privacy; and warranty information. They also encourage merchants to participate in third-party dispute resolution mechanisms that are fair, timely, and affordable. Alternative dispute resolution procedures are not meant to inhibit consumers addressing complaints directly to merchants or interfere with any legal rights of merchants or consumers.[36] Similarly, BBBOnLine and the Global Business Dialogue for Electronic Commerce have made great progress in developing guidelines for merchants and for trustmarks upon which consumers can rely as they deal in cyberspace.

Intellectual Property

The WTO agreement on Trade Related Aspects of Intellectual Property (TRIPS) is one source of intellectual property protection and regulation online. The TRIPS accord requires all WTO member states to guarantee strong protection of all intellectual property, including confidential information, on the basis of national treatment (i.e., treating a state's own nationals and foreigners equally) and most-favored nation treatment (i.e., equal treatment for nationals of all WTO members).[37]

As was noted earlier, the World Intellectual Property Organization also oversees international treaties and policies with respect to copyright, trademarks, and patents. WIPO has already begun to specifically address issues of intellectual property as they relate to electronic commerce. WIPO convened the first International Conference on Electronic Commerce and Intellectual Property in September 1999.[38] WIPO plans to hold its second international conference, the WIPO Expo on Electronic Commerce and Intellectual Property, in September 2001. WIPO has also produced a "Primer on Electronic Commerce and Intellectual Property Issues,"[39] which addresses a wide range of evolving issues in trademarks and unfair competition, domain names, and patents. It also speaks to special issues with respect to intellectual property and developing countries.

Since the United States is the largest producer and exporter of intellectual property, the role of U.S. copyright law takes on a special relevance. Expanded use of the Internet by businesses has spawned a variety of complex issues, as old laws need to be adapted to new technologies. The range of issues of which business executives need to be aware includes:

■ *Copyright Infringement.* The nature of the Internet allows individuals to make perfect reproductions of copyrighted works and to distribute such works almost instantaneously throughout the world with ease and anonymity at virtually no cost. A particular aspect of the Internet is the issue of copyright liability for the infringing acts of third parties using chat rooms and bulletin boards. This issue is still being decided on a case-by-case basis. New business models, such as Napster's peer-to-peer model that involves "sharing" of intellectual property, are also the basis of current litigation.

■ *Framing and Linking.* Infringement by linking, infringement by caching, and infringement by browser (copying into RAM) have all been issues.

■ *Trademarks and Domain Names.* These issues have been the source of many complaints, including against "cybersquatters" who register the trademarks of others for use online. Another area is "hidden trademark infringements" through the use of invisible (to the viewer) "metatags" that identify websites to search engines and for other purposes.[40]

The U.S. Digital Millennium Copyright Act (DMCA), passed by Congress in 1998,[41] clarifies the liability of Internet service providers for acts of infringement committed through the use of their facilities. The Act offers broad protections for ISPs that unknowingly transmit or store copyrighted material, but also requires ISPs to take specific action in order to qualify for those protections. The Act requires an ISP to remove, or disable access to, any linked, stored, or cached material when the ISP receives a written notice concerning that material, provided the notice meets certain requirements. The Act exempts the ISP from liability for taking down or blocking access to such material in response to the required notice, but also provides that failure to take down or block access pursuant to notice will result in loss of the ISP's statutory exemptions from liability. There is a further provision for counter-notification by the alleged infringer seeking to have the material reinstated.

Intellectual property is a highly specialized area, requiring expert advice. But it is up to executives to be able to spot potential issues so that they can be addressed early on, both to protect their companies' own intellectual property and to avoid crossing the line into violation of the rights of others.

Content Regulation

Issues of content regulation arise in several ways in the context of e-commerce. These include:

■ Commercial speech (e.g., advertising, marketing, and promotion)
■ Content concerning regulated products (e.g., alcohol, tobacco)

- Defamation (i.e., libel)
- Rights of privacy and use of name and likeness
- Securities regulation
- The control of licensed professions
- The protection of children
- Prohibited content

In a number of countries, access to the Internet for any reason is discouraged.

The United States is almost unique in the scope of its Constitutional protections of speech under the First Amendment, but traditionally some speech, such as outright fraud, libel, and obscenity, has been unlawful. It is safe to assume that speech that would traditionally have given rise to criminal or tort proceedings offline will be likely to do so online. But even in those cases, it may be defined differently in different jurisdictions; the jurisdictional question hangs over all of these issues.

While it is presumably not your company's plans to violate the law, challenges to your actions may arise indirectly through linking, chat rooms, or use of your site as a portal or ISP. For example, the head of CompuServe in Germany was charged—and ultimately acquitted—of violating German laws against child pornography because German citizens could access through CompuServe certain websites that displayed such materials.[42]

Scandinavian and some other European countries have laws that apply to advertising generally, with respect to amount, timing, content, and audience. These laws were created with traditional media (e.g., broadcast and print) in mind, but you should be aware of the possibility of their being interpreted to apply to online marketing or even a finding that the simple existence of a website itself constitutes an "advertisement."

If your business is online and directing the marketing of your product or service at a particular country or language group, then the conservative assumption is that you may be subject to the laws of that area with respect to advertising, marketing, and promotion. These could include rules about product claims, competitive claims, and promotional activities, especially games of chance and lotteries. And you need to be especially careful to ascertain the rules if you deal in what are often regulated products: alcohol, tobacco, cigarettes, firearms, and pharmaceuticals. In these circumstances, the fact that you are online and located outside the country may not protect you.

While (it is hoped) your company will not engage in intentional direct defamation, there is a substantial risk online from claims against you with respect to defamation by third parties who use your website's chat rooms, bulletin boards, and product review spaces. Some countries, such as the United Kingdom, have plaintiff-friendly libel laws, and under some circumstances, you could find your company being sued there. The law in this area is still evolving, but not being aware of the allegedly libelous content may be some defense (much like a common carrier is protected for unknowingly transmitting or storing copyrighted material). If your company has actual knowledge of libelous content or should, under the circumstances, have known, then liability may well arise.

Aspects of the traditional tort law of privacy may also come into play in advertising, especially with respect to individuals' right to control the use of their name and likeness. Creating images of persons that imply endorsements, or even using their voice (or sound-alikes), unique characteristics, or likeness (including look-alikes) without their (or possibly their estate's) consent, may create liability. The ability of the computer to manipulate images makes it tempting to generate "celebrity" endorsements, but they could turn out to be more expensive than anticipated.

Virtually all countries have laws with respect to some forms of prohibited content. There are categories that are close to universal (e.g., child pornography)—but even here legal definitions may differ. And there may be countries where casting aspersions on certain groups or religions or practices (i.e., "hate speech") or criticism of the government may be expressly prohibited. In addition, some countries have laws with respect to the protection of children from advertising and commercialism, so companies that could be considered to be marketing products to minors or attempting to attract minors to their websites need to be especially wary.

Other, more narrow areas that are subject to regulation include the issuance of securities and the practice of certain professions, typically licensed professions such as medicine and law. However, other areas may also be subject to certain regulation, including securities advice, real estate, and brokerage practices. Providing certain advice across national (or, in the U.S., state) borders is therefore somewhat risky. Again, laws that apply offline are not suspended just because you happen to be online.

Finally, there are general issues with respect to free speech (especially political speech) that may arise, intentionally or unintentionally (e.g., an advertisement for a favorable movie about Tibet may cause considerable consternation in China). Furthermore, there are a few countries that are concerned about the introduction of modern (no longer just "Western") values generally. These include countries in the Middle East and North Africa and some other Islamic countries, as well as autocratic countries such as Myanmar.[43]

Content regulation is an area that is still evolving. While there are, as yet, no final global answers that fit all situations, it is appropriate for responsible executives to be aware of where their customers are (or where the company is seeking them) and understand that the company may have the responsibility to abide by the laws, rules, and regulations related to commercial communications and other content of that place. It may also be important to consider joining with other businesses to seek to establish rules that will maximize the ability of Internet users to have access to the widest array of content while ensuring that users have access to tools so that they can control their own communications rather than encouraging government controls that may vary and may lead (a la Yahoo!) to a virtual French net, Chinese net, etc.

Global Digital Divide

Some senior corporate executives have already recognized that the impact of information technology (and its corollary, electronic commerce) reaches beyond the marketplace. A good example of early sensitivity to the environment was set forth in IBM Chairman Louis Gerstner's keynote address to the COMDEX conference in 1995:

> A few decades ago, there was another "defining" technology. You may remember it: nuclear power. It, too, was going to change the world. It was going to make energy as cheap as water . . . bring air conditioning to deserts, heat to frozen tundras. Reactors would power cars and ships, airplanes and spacecraft. Inexhaustible energy. But what happened? The nuclear power industry is a dormant industry today. Those grand visions were never realized. Why? Was it because of bad science, disappointing technology? Not really. While that industry was focused on megawatts and reactor cores, communities and governments were worried about the implications of that technology. They stopped the industry dead in its tracks.
>
> Today, our industry has grand visions. . . . And they are grand. And very ambitious. We're talking about no less than changing the world in very fundamental ways. Yet, too often what are we focused on?. . . Megahertz, gigabits, and multitasking. There's a disconnect between our priorities and those of a lot of people and governments. . . . [T]he time has come to step up to these challenges. Even as we continue to innovate and create, we must now also think about the broader implications for the future we are creating.[44]

How prescient those words sound now in light of the negative responses to globalization and the WTO. These are the words of a strategically sensitive businessperson operating in a global environment of e-commerce, responding to the enlightened long-term self-interest of his company and industry.

Businesses have the opportunity to demonstrate the potential of the

Internet—to open new markets, create new classes of customers, raise standards of living, and improve working conditions while expanding the trained workforce. This has led many leading businesses to support international efforts to reduce the global digital divide.

Assuring equitable access to digital technology to bring the benefits of the new economy to developing countries is now widely recognized as one of the most significant challenges of the new century. The concept of the global digital divide is an integral part of the public discourse about globalization and the impact of information technologies. Countries and regions face complex challenges in the allocation of scarce public resources to find the best path (or paths) to successfully integrate into the global economy, and to find the capital, equipment, and expertise necessary to achieve their goals.

The G-8, at its July 2000 meeting in Okinawa, extensively addressed the issue of bridging the digital divide and promoting global participation, especially for emerging and developing economies. It called for bilateral and multilateral assistance and support from international financial institutions, as well as from the private sector, naming specifically the Global Digital Divide Initiative of the World Economic Forum and the Global Business Dialogue on E-Commerce. The members agreed to establish and sponsor a Digital Opportunity Task Force to integrate these efforts.

Other international institutions also recognize this issue and are preparing to help. World Bank President James D. Wolfensohn, at the conclusion of the 2000 spring meetings of the World Bank and IMF in Washington, D.C., said that closing the digital divide is a "central aspect" of the World Bank's work. He said the Bank needs to ensure that the digital divide doesn't make the gap between rich and poor countries even wider.

Likewise, the administrator of the United Nations Development Program (UNDP), in remarks to a gathering of world leaders in Davos, Switzerland on January 31, 2000, noted that "the goal must be for information technology to deliver revolutionary breakthroughs in terms of giving the world's poor access to the global economy. If it is not addressed, the digital divide will grow. Corporations will stick to markets they know. Developing countries will keep their doors closed, and opportunities and access will be denied to millions of small entrepreneurs in the developing countries."

Conclusion: A Guide for the Perplexed

For a businessperson, this is an exciting time to take advantage of the opportunities of e-commerce. However, it is in many ways a new area, requiring new approaches—and new rules. And in the case of electronic commerce, international, regional, national, subnational, and sometimes local bodies are still formulating those rules. Having a business presence effectively everywhere in the world simply by virtue of having a website and doing business online can create many traps for the unwary. However, being too conservative about developing this area can be a distinct competitive disadvantage. What's a prudent businessperson to do? What can he or she do about issues that seem very broad and, perhaps, remote?

Rule 1: Be proactive. E-commerce is an important part of your corporate strategic, regulatory, and legal planning. There are many developments in the area of policy and regulation that can have a profound impact on your business. Learn what they are, try to understand the alternatives, and locate the appropriate place to join the public policy discourse. Advocate for uniform, clear, and consistent rules that promote—not hinder—commerce.

Rule 2: Be aware. Know the international implications of your enterprise's behavior. Be aware that it is important to identify all of the places in which you are doing business, and understand the rules that apply there. On the other hand, there may be places where you specifically do not want to be doing business. Make it expressly clear that you are not holding yourself out to do business in those places. Be aware of areas of particular sensitivity in content and in advertising and marketing techniques.

Rule 3: Be current. Regularly monitor the changing global environment. If your organization is not set up with internal resources to regularly track developments, rely on your trade association, the trade press, and other sources. Use industry groups both as resources for advice and as spokespersons for views. Take advantage of opportunities of industry meetings and trade shows to learn and to advocate appropriate positions. Join and support groups that share your views. Support research and white papers on emerging e-commerce subjects.

Rule 4: Be willing to ask for help. Get expert help when you need it—and develop the skill of spotting red flags so that you know when that is! A senior executive doesn't have to know all the answers—but does have to know when and how to get them. Areas of policy, law, and taxation all have specialist practitioners who are available to provide insights and counsel.

Rule 5: Be a leader. Never forget that if business fails to lead in these areas, and to self-regulate responsibly, there are others who are willing—indeed eager—to step in and have governments and regulatory agencies assume responsibility, which they may do with a heavy hand. Subscribe to various codes of good conduct, whether based in your industry or general, with respect to concerns such as privacy and consumer protection. This is not just good behavior, it is common sense—*trust* is one of the most important assets for success in electronic commerce, and having a good reputation is worth more than diamonds.

In the end, the lesson for executives in the environment of electronic commerce is that actions taken by government do matter. Government can help and enable, or control and channel. It can affect deeply what you can do and the success of your enterprise. It can impose rules that are constricting, or it can act to increase the confidence of all users—consumers and businesses alike. It is worth knowing about because it is important. Because it is important, it belongs in the strategic plan. And if it's important enough to be in the strategic plan, it's important enough to try to affect.

What the future e-commerce environment will look like is in large part in the hands of the business community. For better or worse, it's your future, and you need to engage in the process of shaping it. In part, it means participating in the public policy discourse, and in part, it means meeting or exceeding the expectations of consumers. It is the classic opportunity to do well by doing good—and the consequences of not aspiring to do well are very unattractive to consider. It's in your hands.

Endnotes

1 L. Lessig, *Code and Other Laws of Cyberspace* (New York: Basic Books, 1999).

2 "Anti-Capitalist Protests: Angry and Effective," *The Economist* (September 23, 2000), p. 85.

3 United States, The White House, "A Framework for Global Electronic Commerce" (Washington, D.C.: The White House, July 1, 1997). Available from: http://www.ecommerce.gov/framework.htm/ (October 22, 2000).

4 U.S. Department of Commerce, "The Emerging Digital Economy Report" (Washington, D.C.: Department of Commerce, April 15, 1998). Available from: http://www.ecommerce.gov/letter.htm/. (Access date October 22, 2000.)

5 World Trade Organization, "Special Studies: Electronic Commerce and the Role of the WTO" (Geneva: WTO, 1998).

6 Organization for Economic Cooperation and Development, "The Emergence of Electronic Commerce: An Overview of the OECD's Work," OECD Policy Brief No. 1 on Electronic Commerce (Paris: OECD, 1997). Available from: http://www.oecd.org/subject/electronic_commerce/documents/emergence.htm/ (October 21, 2000).

7 Available from: http://www.dfait-maeci.gc.ca/foreignp/g7/2000/Okinawa_Charter_GIS0722-e.asp/. (Access date October 2000.)

8 International Telecommunications Union, "The Valetta Declaration and Action

Plan: A Strategic Plan for the ITU Development Sector" (Geneva: ITU, 1998). Available from: http://www.itu.int/newsarchive/press/WTDC98/VAP1.html/ (October 23, 2000).

9 Available from: http://www.itu.int/ECDC/WTDC98-Article-on-ECDC.pdf/. (Access date October 22, 2000.)

10 U.N. Commission on International Trade Law, "UNCITRAL Model Law on Electronic Commerce" (New York: United Nations, 1996). Available from: http://www.uncitral.org/en-index.htm/ (October 21, 2000).

11 "International Commercial Transactions: 1998" (The Uniform Commercial Code Survey), *Business Lawyer* (August 1, 1999), p. 2001.

12 Available from: http://www.wipo.org/treaties/index.html/. (Access date October 22, 2000.)

13 All WIPO-administered treaties are available from: http://www.wipo.org/treaties/ip/index.html/.

14 Available from: http://ecommerce.wipo.int/primer/index.html. (Access date October 22, 2000.)

15 U.S. Department of Commerce, "U.S.–E.U. Joint Statement on Electronic Commerce" (Washington, D.C.: Department of Commerce, 1997). Available from: http://www.ecommerce.gov/ecomnews/useu.html/. (Access date October 22, 2000.)

16 Available from: http://www.apecsec.org.sg/ecotech/apecbec.html/. (Access date October 22, 2000.)

17 Available from: http://www.ftaa-alca.org/. (Access date October 22, 2000).

18 As of October 2000, the Global Business Dialogue on Electronic Commerce was emerging as a leading voice in regard to nongovernment, business-driven policies on e-commerce. More information is available at http://www.gbd.org/.

19 In a case that moves in this direction, *Cody* v. *Ward,* 954 F. Supp. 43 (D. Conn. 1997), a Connecticut court found that the bare existence of a website accessible to Connecticut citizens, combined with the availability of an 800-number that they could call, was sufficient to establish jurisdiction over an out-of-state company. In a German trademark case, it was held that, under German law, any activity on the Internet that is visible in Germany brings the actor under the jurisdiction of the German courts. A court in Berlin in 1997 enjoined use by MCN—a Kansas City web design, Internet service, and domain name brokerage firm—of concertconcept.com, concertconcept.de, concert-concept.com, and concert-concept.de as violating the rights of a German company in its trade name and mark. This case, *Landgericht Berlin,* November 20, 1996, 5 U 659/97, 97 0 193/96, was upheld on appeal March 25, 1997. The court specifically noted that it is irrelevant to German jurisdiction whether the defendant's host computer was in the United States or whether the domain was registered there. The only relevant criterion is that the website can be read in the district of the court.

20 J. Delaney and W. Schwartz, "The Law of the Internet: A Summary of U.S. Internet Caselaw and Legal Developments," in *eCommerce: Strategies for*

Success in the Digital Economy 2000 (New York: Practising Law Institute, 2000), pp. 185 et seq.

21 M. Mangalin and K. Delaney, "French Court Orders Yahoo! to Block Sale of Nazi Items," *Wall Street Journal* online edition, November 21, 2000. (Accessed November 22, 2000.)

22 Eduardo Cue, "National Boundaries: Latest Frontier in Cyberspace," *The Christian Science Monitor,* January 10, 2001, p. 1. (Accessed through *The Dow Jones Publications Library,* January 11, 2001.)

23 K. N. Cukier, "Virtual Exceptionalism: Cyberspace Meets Sovereignty," *The Wall Street Journal Europe* (August 17, 2000), p. 6.

24 Available from: http://www.abanet.org/buslaw/cyber/initiatives/jurisdiction.html/. (Access date October 22, 2000.)

25 R. Plesser and Marbury, "Developing a Global Legal Infrastructure to Support E-Commerce: Reconciling Jurisdiction and Consumer Law Uncertainties on a Global Basis," *The Global Digital Explosion* (Washington, D.C.: The Computer Law Association, Inc., 2000).

26 Delaney and Schwartz, "The Law of the Internet," provides an extended discussion and list of cases.

27 Organization for Economic Cooperation and Development, "OECD Guidelines on the Protection of Privacy and Transborder Flows of Personal Data" (Paris: OECD, 1980).

28 European Commission, Data Protection Directive (95/46/EC), 1995.

29 A summary of Federal Trade Commission activity with respect to consumers and privacy is available from: http://www.ftc.gov/privacy/index.html/.

30 A discussion of the details of each of these principles is available from: http://www.ftc.gov/reports/privacy3/fairinfo.htm#Notice/Awareness/. (October 22, 2000.)

31 Available from: http://www.privacyalliance.org/resources/ppguidelines.shtml/ (October 22, 2000).

32 Federal Trade Commission,"Privacy Online: Fair Information Practices in the Electronic Marketplace: A Federal Trade Commission Report to Congress" (Washington, D.C.: FTC, May 2000). Available from: http://www.ftc.gov/reports/privacy3/fairinfo.htm#Notice/Awareness/.

33 L. Vaas, "Customer Privacy Lockdown," *eWeek* [online], October 15, 2000. Available from: http://www.zdnet.com/eweek/ (October 23, 2000).

34 U.S. Treasury, Department of Tax Policy, International Tax Bulletin, "Selected Tax Policy Implications of Global Electronic Commerce" (Washington, D.C.: U.S. Treasury, December 1996). Available from: http://www.pmstax.com/intl/ustdnet9611.shtml/ (October 25, 2000).

35 Available from: http://www.oecd.org/dsti/sti/it/consumer/prod/CPGuidelines_final.pdf/. (Access date October 21, 2000.)

36 European Commission, Directive on Protection of Consumers in Respect of Distance Contracts (97/7/EC), May 20, 1997.

37 "Internet and E-Commerce Group Proposes Guidelines for Consumer Protection Online," *PR Newswire* [online], June 6, 2000.

38 Further information is available from: http://www.wto.org/english/tratop_e/trips_e/trips_e.htm/.

39 Further information about the WIPO International Conference on Electronic Commerce and Intellectual Property, including the program, speakers, and papers, is available from: http://ecommece.wipo.int/meetings/1999/. (Access date October 22, 2000.)

40 Available from: http://ecommerce.wipo.int/primer/introduction.html/. (Access date October 22, 2000.)

41 Delaney and Schwartz, p. 82.

42 U.S. House, 105th Congress, 2nd Session. *H.R. 2281, U.S. Digital Millennium Copyright Act.* Public Law 105-304, signed on October 28, 1998.

43 CompuServe Deutschland, Bavarian District Court (November 17, 1999).

44 A good source for information on developments in the area of content regulation is Electronic Frontiers Australia Inc. (http://rene.efa.org.au/liberty/debategl.html). Other resources include the Electronic Frontier Foundation (http://www.eff.org) and the Global Internet Liberty Campaign (http://www.gilc.org). These sources have contributed information to this section of our chapter.

45 L. Gerstner, Keynote Address (delivered at COMDEX '95, Las Vegas, Nevada, November 13, 1995).

Rebalancing Management in the Emerging E-Marketspace: From Control to Leadership

David Partridge, e-Business Innovation Institute, IBM Corporation
Nirmal Pal, eBusiness Research Center, The Pennsylvania State University

At a time of very rapid and profound change, as we are witnessing with the global e-business (r)evolution, it is very important to provide continuous leadership that causes organizations to adopt and accept change both efficiently and effectively. In the last several decades, organizations hired people whom they expected to be their lifetime employees. Current studies show that the college graduates we hire today will change their jobs on the average of seven or more times in their lifetime, which means changing jobs every five years. That is just one aspect of the change. At the same time, there are profound changes going on about the way we work, the way we learn, and the way business and commerce are conducted, which is brought about by the phenomenon we call e-business.

Therefore, business leaders must develop an organizational culture that is used to continuous change and relentlessly leverage change to their advantage, allowing them to attain and then sustain competitive advantage.

Note: The authors of this chapter acknowledge that much of the thought leadership for this chapter came from their association with the IBM Consulting Group.

Changes to the Elements of Management

We have a "management gridlock" in today's business environment. The combination of management processes, organization structures, assigned responsibilities and authorities, and the supporting information infrastructure enables today's managers to systematically achieve near-term financial and marketplace performance optimization (see Figure 5-1).

The great winners of the current generation of managers are those who are able to manipulate this systematic management environment in a reasonably predictable world. These winners are efficient optimizers of the current "ecosystem of commerce." They understand cost control, cost reduction, automation, and optimization very well and are the best project managers, best controllers, and best general managers in the context of today's business. There is, however, a clear requirement for rebalancing management to reflect the dramatic shift in the overall context of commerce driven primarily by the emerging e-marketspace.

Next-generation great managers will be called "migration-experts" for their ability to continuously "move cows from here to there without losing any cows."

This rebalancing will give rise to several different changes to the elements of management:

■ *Management Process Architecture.* Fundamental changes to performance measures within management performance itself will be a

FIGURE 5-1
Four Elements of Management

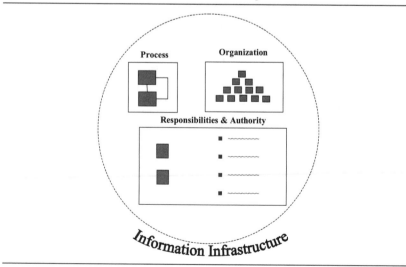

primary agent of change. The traditional focus on near-term financial performance measurement must be modified with the addition of customer propensity-to-buy measures; we discuss this concept more toward the end of this chapter under the heading Metrics.

■ *Organization Structure.* Flexible communities of teams assembled from task groups and organizations flattened around a network structure are emerging as a more prevalent form of organization structure. Gone are the days of rigid hierarchical organizations surrounding vertically integrated business models as the norm.

■ *Assignment of Responsibility and Authority.* We are now witnessing a basic redefinition of executive-level management success criteria. Where once executives believed "success is control," today "success is vision, empowerment, and enterprise migration management." Concurrent with this change is the emergence of the truly customer-centric organization and a new class of managers able to create working environments based on "value capture through context," which is fundamental to this new business model. In such an environment, organizations must understand the specific needs of individual customers at a given point in time and within the context of that need. The way we select, assign responsibility and authority, and evaluate these managers must therefore undergo fundamental change.

■ *Management Information Infrastructure.* Again, a basic change in purpose is begun: from a control measurements focus to a market intelligence and opportunity identification/quantification emphasis, and from hierarchical, vertical flows of communication to "continuous dialogue" among all layers of management (and there won't be many) to achieve sharing of information.

In addition, web-based technology allows, and arguably requires, us not only to automate and real-time link our global business processes and supporting management information infrastructures, but also to extend these to all key stakeholders, including those in our key business processes.

Market Maturity and Business Model Evolution

Figure 5-2 shows the standard bell curve of business/marketplace stages from embryonic through growth and maturity to aging. In the embryonic and early part of the growth stages, market growth is rapid as new customers discover the products/services being offered, demand often exceeds supply, and a "products offered" business model is typical. Success in this phase of marketplace maturity is dangerous because a "build it and they will come" mentality can become ingrained in management culture. Often, performance management in

FIGURE 5-2
Market Maturity

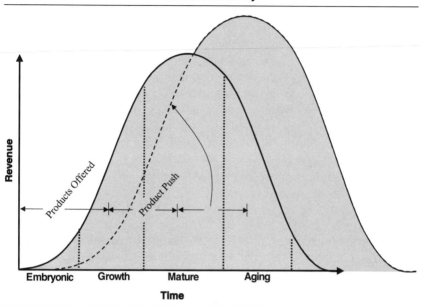

this environment is focused on production; shifts in customer demand and competitor responses reflect this as well: "Manufacturing" product design and supply chain/sourcing are dominant.

In the latter part of the growth phase and the major part of the mature phase, slowing demand growth and/or increasing competition reduce profit margins. In response to this first "crisis," management shifts to a sales emphasis. Organizations are aligned around go-to-market selling groups, and key management information systems are those that track sales and delivery. Successful managers are those who deliver on assigned quotas, independent of market conditions. The typical business model embodying these characteristics is referred to as "product push." In this type of competitive environment, a product-push business model when competing with a products-offered model will win, and many of the great commercial enterprises of the last decade of the twentieth century typify this approach to management.

In the latter part of the mature phase and as competitors begin to experience the shrinkage in overall market demand and resultant margin shrinkage, a race for size/scale generally breaks out, and industry consolidation merger/acquisition is common—M&A activities and industry consolidation have been big stories for the business media over the past ten years. From a management mind-set perspective, most industries throughout most of the aging phase experience what we call the Last Iceman syndrome—that is, the belief that "if we're the last one standing in our industry, we can charge anything we want because some demand will always be there" (see Figure 5-3). To win this end-game competition, a tremendous focus on cost-efficient production and distribution becomes prevalent, reflecting the belief that only the lowest-cost producer can survive. Often in this environment, the actual wants and needs of the customer are ignored in the belief that price is all that matters.

An alternative, the "customer-centric value capture" model, has operated successfully in those businesses or markets where selected customer segments will pay for it. These customers are those whose business is sufficiently valuable to make the cost of "customer-centricity" affordable; private banking is a classic example of this business approach. Excellence in this model requires an organizational structure that reinforces the paramount need to anticipate customer needs and to ensure that the customer experience of the relationship with the commercial enterprise is that the customer's interests are being put first. Relationship-based value realization is central to this business model, and management systems track its accomplishment. The relationship manager is king in this model; the skills and aptitudes required for successful execution are highly valued and compensated.

The great shortfall to this model historically has been its limited applicability to commerce in general, given its prohibitive cost to deliver in mass markets. Put simply, while many middle-market consumers would very much like to enjoy private banking–quality service, none are willing or able to pay for the cost of the customer-centric version of it.

FIGURE 5-3
Business Model Evolution

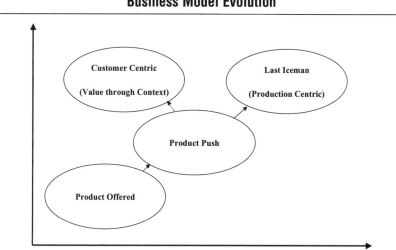

The arrival of the e-marketplace and its underlying technologies, however, will make this business model feasible in a wide variety of industries by enabling "virtual agency"–based offerings that can serve a customer "where I am, where I live, where I work, where I shop." The resultant impact on the fundamental structures of industries will, we believe, upset the competitive balance that has existed throughout much of the latter half of the Industrial era. The old game is ending and a new one is beginning. The winners will be those who can manage successfully in the emerging e-marketspace.

The Context of the E-Enabled World (E-Business)

It is important to be clear with our readers about our definition of e-business. In Figure 5-4, the smaller circle represents business-to-consumer (B-to-C) e-commerce, which is commonly referred to as e-retailing or e-tailing. If we take today's world economy to be approximately $32 trillion, the total potential B-to-C market opportunity is about $12 trillion. The estimate of e-tailing in the year 2000 is $30 billion worldwide, a big number by itself, but very small in terms of the total size of the opportunity.

The middle circle represents the size of e-commerce, which includes both B-to-C and business-to-business (B-to-B) markets. The total size of B-to-B e-commerce is about $12 trillion in the year 2000. Of this, the electronic component is about $200 billion.

FIGURE 5-4
Relative Market Position of E-Business, E-Commerce, and E-Tailing

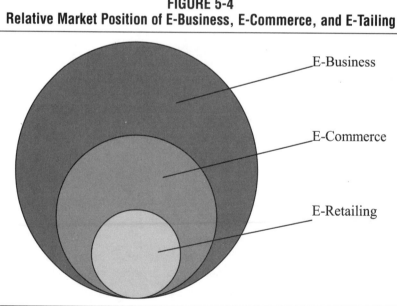

E-Business

E-Commerce

E-Retailing

As we can see from this analysis, the penetration of electronic commerce in both business-to-consumer and business-to-business markets, while substantially more for B-to-B, has not yet reached the critical mass of 10 percent of the opportunity. While the world economy is increasing by 3.2 percent each year (up from 2 percent per year in the mid-1990s), both B-to-C and B-to-B e-commerce is exploding exponentially. According to U.S. Commerce Department estimates, electronic commerce will hit the 40 percent mark in year 2005. From this we can conclude that 2000 and 2001 are at the inflection point in the growth curve of e-commerce.

The outer circle represents what we call e-business, which is e-commerce plus all other business processes that are, or can be, leveraged by web-related technology. We believe that e-business has become pervasive, that the whole of commerce will be embraced by Internet and related technologies that enable, extend, and integrate all key business processes: supply chain management (SCM), customer relationship management (CRM), enterprise management, and other supporting business processes. Thus, e-business is about leveraging business value from your relationships with suppliers, partners, employees, customers, and other key stakeholders. Taking maximum practical advantage of e-business is a key management mandate and responsibility. Success in management of the "migration" to e-business will become a primary measurement of management effectiveness in the near future.

If we look at the extent of this change, it is affecting the way we work, the way we learn, and the way we conduct business (see Figure 5-5). In the United States, among white-collar workers, the ratio of computers (desktop or otherwise) to workers already exceeds 1:1. Ford Motor Company recently initiated a program that will require all of its workers worldwide to have computers. The changes are affecting us in every walk of life, from buying an airline ticket, to reserving tickets for a Broadway show, to scheduling school activities, to paying our taxes and bills and renewing our driver's licenses.

If we look at any organization in any industry, and look at its key business processes, we find that there are opportunities to leverage e-business in each of these key processes. This leverage is providing significant efficiency and effectiveness gains, and a greater number of organizations are adopting e-business, with some organizations already being in their second or third generation of this change.

Management and Leadership

Now, what is the difference between management and leadership?

In Webster's dictionary, management is defined as "the act of managing, controlling, or conducting." The word *manage* is defined as "to

FIGURE 5-5
Changing Nature of Work, Business, and Learning

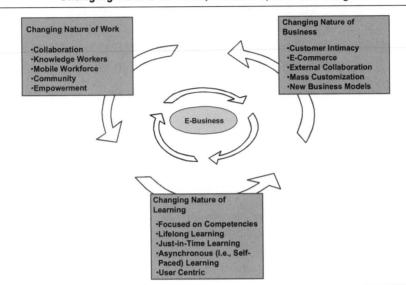

direct or conduct the affairs of a business, and to control the operations." Control is a key parameter in this definition, and in the traditional sense, the term *management* is given to mean control-oriented management.

Leadership is defined as "the act of leading or guiding." The word *lead* is defined as "to go with or ahead of so as to show the way."

These terms are closely related, but each provides a different focus and dimension, as presented in Figure 5-6.

Management primarily deals with planning, budgeting, organizing, staffing, measuring, controlling, and problem solving.

Leadership, on the other hand, is primarily an intellectual task. The intellectual task is to create and communicate vision, strategies, directions, and priorities. A good leader must also be a good coach. The coaching task is to get everyone energized and committed to execute the strategies, priorities, and direction.

Management deals mostly with status quo and is effective at each layer of an organization hierarchy. On the other hand, leadership deals mostly with change and must be effective throughout the organization during a period of change. Since change has become the way of life in every sphere of our work, commerce, and industry, one of the most important aspects of strong, continuous leadership is the ability to help people develop a sense of belief that change is in their best interest; adapting to change and relentlessly leveraging it is key to their success.

FIGURE 5-6
Management and Leadership

Leadership	Management
Communicate Vision	Plan
Strategize	Measure
Enable	Control
Empower	Structure
Inspire	Reward/Punish
Mentor	Command
Network	Operate
Show Intent	Execute
Transform	Improve
Establish Community of Practice	Organize Task Groups
Lead by Principles	Execute Plans
Energize	Monitor Status

IBM: A CASE STUDY

The story of IBM Corp. provides rich insights into the issues of management and leadership in the New World.

IBM in 1993—When the Bottom Fell Out

In 1993, IBM lost more than $8 billion in one year, and the stock price came down to the low $40s. IBM had made investments in people, plants, and machinery in the previous years to cater to business growth that would have far exceeded the $50 billion of revenue that IBM made in 1993. For example, IBM had 425,000 employees in 1993, and only about half of that number could be justified for the business volume in that year.

The Management Challenge—Stop the Bleeding

When Lou Gerstner joined IBM as chairman and CEO, he was asked about his vision. He said that IBM did not need a strong technology vision for its future; he needed to address the more immediate problems facing IBM. His comments were misunderstood by the media, but not by IBM's senior management. IBM executed a plan to balance its people and infrastructure investments with its business base. More than 200,000 employees had to be removed, and many manufacturing plants and operations had to be closed forever. IBM needed a decisive leadership vision to think through the change and a powerful management structure to execute it.

IBM in 1995 and Beyond—Sustain and Grow

IBM's focus was now on growth, while sustaining resource actions and other cost reduction and control measures. Key business processes were critically examined and transformed to meet the new set of business parameters. This refocus also needed key leadership vision and follow-through. IBM was run as what many consultants called a multilocal corporation. Country operations were more or less autonomous, with each having its own information technology infrastructure and set of business processes. It served the company well when business was booming and cost was not an issue.

IBM took decisive action to establish a global management system to have common business processes supported by a common information technology infrastructure. Instead of thirty-five CIOs, IBM changed to one CIO and one global business process owner for each of the key business processes. This change, while it sounds simple, was very difficult to execute. No country management team wanted to give up its control of the two key infrastructure foundations of information technology and business processes, but IBM's senior management team remained committed and provided the leadership to make it happen.

The Leadership Challenge—IBM's E-Business Vision

In October 1995 at the Internet World Exposition, Lou Gerstner talked for the first time about his vision about web technology and a network-centric world. He energized the whole company to work around his grand vision, and in early 1997 the e-business phrase was created. From 1997 to 1999, IBM spent a few hundred million dollars in a media blitz to gain mind share. Today, everyone from housewives to corporate CEOs knows about e-business.

IBM's business in 1999 exceeded $80 billion worldwide, and the value of IBM stock was equivalent to $500, taking into consideration two stock splits during this time frame. This transformation was only possible through the strong leadership and commitment provided by the senior management team.

IBM in 2000—Positioning for the New Millennium

In August 2000, IBM announced a series of significant changes in its top management positions. Leading the pack was Sam Palmisano, a long-time IBMer, who was named chief operating officer and president. While announcing the changes, Lou Gerstner said that for the past several years, IBM formulated and crystallized its vision and created a mind share for e-business; now was the time to create a market share.

The Execution Challenge—Mind Share to Market Share

IBM now has a clear vision and has established a governance framework to realize that vision. During the August 2000 announcement, Gerstner said, "It is now time for superior and flawless execution. This is where a strong management team overseeing IBM's day-to-day operations is key to this flawless execution."

Creating and communicating a compelling and shared vision is the first step toward a systematic approach to set the strategy, directions, and priorities of any organization.

The Leadership Pyramid

The leadership pyramid (shown in Figure 5-7) is a useful framework for discussing leadership and management focus at three stages: vision and values, governance, and execution.

FIGURE 5-7
The Leadership Pyramid

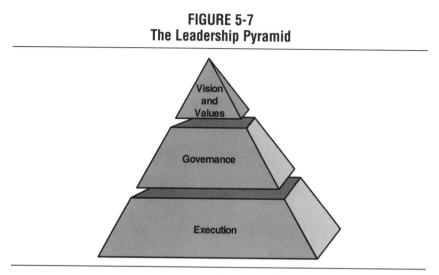

To begin, we have to think about what new values we want to deliver to our stakeholders. This can be done by first identifying the stakeholders of the organization. They are our customers, business partners, suppliers, distributors, employees, shareholders, and a general category called "influencers." The vision must be seen as delivering new values to this set of people, both individually and collectively. Creation of a powerful and compelling vision is the intellectual task that we referred to before. This is where leadership plays a key role.

Shareholder value is the most important consideration for the leadership team. What needs to be done to meet and exceed analyst expectations on Wall Street is at the top of every senior leader's mind at all times. Also, analysts' expectations and focus seem to change periodically. For example, a few years ago nobody worried about missing a sales forecast, as long as there were no dents on the profit margins. But of late, analysts are focusing on sales growth, because the growing view among the analysts is that in recent years profits have been boosted by productivity and cost cutting that may no longer be sustainable. A case in point is the stock market performance after Intel Corp. announced that sales in the third quarter of 2000 would fall well short of expectations, sparking a 22 percent downturn in this company's stock on September 22, 2000. That was the biggest one-day drop to date in Intel's history.

Creating visions to continuously deliver new and differentiating value in all lines of the business is one of the key activities of the Leadership team.

Vision

In the previous section on management and leadership, we talked about the various dimensions of each. As we discussed before, they are related, but each puts forth a different focus and activities. In formulating a powerful vision, strong leadership is key.

While creating vision for the e-world, it is important to remember that we are mostly in unknown territory, in the sense that we do not have much historical data and analysis to predict the future. Therefore, we suggest an iterative vision-building approach that allows for repeated examination of the vision every few months, so that one can fine-tune the vision as market forces dictate change.

The key considerations are to repeatedly examine what business we are in and what business we will be in the future. What are our goals for growth, and what values will we deliver to our targeted market segments? What segments should we target and pursue, and what would be the most appropriate delivery channel for that segment? Finally, what strategic capabilities do we need to build to realize this vision?

It's essential for the senior management team to meet and examine the current industry leaders and then do scenario planning to explore the future possibilities and potentials. During the scenario-planning session, key assumptions in terms of trigger events must be noted. It will be useful in future iterations of the vision to reexamine these trigger events and tune the vision appropriately. Scenario planning must include new products and services in relation to the chosen customer and market segments. The focus should include enhanced and new products and services for existing and new customers and markets.

The problems most frequently encountered in building the most appropriate vision are lack of imagination, inappropriate risk-aversion mind-set, failure to understand the brand management requirements for the e-marketspace, and lack of articulation of the required portfolio of businesses for the converging economies.

Once the vision is created, it needs to be communicated to all stakeholders to get their buy-in. In addition, it is important to capture the mind share of the masses and increase their awareness. IBM did that very well in the late 1990s. IBM spent hundreds of millions of dollars to advertise its e-business message in all major media around the world. During the 2000 Olympic Games in Sydney, both AT&T and IBM spent significant money to get their wireless technology message to the masses very effectively.

Governance

After the vision is created, the leadership team needs to think through the governance aspects before execution of the vision can begin.

An effective governance framework (see Figure 5-8) allows for thinking through the strategic implications of the vision in relation to the overall business goals of the organization. Quite often, individual

FIGURE 5-8
Governance Framework

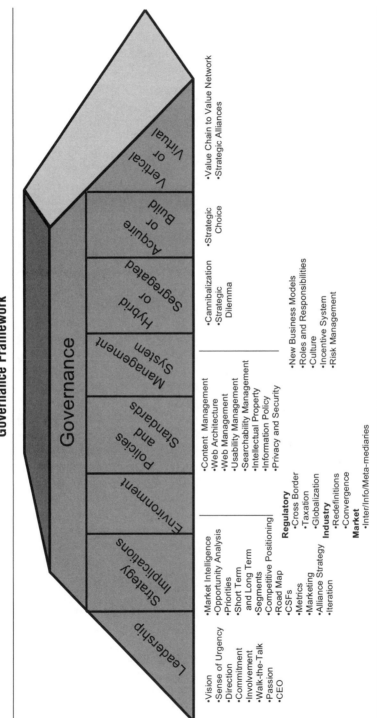

Leadership
- Vision
- Sense of Urgency
- Direction
- Commitment
- Involvement
- Walk-the-Talk
- Passion
- CEO

Strategy Implications
- Market Intelligence
- Opportunity Analysis
- Priorities
- Short Term and Long Term
- Segments
- Competitive Positioning
- Road Map
- CSFs
- Metrics
- Marketing
- Alliance Strategy
- Iteration

Environment
Regulatory
- Cross Border
- Taxation
- Globalization
Industry
- Redefinitions
- Convergence
Market
- Inter/Info/Meta-mediaries

Governance

Policies and Standards
- Content Management
- Web Architecture
- Web Management
- Usability Management
- Searchability Management
- Intellectual Property
- Information Policy
- Privacy and Security

Management System
- New Business Models
- Roles and Responsibilities
- Culture
- Incentive System
- Risk Management

Hybrid or Segregated
- Cannibalization
- Strategic Dilemma

Acquire or Build
- Strategic Choice

Vertical or Virtual
- Value Chain to Value Network
- Strategic Alliances

divisions or strategic business units (SBUs) develop e-business initiatives that provide short-term benefits to the division or the SBU, but do not advance the overall goals of the organization as a whole. This often creates dissatisfaction among the stakeholders and results in redundant efforts.

This happens often, and even in many Fortune 500 companies. When we, the authors of this chapter, both worked in the IBM Consulting Group's e-business practice, we received many inquiries from the senior management of our client organizations about their overextended and inconsistent e-business initiative portfolios. These queries often resulted in e-business strategy engagements for us. In most of these situations, individual divisions or SBUs would initiate execution of initiatives without thinking through the governance aspects. Therefore, it is very important to provide a framework that not only allows, but also requires, a systematic analysis of all areas of governance before execution can begin.

Leadership

All aspects of governance require strong leadership. Governance provides the framework through which strategy, priorities, and directions can be set and then revisited in different iterations of the vision.

Another aspect of successful transformation of an organization to e-business is strong leadership from the CEO. As shown in the IBM example, Lou Gerstner provided strong leadership, secured the commitment of his senior management team, and constantly demonstrated his own personal commitment every time he spoke in external and internal IBM meetings.

Demonstration of senior management commitment also comes in the form of another decisive action—the appointment of a senior executive to lead the change, one who is highly visible in the ranks of the organization and has the passion and leadership qualities to make the change. We, and many others, call this position the CeO, or the chief e-business officer. In the case of IBM, this role is given to a senior executive who is vice president of business transformation/chief information officer (BT/CIO). This executive is in charge of business transformation for IBM, as well as responsible for the information technology infrastructure and strategy. This senior executive reports to the senior vice president of strategy. Traditionally, you will find the CIO position reporting to the chief finance officer, as information technology is primarily seen as a cost issue. More often, and especially in the world of e-business, information technology is seen as the driver of business value and growth, and in many organizations, as in the case of IBM, the CIO now reports to a business function. This change in reporting is subtle but very fundamental, because it demonstrates the profound change in senior management mind-set.

Market Intelligence

One of the primary activities of the leadership team is to engage in continuous market intelligence. This enables the executives to understand their competitive positioning in the market, the changing needs and wants of the customer segments that they serve, and the emerging opportunities in the marketplace that they can leverage. Competitive positioning analysis not only includes current competitors, but also prospective ones. There is a need to continually understand how others are delivering value to the targeted market segments that an organization serves.

Market intelligence was always regarded as a key function, but its role in the changing world of e-business has become the most important management tool in determining short-term priorities and long-term goals. The problems that most organizations face in e-space are limited out-of-the-box-thinking capability, limited understanding of changing customer buying behavior, explosion of available data, and limited understanding of what emerging technologies will enable. That is why market intelligence has become a key function. Its job is to continually keep a finger on the pulse of the market and customers the company serves, as well as keep an eye on both traditional and nontraditional competitors.

Environment

Another key element of governance is being able to think through the environmental issues. These are primarily in (but not limited to) three specific areas:

- Regulatory
- Industry
- Marketspace

Regulatory issues are related to cross-border implications of differing taxation, privacy, security, and related policies within the various states of a country such as the United States or between countries around the world. The main management issue here is the limited understanding of current and anticipated changes to the regulatory environment.

In addition, any presence on the World Wide Web is, by default, a global business. Therefore, even though a business may primarily be within one country, the global implications need to be thought through. A case in point: When Lands' End went live with its website in late 1997, it started getting orders from college students in Taiwan, Japan, and other Asian countries, for which it did not have a delivery and distribution mechanism at that time. Distribution, inventory management, and customer service are key issues with all business-to-consumer businesses within a country. Many businesses suddenly found themselves in the export business for the first time through their B-to-C websites and were caught unprepared.

Other issues of environmental concern include the industry and the e-marketspace. Industry is going through a rapid phase of redefinition and convergence. Take any industry, for example, financial services, and let us see what is happening to that industry. We know that banking and insurance are coming closer. We know that many typical banking functions can now be done at and through your local supermarket. In some European countries you can conduct most of your banking transactions by using a cellular phone. All of these and other factors are changing the very nature of this industry.

In the e-marketspace a revolution is taking place. It started with one-to-one marketing through organizations such as Amazon.com. The second wave of change brought about the eBays of this world that allowed for one-to-many marketing through auctions. In the third wave of this change, we are witnessing the emergence of trading networks or exchanges for both the vertical and horizontal markets. Many research firms are predicting there will be as many as 10,000 such trading networks by the year 2004. The buyer-seller matrix in Figure 5-9 shows a two-by-two chart with the relative positioning of these e-markets.

All of these issues play significant roles in the strategy formulation of any organization.

FIGURE 5-9
Buyer-Seller Matrix

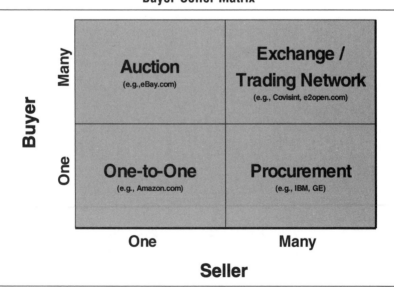

Policies and Standards

While it is important to make sure that individual creativity and innovative ideas for e-business are respected and allowed to be tested, it is also important to make sure that organizations create a set of policies and standards as guidelines. These are important for maintaining consistency and a common look and feel for all of the e-activities and formats. These areas of policies and standards include, but are not limited to:

- Content management
- Web architecture
- Intellectual property
- Information policy
- Privacy
- Security

Management Systems

In almost all situations we find structural resistance to change or an organizational inertia that inhibits change that is essential to moving forward with speed in e-business implementations. Also, in many cases the organizational responsibility assignments are out-of-date, and the key business processes are slow to respond.

A key question to ponder is, "How does our culture compare with those of our current competitors?" Other related issues are: How does the culture affect employee loyalty, quality of customer service, and employee productivity? We must also investigate the incentive systems. How do they compare with our competitors?

The other key area to consider in management systems is the issue of risk management. Are we too oriented toward risk aversion? Is there a way to balance risk taking with appropriate steps for iterative vision development and strong market intelligence? In the e-marketspace, new ideas and innovations need to be constantly experimented with, even if you do not want to be a leader. The management system should provide for such experimentation. Otherwise, you will be left behind.

A good case in point is a package-delivery company. The company excelled in innovations when it gave customers access to package-delivery data through its website. Customers were happy to take over a function done by the delivery company before, and a great saving of call center operating staff resulted from this innovation. Many experts cited this company as the leader in its industry. Others in the industry, however, soon copied this idea and went beyond by providing service excellence to the extent that during the 1999 holiday period, the share of the package-delivery business for the first innovator dwindled to 10 percent. The moral of this episode is that you cannot just do one innovation and expect to leverage that forever or even for a long time—you need to provide a management system that encourages relentless innovation to reach the top and stay there.

Strategic Choices

A common strategic dilemma in moving to e-business with speed is whether to build a separate, hands-off operation for the e-space or a hybrid organization that combines the physical and the digital world.

The Charles Schwab Corp. initially chose the segregated route and created e-Schwab as a separate operation that required Charles Schwab customers to open new e-Schwab accounts to deal with them through the Web. In 1998, the company made a management decision to combine the two operations. It was a bold and decisive step, since the conventional wisdom at that time was to separate the two operations. In fact, the company's stock value took a dip for a while, but the rest is history.

Similarly, Barnes & Noble had separate operations for its traditional and dot-com business but has now launched plans for extensive integration of its superstores and website. Customers can go to a superstore for the pickup or return of books ordered through the dot-com business. In addition, Internet service counters will be set up within the superstores for customer ordering.

The other strategic issue is whether to acquire or build. To build and grow takes a long time, and many incumbents are taking the shorter route of acquiring the expertise they need for e-business. Since 1993, Cisco Systems acquired (or announced its intent to acquire) sixty-five companies. It is a great example of growing by acquisition.

The third strategic choice issue is that of building strategic alliances either to offload noncore functions or to have access to new talent, new markets, and new technology. There are many examples, one of which is Deutsche Bank, a late arrival to the e-business game. However, when it decided to move, Deutsche Bank speedily built alliances with several organizations as follows:

Deutsche Bank Alliance/Partner	Purpose
eTimeCapital	Handles B-to-B commercial transactions
Nokia capabilities	Provides mobile commerce (m-commerce) and mobile banking
AOL.com	Provides a platform for Deutsche Bank products
Yahoo!	Helps Deutsche Bank gain new customers and e-cash functionality

| mySAP.com | Provides an e-business platform, products, and services |
| Mannesmann | Provides mobile banking and pan-European access |

The new economy has driven strategic alliances to the top of many boardroom agendas around the world. In this environment, establishing and managing alliances becomes critical to success. It requires a new skill that most firms do not have today. Also, for a traditional firm, it means giving up something the firm has always done. This is what we meant by cannibalization in our governance framework in Figure 5-8. It requires a strong leadership vision and execution to make it work.

We can now begin to see how the value chain of a vertically integrated firm can effectively disaggregate into a value network of a virtually integrated firm that provides for significant improvements in time to market, product and services innovations, efficiencies in scale and scope, and mitigating competitive forces.

In conclusion, many Fortune 500 firms have jumped to execution for expediency without spending time to think through the governance issues discussed here, and in most, if not all cases, they ended up spending a lot of time and energy in redundant efforts and engendering customer dissatisfaction.

Execution

As we move down the leadership pyramid from vision and values through governance to execution (see Figure 5-10), it is important to have an effective structure that reinforces and complements the governance framework. To succeed, a business must have a focused execution capability. This is where the management task becomes very important.

Competencies and Skills

The new business vision that we developed must now be translated in terms of new competencies and new skills of e-business professionals. As there is a tremendous shortage of e-business professionals, there is considerable difficulty in attracting and retaining qualified and experienced talent. The Information Technology Association of America (ITAA) has stated that in the year 2000, U.S. industries would create 1.6 million new jobs for IT workers. Of this number only about 800,000 can be filled through students graduating from technical schools and universities in the United States. The question of whether the United States is producing an adequate supply of IT workers continues to be a subject of much debate. We believe that an imbalance in supply and demand will continue in the near future.

FIGURE 5-10
Execution Framework

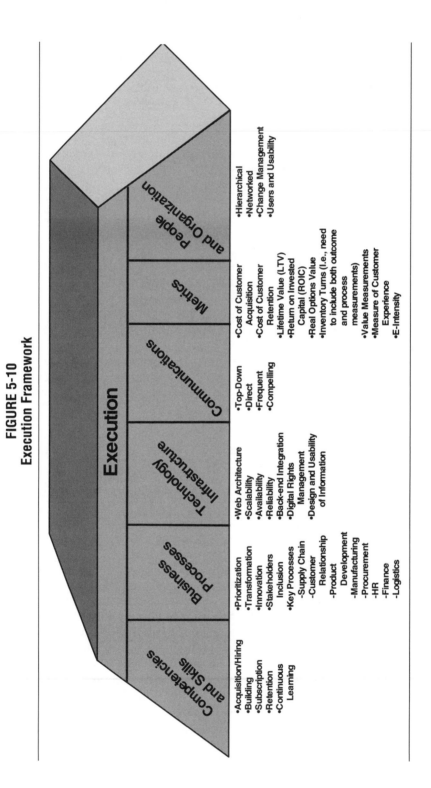

There are some key questions that an organization must answer to address the problems in this space. These are:

- Does our compensation and rewards system attract, motivate, and help retain the required skills?
- Do we have a skill management system that has an accurate inventory of staff skills and abilities?
- Do we have plans in place for just-in-time education as well as lifelong education?

When the CEO of Cisco Systems was asked what keeps him awake at night, he said attracting and retaining key talent was his primary issue.

New Business Processes

To realize our vision and convert business strategy into operating reality, we need to transform our key business processes and align them with business objectives. We need top management attention and focus to create a strong transition management team. The team should systematically look at where in the company's delivery system specific tasks and activities need to be performed, as quite often the legacy processes contain structural design flaws that lead to ineffective role and responsibility assignments. IBM traditionally had a separate product development process in each of its strategic business units. This situation not only caused redundancies and excessive cost, but also longer time to market for new products. Quite often different groups would design products that would have different architectures that would not be operationally compatible. It was quite a well-known fact in the industry that the System 34 through System 38 series of products from IBM's Rochester development laboratory were very innovative in design but incompatible with the System 360 to System 390 series of products from IBM's Poughkeepsie laboratory and plant. Today, IBM has one common Integrated Product Development (IPD) process across all operating units worldwide. IBM has gained significant efficiencies in scale. Its time to market for new products is down to a few months from a few years.

IBM has made similar gains in all of its key business processes by transforming these processes, automating them by using the broad reach of the Internet, and including its key stakeholders in these processes.

Jack Welch, the celebrated CEO of General Electric Company, was late to the game of e-business. There are numerous articles on the subject of how Jack Welch is revitalizing GE with e-business initiatives. One of the many things that he has done is to appoint a team of hand-picked individuals in each of the GE divisions called "Destroy-your-company.com." Their job is to go through their division and basically cannibalize everything that is no longer providing value. Many other firms have taken similar initiatives and have implemented the creative destruction process as their core strategy.

Typical questions that management needs to ask are:

- What are the current capabilities for our key business processes?
- How do our process capabilities compare with our competitors and customers?
- Have we benchmarked our key process performance indicators against the best of breed in our industry and beyond?
- Where in our delivery systems should tasks and activities be performed?
- How should these tasks and activities be grouped and tiered?
- Do our business processes help achieve and sustain competitive advantage?

Technology Infrastructure

While discussing information technology infrastructure, we have always talked about scalability, reliability, and availability. However, the e-business environment has given new meaning to these terms. E-commerce websites of major organizations such as IBM, Yahoo!, or Amazon.com are basically hundreds of very powerful computers connected together with an ability to add new processing power as needed. In addition, they often use replicated sites around the globe to offer acceptable response times to their global consumers. These front-end processors then have to be integrated with the back-end processors, which increases the complexity of the overall system by an order of magnitude.

This environment causes an explosion of data that needs to be processed and presented in a manner dictated by the new business models and the new management systems. One of the key areas is market intelligence, where the information technology infrastructure becomes an integral part of the business decision-making process. This requires a continuous monitoring of competitive activities and end-users' changing needs and wants, and an ability to identify opportunities for new products and services and new customers and markets.

The typical problems that organizations face in e-space are limited understanding of outsourcing and insourcing opportunities, limited e-technology management experience and expertise, and an inability to move at "web speed."

Typical questions that management needs to ask are:

- What types, format, and frequency of information do the new business models require?

- Will our current information systems and technology infrastructure adequately support our current and future business management requirements?
- What are the emerging best practices for technologies in use and for technology management?
- Does our information technology support achievement of competitive advantage?

Communications

One thing that all successful leaders of transformation have in common at the time of change is effective, top-down, frequent, and compelling communications directed to all members of the staff. Lou Gerstner and his divisional general managers send direct communications to employees periodically with details on IBM's state of the business and whenever any key change occurs. Previously, information flowed through the organization hierarchy with stages of filters at every layer. Quality and timeliness of information dissemination suffer greatly if information has to flow through the hierarchy. As chairman of AT&T Wireless Services, John Zeglis practices similar and frequent direct communications to employees and uses voice mail to all employees to supplement e-mail, so all employees can hear him directly on key issues and performance.

Typical questions that management needs to ask are:

- Does top management communicate with all employees clearly and frequently about business issues and status?
- Does top management communicate with other stakeholders (e.g., suppliers, distributors, business partners, key customers, and key influencers) clearly and frequently?

Metrics

New business models bring with them new ways of looking at key performance indicators. Old ways of evaluating and tracking organizational and individual performances are no longer valid. A good example of new metrics is cost of customer acquisition. In the web environment, if your new customer spends $100 and you spent $1,000 in acquisition cost, per customer, in advertisement and commissions to others, then you will not know where you stand unless you start measuring this new parameter.

We addressed strategic alliances while talking about governance issues. E-business brings about new opportunities to build alliances to offload noncore functions, to build access to new technology and talent, and to gain access to new markets and customers. New metrics need to be developed to track and evaluate the performance of these alliances.

The problems here are always the legacy mind-set and weak quantification of financial and nonfinancial key performance indicators.

Typical questions that management needs to ask are:

- Do we track and evaluate organization and individual performance accurately?
- What are our key performance indicators? Are they defined by each of our business units, products, markets, and customer segments?
- How do we get information on performance?
- How do we link individual and organizational goals?
- Does our measurement system generate desired behavior by our employees?
- Does our measurement system allow us to track and evaluate the performance of our strategic alliances?

Five Principles of E-Business Leadership for Traditional Firms Converging with the New Economy

If we summarize our discussions in this chapter of moving from control-oriented management to leadership-oriented management, then it boils down to the following five principles:

1. *Traditional firms must master relentless innovation.* Marketspace is hyperdynamic, with performance bars rising every 90 to 120 days. To stay ahead and succeed, the focus has to be on management speed and agility. All management systems require revision to keep pace in such a highly volatile environment, and leadership must provide an environment where relentless innovation can thrive. The focus must always be on new value delivery to key stakeholders.

2. *Traditional firms must embrace creative destruction as a core strategy.* Assets are constantly revalued, with physical assets losing relative value and knowledge assets gaining value. New entrants leverage state-of-the-art technology and business design, while incumbents struggle to migrate. Self-directed customers handle work formerly done by employees, shifting the nature of interaction between the firm and its customers. The leaders of the industry are going to be those who have the courage of their conviction to follow through on new ways of doing business. The focus here must always be on value-creating process capabilities and on lines of business portfolio.

3. *Traditional firms' advantage lies in the ability to sense and respond.* Power changes hands as search costs fall dramatically, allowing

customers to easily compare offerings and act on choices. Personalization and collaboration are key to empowering customers and building loyalty. Powerful tools of information technology and telecommunications can deliver real-time market intelligence to leaders to sense yet unforeseen changes in market forces and reinforce organizational agility to respond effectively and continuously. The focus here must always be on speed and agility.

4. *Traditional firms must pursue experimentation and partnerships.* In the converging economy, value propositions disaggregate and reaggregate, as customer advocates emerge to facilitate choice and provide "objective" advice and "free" information. Radical shifts are beginning to occur between buyers and sellers, causing new business models to emerge to supplant existing ones. In this environment, partnerships and affinity selling flourish. Today's customers have unprecedented reach to global markets and electronic channels, and to cater to this environment and remain competitive, a company needs to broker relationships that never existed before, sometimes even with traditional competitors. The focus here must always be to think of the Web as a channel, and how your company can leverage this channel to pursue experimentation and new partnerships.

5. *Traditional firms must adopt customer-centric design of products and services.* Brands and customer relationships are key drivers of economic value capture. New entrants thrive or perish based on their ability to build their brand and attract customers. The online customer expects much higher service levels, and the inability to meet these expectations tarnishes both online and offline brands. The focus here must always be to think of the Web as an extension of your brand, and how to exploit it to include your customers in the design and delivery of your products and services.

Conclusion: E-Business Adoption Index

In conclusion, vision, governance, and execution play significant roles in successful and sustained achievement of competitive advantage by the adoption of e-business for tomorrow's converging economies.

It is also important to achieve a harmony and balance between these three parameters. Your governance framework must reflect the achievement of your vision and values. Your execution structure must be appropriate and adequate to your governance.

We propose to build a ten-point scale for each of the three leadership parameters that managers can periodically measure to see if the three are synchronized with each other. We used Charles Schwab as an example in order to illustrate how to plot the three parameters against a hypothetical scale, as shown in Figure 5-11. We took into consider-

FIGURE 5-11
E-Business Adoption Index

Example: Charles Schwab

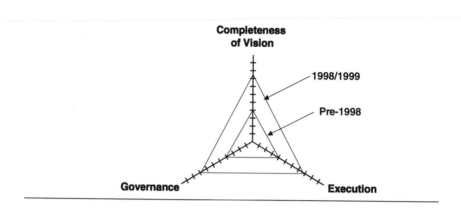

ation the company's situation before and after e-Schwab was converged into the mainline Charles Schwab operations. Our premise here is that Charles Schwab's completeness of vision in terms of sustained value delivery to its constituents reached a significantly higher level when they decided to combine the two operations. They then built an appropriate governance framework and a complementary executive structure to realize their vision.

The balance can only come from repeated and systematic management assessments and iterations of the three leadership parameters of vision, governance, and execution. Beyond these parameters, organization must seek also to rebalance management from control to leadership, as described throughout this chapter.

Growing Pains: The Precarious Relationship between Offline Parents and Online Offspring

Michael E. Brown, The Smeal College of Business Administration, The Pennsylvania State University
Kevin G. Corley, The Smeal College of Business Administration, The Pennsylvania State University
Dennis A. Gioia, The Smeal College of Business Administration, The Pennsylvania State University

In the old days of e-commerce, pure play start-ups battled each other in frenzied excitement, investors gorged on anything that was dot-com, and Internet stocks traded at almost incomprehensible multiples. Internet commerce presented many new possibilities and promises, and although there was a sense of uncertainty surrounding the great unknown, the opportunities for growth seemed limitless. Since then, traditional bricks-and-mortar companies have fought back, a trend popularized in the business press as a bricks-and-clicks strategy[1]—where offline parent companies create online children and either nurture them in a collaborative and harmonious relationship or raise their offspring as cannibals, capable of devouring the competition and potentially the parent that helped it to grow in the first place.

Making a successful transition from bricks-and-mortar to bricks-and-clicks presents both challenges and opportunities for traditional old economy companies. Although much has been written about the financial possibilities of a bricks-and-clicks strategy, there has been scant attention given to the practices and pitfalls of managing this transition. What are the key issues associated with a bricks-and-clicks transition?

What can prevent a company from realizing the potential promised by such a strategy?

Although many bricks-and-clicks companies may already have addressed some obviously important issues surrounding this transition (e.g., strategy formulation and implementation, financing an Internet endeavor, managing Internet logistics, cross-channel marketing), few have given adequate consideration to the more subtle, but arguably more fundamental, issues of organizational identity and organizational learning as they apply to the relationship between offline parents and online children. For example, questions confronting the parent organization such as "How does the addition of this online offspring affect our organizational identity and image in the marketplace?" and "What should we learn from this online child of ours?" inevitably affect the emerging relationship between parent and child. Similarly, basic questions arise for the child organization, too: Who are we as an organization? How do customers, vendors, investors, and our own parent company see us as an organization? What do we need to do to innovate and become a learning organization in the complex and dynamic e-business world? Such questions that are endemic to a bricks-and-clicks endeavor are often given scant attention or are ignored altogether. Implicit or unilateral answers to such questions, however, can be a source of unrecognized and unresolved friction between parent and child that can hinder even the best-laid plans and strategies.

How can companies successfully manage a bricks-and-clicks strategy? How can the Internet child obtain the benefits of collaboration with the parent organization while avoiding the risk of being tied too closely to the old economy ways of the parent? To explore such questions, we conducted an in-depth study of the top executives of a prototypical Fortune 500 company's online division. To find out more about the challenges of leading a transition to bricks-and-clicks, we engaged the president of this new enterprise (who came from the parent company) as our primary informant. We tracked and interviewed the president and other members of the dot-com organization's top management team over a period of nine months during the implementation of the bricks-and-clicks strategy.

The context and people we studied provide an ideal setting for a study of the key issues involved in managing a move to bricks-and-clicks. All of these executives began their careers in the offline world and now find themselves managing in the e-business environment. These individuals are living the transition and, therefore, are in a unique position to offer insights from the perspective of leaders who have experience with both the old and new economies. This is an especially important topic at this time because of the number of traditional companies now more aggressively competing in the Internet domain.[2]

A Continuum of E-Business Restructuring Relationships

Companies aspiring to Internet play can choose from a wide variety of options for structuring their e-business operations: from treating the Internet division as just another branch of the company to developing a (quasi-independent) wholly owned subsidiary of the company, issuing a "tracking stock" that separates out the performance of the e-business operations from the main financials of the company, or completely spinning off the e-business as an entity independent of the parent company. As illustrated in Figure 6-1, these options lie along a continuum of restructuring options that range from a high level of control by the parent company (new division) to a state of relative independence from the parent (new entity).

Of these options, two, in particular, seem to be most prevalent in recent bricks-and-clicks restructurings. The first involves the creation of a wholly owned subsidiary—one that is spatially separated from the core business and functions with some independence while maintaining close financial ties to the parent—that gradually moves toward complete independence culminating in an initial public offering (IPO). This approach has the purported benefits of allowing the online child more freedom to create its own business processes and culture while still taking advantage of the economies of scale available as part of the larger parent organization (e.g., supply chain, distribution channels, advertising, legal expertise). The move toward complete independence occurs as the child becomes more self-sufficient and the market accepts its viability as a stand-alone entity capable of turning a profit and surviving in the face of growing competition. The owners/executives of the parent company usually retain some stake in the online child, thus allowing them to take advantage of the often-lucrative IPO market for new e-commerce companies.

The other favorite of bricks-and-clicks restructurings is the issuance of a tracking stock. Tracking stocks function essentially like spin-offs except that the parent and child do not actually separate as in a true spin-off. A corporation issues a tracking stock for an attractive piece of its business, unlocking the hidden value for investors, but without relinquishing control over these important assets.[3] Thus, one important

FIGURE 6-1
Continuum of E-Restructurings

New Division	Wholly Owned Subsidiary	Tracking Stock	Independent Entity

difference between the tracking stock option and the creation of a new department is the image of independence projected to external stakeholders. The online child is often perceived as being more independent from the parent company, thus affording the organization some wiggle room in its relationship with the media and investors. Of course, tracking stocks have been criticized for creating the appearance of a spinoff—one where investors think they are buying a pure play company without realizing that their investment is contained inside and tied to the fortunes of the larger company (for better or worse).

The Internet child organization we studied is representative of many other bricks-and-clicks companies among the Fortune 500 in that it is not yet spun off from its parent and is currently operating like a wholly owned subsidiary. Thus, it lies more toward the high control end of our restructuring continuum. In many ways, the relationship between our offline parent and online child is like any human parent-child relationship. It is characterized by growing pains caused by a child's need to establish its own identity and modes of learning.

Because we have agreed to preserve the anonymity of our informant executives and the company they work for, we will refer to the parent company as Vertex, Inc. and its online child as Vertex.com in reporting our findings that follow.

Life in an Online Offspring

Engaging the top management team members of Vertex.com provided us with an eye-opening understanding of the harried world of Internet executives.[4] The outright pace of activity in great part defined this world and affected almost every other managerial process. It is a domain where things happen at lightning speed, decisions must be made now, yet the tasks at hand are highly ambiguous, complex, and changing. These two aspects of the dot-com context, speed and ambiguity, are key to understanding the relationship between offline parents and online children, as well as to gaining insight into larger issues associated with conducting business in the e-commerce arena. To enrich the "presence" and vividness of our findings, we have employed many direct quotes that capture the essence of the e-commerce experience.

"Everything Happens So Incredibly Fast!"

Modern business moves at a fast pace. We know that. Those of us engaged in the study and/or practice of management are by now accustomed to talking about high-velocity environments, those characterized by fast-paced, discontinuous change and inaccurate or unavailable information.[5] Yet, by the standards of the dot-com world, such environments now seem almost pedestrian. The executives in our study, all of whom came from fast-paced environments, described their experience in Mach speed or "warp speed" terms. The executives of Vertex.com perceived the difference between the offline and online world as that dramatic.

Speed compresses time and perhaps affects decision making most of all. There is never time to evaluate alternatives adequately. Heuristics and information sources applicable in the offline context are simply irrelevant or unavailable in the online setting. Decision-making speed becomes notably more valuable than precision. Furthermore, making and implementing decisions become virtually simultaneous activities, so the online world also becomes an improvisational world. Optimizing just takes too long; satisficing, settling for something that's good enough rather than pushing for the optimum result, is necessarily sufficient. The director of human resources noted:

> Some people can get tied up in knots with the tempo, with the constant change, with the unknown, and it makes them miserable. Those people hate it here.

The rapid pace of the dot-com organization and the relatively more routine tempo of the core business led to divergent (and disruptive) conceptualizations of time for members of the two organizations. "Doing things quickly" in the offline organization had an entirely different meaning than in the online company, as the chief marketing officer recounted:

> Recently we needed an analysis. We needed very quickly to find out what was working in market . . . and so we went to the corporate IS function and said we need these three pieces of information. And they said, "Okay, fine." Two days later, we are expecting the results, and IS send us this form saying, "Sign this, and we will start the process, which may take up to six weeks." We said, "We thought this was going to be done today!" And they answered, "No, this is the way it has to be done; what world are you living in?" We can't live like that.

Even though the pace was relentless, its effects were compounded by the ill-defined and complicated activities required to lead the effort to become a player in the online arena.

"It's Crazy Because Your Competitive Constructs Get Blown Apart"

Not only must Vertex.com executives operate at a frenetic pace, but they need to deal with an almost overwhelming variety of complex, changing activities and a highly ambiguous competitive environment undergoing continuous redefinition. The high degree of change in this environment gives time an almost fluid-like quality that makes not only something like tracking competitors a complicated exercise, but also something as simple and mundane as managing a daily calendar. The director of human resources noted, "I have learned to keep as much blank on my calendar as possible because 50 percent of it gets changed anyway." Overall, the rapidly changing environment meant that coping with ambiguity was one of the greatest adjustments facing the organization as it jumped into online competition.

> Before there was an Internet, it was a very competitive but finite universe of competition. In the online world . . . there are just so many [business] models out there crashing into so many other models.

The need for rapid implementation forced Vertex.com team members to overlay strategic activities that once were handled in an orderly, sequential manner in the offline world into a process that bordered on chaos with little semblance of temporal order. The chief marketing officer provides us a particularly vivid example:

> What we do isn't linear. Typically in a marketing organization, when starting up, you would write a strategy, develop a go-to-market plan, then test and execute. Then, based on the results, you would make some decisions and also build a database. The interesting thing about operating in a dot-com . . . is that we are doing [all these things] at the same time . . . they all have to be done concurrently or you are not going to be successful. That is a huge challenge.
>
> In contrast to the offline world, where boundaries are more finite, the Internet offers the possibility of competition from unknown sources, start-ups as well as established online organizations, who can quite easily compete in the market domain. Barriers to entry are minimal. Targeting customers can also be a challenge, because a web page can be accessed by diverse customers from anywhere at any time. Trying to get a handle on such fundamental concepts as who our customers are and who our competitors are is made more problematic by this environment's complexity and dynamism. The problem is compounded because the wisdom, heuristics, and technology of traditional business do not always apply to the Internet arena.

Furthermore, as the president of Vertex.com explained, the variety of business models often precludes the development of a coherent approach to coordination and competition:

At any given moment you have five or six or seven different business models, and for our new business development effort, half the battle is explaining to people the various models for doing business. . . . There are media models, shopping models, auction models. It's scary. There never used to be that way offline.

Responding to the Demands of Life as an Online Offspring

Vertex.com executives adopted strategies to cope with this extraordinarily dynamic and difficult-to-navigate environment. The pace of communication is fast, fragmented, and furious; meetings happen on top of other meetings, and decisions are made with minimal information. The president recalled experiencing initial Internet culture shock:

> At first, I couldn't understand why these Internet people had their cell phones on all day. I was thinking to myself, "That is so weird, they are in the building; it's not like they are traveling. Why do they leave their cell phones on in their home office building?" Well, the reason they do is because if they are not at their line, or their assistant can't find them, they are still instantly accessible. They all call each other on their cell phones. . . . Now I realize if I am in a meeting and Joe Blow hasn't shown up yet, I can call him on his cell phone, no matter where he is. Sometimes I find that he is in another meeting scheduled at the same time, so we just do two meetings at once by cell phone.

Members of this organization take multitasking to the extreme. Double-booking meetings is normal, and triple-booking is not uncommon. They either attend one meeting for a brief period of time, make their contribution, and hustle off to join the other meetings in progress, or they make arrangements to "be present" by phone so they can juggle the complex requirements of the job. Even the office space has been restructured to facilitate quick communication among the top management team members. The president observed:

> I gave up my nice corner office for a cubicle. I had never sat in a cubicle in my life. And so here I am in the cubicle—and I really love it. . . . I frequently got thirty to forty voice mails a day. Now I am down to about a dozen a day (and most of those are external) because the people I work with, surprise surprise, talk to each other in person on the fly; we make decisions right then and there and then we move on. There is none of this back-and-forth voice mail . . . cubicles just work wonders in facilitating communication

and speeding it up . . . plus I hear and see a lot of things and I can pick up on the tempo and the flow of things around me.

The demands of catching up to online competition, operating in an e-business environment that often disguises new competitors, and trying to anticipate innovative business models unfamiliar to the core business produced a palpable tension with the parent company, Vertex, Inc.. This tension was traceable to the differing identities held by members of the two organizations. Although the informants referred to Vertex, Inc. and Vertex.com as part of a family, there was constant conflict over vision, resources, strategy, and ways of competing. According to the dot-com president, working together was a frustrating, ongoing endeavor:

> I never thought there would be this conflict with the core business, and now I am realizing that it may be my biggest challenge. . . . I feel like we are part of the family, but we are kind of the favored child right now who can get away with a lot of different things. But that's hard, too; it doesn't make it easy working with the rest of the business. . . . We haven't figured out how we are going to work together.

Lastly, the context of the Web world meant that Vertex.com needed not only to attend seriously to issues of organizational learning, but it needed to transform itself quickly into a bona fide learning organization. Change was such a part of the landscape that failing to become a functional learning organization virtually ensured failure of the enterprise. The president of Vertex.com noted:

> How do you institutionalize all that learning across all those functions? We have to develop mechanisms not only to be dynamic, but to have some sort of shared learning ability, and in this environment, it is really kind of ad hoc.

Unforeseen Challenges

The two greatest challenges faced by Vertex.com were fundamental yet not easily apparent to members of either Vertex, Inc. or Vertex.com. These challenges were:

1. *Establishing an organizational identity.* Vertex.com struggled to define itself and establish its own identity as a nimble, e-commerce organization embedded in a bureaucratic Fortune 500 organization.

2. *Creating organizational learning opportunities.* Vertex.com needed to collaborate with Vertex, Inc. to leverage the accumulated wis-

dom of its parent while remaining unencumbered enough to engage in more aggressive, radical attempts to learn and to make sense of the complex and dynamic e-business environment.

Organizational Identity/Image Tensions

We're managing this business within a business, and it's difficult. We're the bratty upstart group that gets to do things. We're in the middle of a firestorm right now because the core business hates us. . . . They don't understand us.

Organizational identity revolves around the basic questions of "who are we?" and "how do we see ourselves as an organization?"[6] Closely related is the concept of organizational image that has to do with insider perspectives on how outsiders perceive the organization. The notion of organizational image is captured by the questions, "Who do others think we are?" and "How do others see us?" For a modern business, there are numerous "others" (i.e., stakeholders) who have different and sometimes conflicting images of a particular organization—investors, analysts, potential employees, customers, suppliers, competitors—and the perceptions of these stakeholders can heavily influence decisions and actions. For Vertex.com, there was one player that dominated above all others, and that was Vertex, Inc. Identity/image tensions at Vertex.com manifested themselves as an issue between those inside and outside the organization, and even more important, in the form of an identity crisis for the online unit, one that strained the relationship between the offline and online businesses.

There is a conflict with the core business around money, space and (stock) options. The options we have are huge compared to the core business. I would say there is space envy, option envy, and fear of cannibalization. The people who are running the other business are afraid that we are stealing their customers.

Members of Vertex, Inc. were jealous of the more generous compensation packages and the greater freedom given to the employees of Vertex.com to deviate from corporate policies and create their own dot-com organization within the larger parent organization. The online organization was allowed to operate under special rules in order to best compete in the more challenging e-business environment. However, tensions arose over the interpretation of these "special privileges," which at a deeper level reflect a conflict in how members of Vertex.com saw themselves as an organization and how they were seen by their counterparts within the parent organization. From one point of view, if Vertex.com is part of the Vertex family, why does it not have to live by the same rules as everyone else? On the other hand, if it is accepted that the unique requirements of e-business require Vertex.com to be distinctive from its parent, then differences in compensation and office space, and a less strict adherence to the penny-pinching ways of the parent, are seen as natural.

These critical questions and answers reveal the depth and complexity of these tensions:

How do members of the online business see themselves?	"We're often seen as the renegades or troublemakers in the family."
How do members of the offline business see the online business?	"They're spoiled children who get everything."

Is the online business separate from or simply part of the offline business? The answer is unclear. Although both parent and child share the same name, the same office building, and many of the same resources such as a shared distribution system, the vast differences between the parent's and child's operating environments call into question any sense of common bonds that tie them together.

Members of Vertex.com discovered that even though they were in the same industry as their offline parent, leading an online business is fundamentally different. This was in sharp contrast with the identity of the parent organization's staff members, who saw themselves as relentless cost-cutters, cautious and methodical planners and executors, strict adherents to the bottom line, and zealots when it came to attention to details. The miserly ways of the parent were in sharp contrast to the spending ways of the online organization, which was more focused on the desired end result of innovative risk taking and fast growth and had no time to focus on the small details that so consumed members of the parent organization. Online organizations (at least for now) have more latitude with investors who would never tolerate such risk taking in a traditional retail business. As an Internet company, taking creative risks leads to more opportunities, ones that might otherwise be missed if the organization were too concerned about incremental progress instead of aggressive growth. As one Vertex.com's manager commented:

> So very much of it is speed to market right now. . . . In mature businesses inches matter; to use a sports analogy, we are still a yards game. . . .

The dot-com organization valued its independence from the offline business so that it could operate more quickly and effectively. It has established its own rules of communication and adopted its own norms for operating that are quite foreign to members of the offline business.

Out of necessity Vertex.com has developed its own identity in order to best meet the demands of competing in the rough-and-tumble world of e-commerce.

As framed by Vertex.com members, some key questions were: Are we part of Vertex, Inc? (Yes.) Do we have similar identities? (No.) Do outsiders see us as the same organization? (Yes and no, depending on whom you ask.) At first blush, such identity and image tensions may seem to be idiosyncratic to the particular organization we studied. We have concluded, however, that these tensions are virtually unavoidable in any online child/offline parent relationship. Any attempts to encourage collaboration between an offline parent and an online child are potentially problematic because of the issue of conflicting identities. Unless the child organization "moves out of the house" (that is, is completely spun off from the parent organization), the possibility for conflict between the parent and child must be recognized and addressed.

As complicated as the internal identity/image tensions may be, they are exacerbated when external observers join the fray. A good illustration of the importance of organizational image occurred when the online unit announced that it was growing at a record pace but had to increase its losses to continue to do so. Wall Street analysts who followed the Internet sector cheered that the company was committed to aggressive growth and doing all that it could to grab its piece of the pie—hallmarks of an energetic Internet company. At the same time, analysts who followed the parent company jeered that the online business was losing so much money and feared that the Internet division would bleed away the profits of the core business. The same company and same results produced diametrically opposed reactions among the analysts depending on their image of the online division. The chief financial officer of Vertex commented on the difficulty of trying to satisfy these divergent expectations:

> It all depends on your audience . . . When I go to a meeting with [our president], I have to remind myself, "Who are we talking to . . . do we have a core hat on or do we have an Internet hat on?"

Becoming a Learning Organization

> We are putting a high premium on learning. . . . In the online world, you have some degrees of freedom [to take risks and make mistakes], but not for long.

Given the unique context that is characterized by speed, complexity, and the aforementioned identity/image tensions, it was imperative that Vertex.com become a learning organization capable of adjusting to the changing e-business environment. Change happens so fast in online competition—changing competitors, changing customers, changing technologies, changing investor expectations—that dot-com leaders are constantly forced to figure out not only how to cope, but also how to fashion structures and processes that can internalize knowledge geared to this kind of dynamism. And that means trying to instill an experimentation stance. Sustainability in this environment means institutionalizing an orientation toward change—and not just reactive change, but a somewhat daring, if pragmatic attitude that encourages proactive risk taking and creative enterprise. The president of Vertex.com admits:

> We have no idea what works, so we are spending much of the next four or five months just putting things out there to see if they work. . . . We know that a good half of it is going to fail; we just don't know which half.

Whereas the core business was in the habit of modifying or adapting existing routines to handle variability, in the online business variability was a defining element of the environment itself. Speed was a driver of that variability, so instilling a stance of experimenting with new ideas became the norm. Comparisons of modes of learning have also characterized learning as incremental versus radical and as exploitative versus explorative. At this stage in the development of the online domain, learning in Vertex.com could only be appropriately understood in radical/explorative terms.[7] Said one manager:

> It is a learn-it-as-you-go kind of business right now. You have to get something out there. . . . If you can get something out there that is "good enough," you can have a chance to come back and make it great. If you don't get something out there, you have no chance at all.

As a result, the facilitation of organizational learning and the creation of a learning organization are primary tasks for a dot-com leader. Learning in new environments is frequently characterized by the questions that demand answers. Some of the salient questions in this domain took the following forms: What technologies will deliver what they promise? Which new tools are hype and which are useful? What technologies are on the horizon that could torpedo us or transform us? Who are our (new) competitors? How can we cope with the expanding demands of an expanding universe of competitors? Additional questions of a more immediate nature give some sense of the dilemmas facing the president:

> Every day is a struggle for me as I think through the decisions that need to be made: Will this slow us down? What is the downside?

What is the upside in learning? Will we still make our numbers? Can we afford to make a mistake? Can we afford not to make a mistake? And can we afford to evaluate it one minute longer?

Leading a learning organization demands courage in risk taking, confidence that risky strategies will work out, and the flexibility to repeatedly reevaluate all of these questions to keep pace with a relentlessly dynamic environment. Becoming a learning organization offspring of a more traditional parent also exacerbates the identity tensions with the core business, so there are nontrivial implications for coexisting with an offline parent that achieved success through exploitative learning.

Advice for Managers of E-Business Parents and Offspring

Here are some recommendations for managing the identity tensions and learning issues that are inherent in a bricks-and-clicks endeavor. These suggestions are directed to both offline parents and their online children.

Don't Assume There Is One Big, Happy Family

One of the first mistakes that occurred in Vertex's bricks-and-clicks implementation was that no one inside the organization foresaw the degree to which family conflict and jealousy would become a serious issue. These conflicts go beyond ordinary organizational politics. The stress of trying to operate an e-business within a traditional bricks-and-mortar corporation places great burdens on members of both the offline parent and online child. Trying to work together while operating under very different circumstances and living up to different expectations creates disharmony that can reduce the overall effectiveness of the bricks-and-clicks strategy. Although these family conflicts are strong enough to disrupt the working relationship between parent and child, they are often invisible to outsiders. For example, in our study, judging by many of the popular press accounts and the statements of Vertex.com's president, the online company has generally been praised as an Internet success story. Yet beneath the rosy picture lay turmoil.

The best way to manage these conflicts is to recognize that first, a bricks-and-clicks context is conducive to creating identity tensions and, second, to address the identity conflicts as soon as they arise. During the time that we studied Vertex.com, the recognition of the identity tensions occurred late, well after the symptoms of the problems had manifested themselves. After the tensions were diagnosed, various formal attempts were made to discuss the issue of identity and its attendant conflict—from a formal memo issued to all employees, to discussion of the issue at a national sales meeting, to multiple roundtable sessions with managers at all levels of both the parent and child organization. The fact that the conflict persisted throughout the duration of our investigation is a testament to the gravity of these issues.

Establish a Mind-Set of "Stay Away, Come Closer"

Such a contradictory statement captures the complexity of the offline parent and online child relationship. On the one hand, parent and child must work together to collaborate, share resources, and compete as one organization with an integrated bricks-and-clicks strategy. On the other hand, the child needs freedom to mold itself into an organization that is best prepared for the fast-paced, unpredictable nature of e-business. Often, our tendency as human beings with limited information-processing capacity is to simplify complex and ambiguous situations. Members of Vertex.com told us that there were many employees in the parent organization who felt that it would have been better for the online organization to relocate to an entirely different site away from the parent organization. Although such a move may have reduced the everyday tensions between the two organizations, it would also have reduced the very synergies and benefits that are provided by a bricks-and-clicks strategy. On the other hand, decreeing that the dot-com organization work very closely with its offline parent would almost certainly doom Vertex.com to an early death, killed by the suffocating constraints imposed by being just another division of the company. Merging "bricks" and "clicks" is difficult and requires an approach that is just as complicated, one that embraces these contradictions between parent and child, old and new.

Any organization that creates a dot-com spin-off simultaneously creates its own rival. Any dot-com leader will struggle with the need to create a distinctive identity and image for the new business to compete with the pure play Internet start-ups and other corporate spin-offs in a sometimes alien competitive environment. Yet creating a too-distinct identity/image can compromise working together in a mutually beneficial partnership with the core business.

Viewing its online child as part of the family, the offline parent organization wants the dot-com organization to live by basic family rules. But members of the dot-com organization see those rules as a potentially fatal hindrance that precludes them from inventing their own systems to compete in the unique environment in which they operate.[8] This is called the law of requisite variety, which is a term borrowed from evolutionary theorists. The clash of image and identity provides a potentially explosive political mix between members of the two businesses.

> I have to create a sense that everybody is a part of it [Vertex.com's growth and success] . . . but you have someone running a five-

minute mile, which is us, and the others running a ten-minute mile. How do you race in the same race competitively and collaboratively?

Because of the preferential treatment that new dot-com spin-offs typically receive, it is important for their leaders to anticipate jealousies and political fallout from the members (and perhaps especially the executives) of the parent business, and to develop a relationship that strikes a balance between the contradictory elements of connection and autonomy, interdependence and independence.

Encourage Your Children to Be Radical (Learners)

One of the most critical survival tasks for the child organization to learn is how to operate in the Internet environment. What tools from the offline world work? What principles of business still apply? Becoming a learning organization is of primary importance for dot-coms. Given the dynamic and complex environment in which it operates, the online child organization needs to have the freedom to take chances, make mistakes, and adjust strategies as conditions change or new data reveals that a course correction is needed. A fundamental aspect of creating this environment involves an organizational identity where members see themselves as "improvisers," capable of moving quickly and adjusting on the fly. Decision making via satisficing is the order of the day, contrary to the usual wisdom of traditional business. There is simply no time to gather and analyze more data. A reasonable possibility will suffice. As the president saw it:

> Sometimes good enough is great. . . . You don't come in to work thinking, "Oh, my God, what if I make a mistake!" Because we are moving so fast, sometimes good enough is just fine. So you make decisions and don't wait to get more data, more data, more data.

In addition to having the latitude to move quickly and take risks, the dot-com organization must ensure that knowledge is distributed more completely throughout the organization so that the "big picture" does not reside solely with one person or remain exclusively at the top. Learning is at a premium, so debate and dialogue should be allowed to flourish in an atmosphere that encourages questioning. A learning dot-com organization is in a much better position to respond more swiftly to constant change compared to more bureaucratic offline businesses. Members of Vertex.com saw themselves as a smart, well-integrated learning community. The physical space occupied by the online organization can help to foster this identity. Vertex.com had no offices, only conference rooms. Executives worked in cubicles, and there were numerous common social spaces that prevented isolationism. Said one manager:

> There is so much more interconnectivity; very rarely should a leadership team member be the only one to know what he or she is doing . . . because so much of what we do cuts across and affects others on the leadership team. There is a lot more cut-across and interconnectiveness than in the offline world we all came from.

An online organization needs the freedom to take risks. It needs to avoid the dangers of overprogramming that can stifle the organization's ability to deal with ambiguity and operate on the fly. Finally, it must learn how to learn. This means that online leaders should actively attend to changes in the operating environment and then foster debate to consider if and how the organization should change to adapt.

This need to learn was seen vividly in the sharp contrast between Vertex, Inc. and Vertex.com. For the offline parent organization, operating in a mature, more static business, the emphasis was on incremental learning—exploiting what is known and programming it into the organization's bureaucratic structure for maximum efficiency. The online offspring, however, needed to engage in more radical modes of learning. Because change in the dot-com world happens fast and frequently, the accompanying uncertainty and ambiguity render many of the old tools and techniques meaningless. Therefore, the entire dot-com organization must adopt a learning approach wherein improvisation is common practice, risk taking is a norm, and learning to learn is required. The concept of the learning organization has never been more relevant, or more necessary, than in the dot-com environment.

Remember That Parents Can Learn From Their Children, Too

We have already said a great deal about the need for the online child organization to establish its own identity and become a learning organization, but we must also highlight the potential learning benefits that can take place for the parent organization as well in a bricks-and-clicks relationship. In the case of Vertex.com, there were numerous occasions when it chose to do something differently from its parent, which provided Vertex, Inc. a chance to learn vicariously from its child's success and failures. The online child was able to provide the offline parent with some frame-breaking opportunities to reexamine its policies and perhaps to uncover new opportunities that would otherwise never have been considered by a parent that was pretty well set in its ways.

One of the best examples concerned the policy of Vertex.com to provide funds for home Internet access for all of its employees to encourage a more wired and intelligent organization wherein employees would scout out the competition, as well as Vertex.com's own website, on a frequent basis. This policy was deemed such a success that soon members of the parent organization were looking for ways to implement it in part or whole in their own organization—something that the otherwise tightfisted parent would never have considered were it not for the explorative ways of the child.

Even in a Hardwired World, the "Soft Stuff" Still Matters

We close by noting that even in a wired world where the latest technologies dominate the headlines, some of the "softer" issues can still make or break a business venture. In managing a successful bricks-and-clicks enterprise, e-business leaders must attend to not only the obvious issues of marketing, finance, and technology, but also to the equally important issues of managing organizational identity and organizational learning. Our study of Vertex.com and its interdependencies with Vertex, Inc., suggests that it is easy to overlook these issues in the now-common bricks-and-clicks relationships that result when offline parents produce online offspring. We have provided some practical suggestions for negotiating some of the pitfalls that come with this new territory. We hope that these suggestions may better enable many bricks-and-clicks organizations to meet the challenges of a complicated and ever-dynamic e-business environment. Accounting for these important issues can help avoid some dysfunctional internal turmoil and strife in an e-business atmosphere that is already hypercompetitive and inhospitable enough, without the added difficulties that come with the precarious relationships between offline parents and online offspring.

Endnotes

1 M. M. Hamilton, "Loud and clear, a silent 'e': Traditional merchants blur lines with seamless integration of 'bricks and clicks,' " *The Washington Post* (April 23, 2000), p. H1; S. McGee, " 'Bricks and clicks' deals may proliferate as firms unlock New Economy assets," *The Wall Street Journal* (February 9, 2000), p. C1; and J. Useem, "Internet defense strategy: Cannibalize yourself," *Fortune* (September 6, 1999), pp. 121–134.

2 E. Brown, "Big business meets the e-world," *Fortune* (November 8, 1999), pp. 88–98; and S. L. Hwang, "Revamping the model—clicks and bricks: Pure Internet stores get a lot of attention, but Net retailers that have one foot in the old world may have the best of both worlds," *The Wall Street Journal* (April 17, 2000), p. R8.

3 For more information on tracking stocks, see F. Barbash, "Tracking a stock gimmick: Tracking stocks' long-term benefits for investors are untested," *Austin-American Statesman* (December 11, 1999), p. B1; B. G. Malkiel, "Manager's Journal: Tracking Stocks Are Likely to Derail," *The Wall Street Journal* (February 14, 2000), p 42A; and S. Sherreik, "Tread carefully when you buy tracking stocks: They're tied to the fortunes of their parent company," *BusinessWeek* (March 6, 2000), p. 182.

4 The general findings and many of the executive quotations in this section are based on M.E. Brown and D.A. Gioia, "Dot-com Leadership: Set Your Watch to Internet Time" (prepared in 2000 for the *Academy of Management Executive* and currently in revision).

5 L. J. Bourgeois and K. Eisenhardt, "Strategic decision processes in high-velocity environments: Four cases in the microcomputer industry," *Management Science* Vol. 34 (July 1988), pp. 816–835; and K. Eisenhardt, "Making fast strategic decisions in high-velocity environments," *Academy of Management Journal* Vol. 32 (September 1989), pp. 543–576.

6 D. A. Gioia, M. Schultz, and K. G. Corley, "Organizational Identity, Image, and Adaptive Instability," *Academy of Management Review* Vol. 25 (January 2000), pp. 63–81, offer a provocative way of looking at identity and image as dynamic and interrelated concepts. Their ideas counter the long-held notion that identity is stable and enduring, as portrayed by S. Albert and D. Whetten in "Organizational Identity," in L. L. Cummings and B. M. Staw, eds., *Research in Organizational Behavior* Vol. 7 (1985), pp. 263–295. Gioia et al. argue that having a malleable identity is beneficial to an organization in order to manage the often changing and conflicting external images it must contend with (what they call adaptive instability).

7 For a discussion of single- versus double-loop learning see C. Argryis and D. Schon, *Organizational Learning* (Reading, MA: Addison-Wesley, 1978). For a discussion of exploration and exploitation, see J. G. March, "Exploration and Exploitation in Organizational Learning," *Organization Science* Vol. 2 (1991), pp. 71–87. For an overall review of the organizational learning literature, see A. S. Miner and S. J. Mezias, "Ugly duckling no more: Pasts and futures of organizational learning research," *Organization Science* Vol. 7 (1996), pp. 88–99.

8 This is called the law of requisite variety, which is a term borrowed from evolutionary theorists and is described in greater detail by Morgan, G. 1986. *Images of Organization.* Newbury Park, CA: Sage.

CHAPTER 7

Managing the Emerging Technology

Hemant K. Bhargava, The Smeal College of Business Administration, The Pennsylvania State University

Jun Lee, Unisys Corporation

Information technologies are transforming work within and across organizations. Technological innovations and widespread adoption of TCP/IP-related standards—the "language" spoken by every computer on the Internet today—have enabled the redefinition of the role of information technology (IT) from a supporting function to a critical and pervasive business process. In line with the firm's transformation into an e-business, these technological innovations have also dramatically changed the relationships, processes, and interactions between the firm and its stakeholders—customers, employees, suppliers, investors, prospects, and government. As the underlying e-business technologies themselves evolve, firms face a constant challenge to change, not to be changed, in order to remain competitive in the marketplace.

In this chapter, we discuss emerging technologies and practices that will help companies remain open and flexible in response to the changing technical environment, so that past and present IT investments continue to remain valuable in the future. E-business touches everything, as shown in Figure 7-1: business models, strategy, customer relations, value chain, fail-proof operation, logistics, and marketing. This raises the challenge of managing the emerging technologies and maintaining harmony with all of the processes and technologies.

FIGURE 7-1
The Complex E-Business Environment

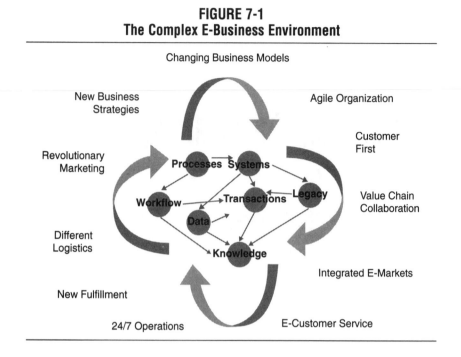

We address this challenge in the following sections. First, we discuss the broad application environment that forms the context within which e-business technologies are deployed. Second, we address the issues with change management in regard to the enterprise information architecture. Next, we discuss emerging technologies that help achieve the goal of an open, scalable, and flexible architecture. Last, we discuss how companies can remain open and flexible with online communities such as trading partners and suppliers by using the open and standard technologies available from software consortia and online trading communities.

E-Business Application Environment

The widespread adoption of Transmission Control Protocol/Internet Protocol (TCP/IP)-related standards for business computing and communication has been accompanied by a wave of technological innovation. Numerous new standards and technologies in streaming media (e.g., QuickTime, Macromedia Flash, RealVideo, immersive video, 3-D video and animation, to name just a few) have helped create a media-rich environment for Internet-based information exchange. Technologies and standards for client-side and server-side computing (e.g., the Java programming language, the Common Gateway Interface, Active X controls, scripting languages) have enabled the seamless deployment of complex computational applications that provide a high degree of platform independence and that can be accessed via a mere web browser. Standards and tools for distributed computing and communication (e.g., CORBA and IIOP, Java RMI and Enterprise Java Beans, DCOM) allow the development of large applications as component-ware, with the freedom to distribute components over a heterogeneous networked computing environment. Finally, development of standards for representation of business information and processes (e.g., XML, RosettaNet, Resource Description Framework) facilitate the exchange of information between organizations in a manner suitable for action by machines and automated agents. Businesses can use emerging Internet-based information technologies in many ways, including to:

- Disseminate information to stakeholders
- Manage relationships with stakeholders
- Conduct business transactions with stakeholders within the organization (i.e., intranet applications), with customers and others (i.e., Internet applications), and across the extended enterprise (i.e., extranet applications)
- Realize efficient allocations of resources and better conduct of marketplaces through improved matching of buyers and sellers

Applications can be simple and text-based or media-rich incorporating beneficial use of streaming media technologies. Applications may largely be broadcast-oriented one-way communication of information, or they may involve two-way information exchange as in electronic customer relationship management. Similarly, applications may involve varying needs for security, privacy of stakeholder information, and standards for management of data. Although applications may be stand-alone involving, for example, only a single process such as order processing, true benefits of e-business transformation are achieved by applications that involve information integration across the firm's internal information systems or across the firm's supply chain.

In each case, the transition from simple to more complicated applications generally provides greater benefits to the firm but is difficult to implement in an open, scalable, and flexible manner. Obviously, no single technology can support such a broad range of applications, and no single technology can remain the dominant choice for a particular application for a very long time. This underscores the need for an enterprise information architecture that helps the company to align the business strategy with the available technologies and to develop new applications and technologies as their business changes.

Enterprise Information Architecture— Blueprint for Change

The biggest challenge for the modern enterprise faced with constantly emerging technology is "change." There are many new technologies available today and in incubation for tomorrow. We can buy handheld computers for salespeople, Oracle for the finance department, Informix for customer support, and so on. The temptations to adopt new technologies and applications are irresistible, but it isn't hard to realize that the company will only achieve more headaches than benefits when these technologies are purchased without much thought to how they will work together and how they align with the business process and goals. Changes in a company's IT structure are sometimes initiated by the temptation of new technologies, but more often by changes in the business process, organizational structure, or the company's vision. How often do we determine the impact of the changes to the information systems before we go ahead and approve the acquisition of new technologies and applications?

Architectural Deficiencies and Frustrations

The average large organization has 150 different applications, tools, and utilities accessible from the desktop, according to Giga Information Group, Inc. In many enterprises, managers and users are frustrated with the current inventory of existing applications, databases, and systems. It is not because there are too many applications, or too few. Nor is it because they are not strategic enough or because they are mainframe, hierarchical, COBOL, or whatever. The frustration arises from uncontrolled changes within the IT structure, a so-called architectural deficiency. John Zachman identifies three types of fundamental architectural deficiencies with their associated frustrations:[1]

1. *Documentation Deficiencies.* In many cases, there is little documentation about the strategic view and plans of upper managers (including CEOs) in regard to the information system. Often the design model of the data, process, and network are not even built and documented. Without explicit formalizations and configuration control of the vision, process, and models—as is done for the actual information system—it is extremely difficult to keep the upper management's plan and intent for the organization's information system in sync with the actual system.

2. *Architectural Legacy.* In general, the data and hardware/systems software were tailored to the application and therefore disintegrated with regard to the enterprise. This creates an enterprisewide discon-

nection among data, process, and files. As a result, the maintenance of this "legacy" consumes the major portion of the IT resources.

3. *Reverse-Engineered Fixes.* The enterprise has simply changed around the existing applications, and these applications were built under the assumption that nothing would ever change. This is clear because the machine-readable codes or uncommented spaghetti programs are the only things left in many cases. If the company changes vision, business process, organizational structure, or the application functions, it has to be reverse-engineered from whatever is left at that level.

Systematic management of technological changes requires the development of an enterprise information architecture that specifies the blueprint for changes.

Enterprise Information Architecture: Definition

An enterprise information architecture comprises vision, principles, process, people, technology, and standards. A well-prepared architecture is a logical organization of information pertaining to corporate-level, enterprisewide elements—in particular, strategic goals and relationships between applications and data elements and technology infrastructure.

The architecture establishes guidelines, standards, and operational services that define the enterprise's systems development environment and govern the acquisition and deployment of technology. As such, it provides the foundation for detailed data, application, and network architectures. An enterprise information architecture is a key component of a mature information system (IS) organization that enables alignment with business goals, consistent processes, and best practices in software reuse. A typical enterprise information architecture is shown in Figure 7-2.

The business architecture defines the business process, roles, and entities from different perspectives, such as the owners of the company and managers. Then, it is transformed to the application model by the architects. The application architecture is driven by business requirements and reflects the strategic intent of the enterprise and some business process issues. These are expressed in the form of models as well as principles and guidelines. The software architecture creates the logical architecture of the application. Then this structure is used to provide the guideline for the design, development, and deployment of application software. Through this layer, the functional view of the business process (i.e., application architecture) is transformed into the view of the software structure (which, in turn, is supported by the technology architecture). The technical architecture identifies the nature and struc-

FIGURE 7-2
Typical Enterprise Information Architecture

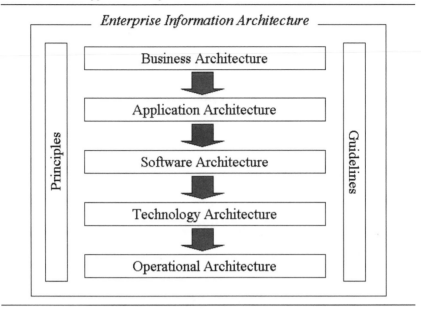

The operational architecture addresses the specific information technologies chosen to support the delivery of the business solutions. The operational architecture addresses the people, processes, and organizational structure required to complete the business solution within the enterprise. Principles and guidelines at every layer of the enterprise architecture are used to communicate and clarify architectural intent. Principles in one view of the enterprise architecture become requirements to subsequent levels. Guidelines are suggestions or recommendations that will result in implementation that is more aligned with architectural intent.

The Giga Information Group performed a cost-benefit analysis of ten companies engaged in enterprise architectural development. All of the companies had annual revenues greater than $1 billion. The overall development includes a planning cost of $3.5 million while the measurable benefits were $600,000. After all of the developments were completed, the ongoing maintenance costs were $100,000 while the yearly measurable benefits were $5 million. Among the benefits: Hardware consolidation makes volume purchasing discounts possible; and reductions in labor and technical support allow staff reductions because of a simplified infrastructure. The company can now use automated tools for network monitoring, software distribution, virus protection, and other tasks made simple by standardization. In addition, having a simpler, more predictable technical infrastructure reduces the cost of developing new systems and the risk of new product deployments, development, and daily troubleshooting, just to list a few.[2]

The well-prepared enterprise information architecture provides huge long-term savings in support and integration costs in addition to better alignment with business strategy and more consistent IT processes. The well-prepared enterprise information architecture can also help companies develop new IT solutions and services faster as the business changes. Developing a good enterprise information architecture isn't simple. It requires time, people, and money. It requires senior-level commitment, flexibility, and a long-term view. Finally, it requires choosing the right enabling technologies that can be used to build open and flexible solutions.

Enabling Technologies for Open, Flexible, and Scalable Applications

Once the "architectural legacy" is taken care of, the next thing to consider in managing the emerging technology is employing open and flexible technologies to avoid the "technology legacy." How do we remain open and flexible with so many past, present, and future technologies? An ideal solution allows us to integrate future technologies with our current and past technology investments, mitigating the risk of developing stand-alone solutions that become obsolete or incompatible soon after they are operational.

Many enabling technologies are now available to deliver this architectural requirement. We shall discuss two sets of technologies:

- Distributed object technologies that allow development of components that can be discovered and executed on several computing platforms and in various applications
- Extensible markup language (XML), a meta-language for creating documents that describe content in a standard, open format, independent of the technology or application

Distributed Object Technologies

There are two principal distributed object technologies, one deriving from the Java-distributed object model and the Enterprise Java Beans (EJB) server-side component architecture, and the second the Common Object Request Broker Architecture (CORBA) standardized by the Object Management Group (OMG). Both the CORBA and Java approaches enable the development of objects with clearly specified interfaces so that these objects are self-describing and may be discovered by other objects. The Java Remote Method Invocation (RMI) protocol is used for communicating between Java objects, whereas CORBA objects communicate using the Internet Inter-Orb Protocol (IIOP).

In evaluating the value of such architectures, it is useful to keep in mind that e-business applications should:

- Be accessible from various types of desktop computing platforms and other devices
- Be able to accommodate changes in the underlying hardware technologies by being platform-independent
- Scale up to support many users, including providing reasonable response times under normal conditions and providing continuous availability even under peak conditions.

Understanding some technical details of these technologies makes it clearer how they contribute to an open and flexible solution.[3]

Java Enterprise Java Beans (EJB) and Remote Method Invocation (RMI)

Java applets and other Java programs provide platform independence via the concept of a Java Virtual Machine (JVM). Java RMI is a distributed object protocol that communicates methods between clients and servers in a networked environment. A Java object whose methods are to be invoked remotely defines its interface as an interface class. This server object is registered with the RMI system, generating server skeletons (a server-side entity that makes calls to the implementation of the server object) and stubs (proxies for the server object), which are then used by client objects to make calls to the methods of the server object. RMI defines a structured and transparent way in which a Java object executing on a JVM can invoke methods of other Java objects executing on (potentially) a remote disparate JVM.

EJBs are reusable server-side software entities that provide application developers the means to encapsulate business logic into application components, independent from the underlying middleware, systems, and hardware. EJBs provide generalized support for low-level services such as transaction, concurrency control, security, naming and discovery, database connectivity, and persistent state.

EJB and Java RMI require communicating objects to be written in Java, but this problem can be mitigated by admitting non-Java applications that are "wrapped" in a Java interface object. Java objects can be executed on any platform that provides a JVM, which includes most desktop computing environments and many other devices including personal digital assistants (PDAs), cell phones, and information appliances. Enterprise Beans can run on any server that implements the EJB specification, thus providing platform-independence on both the client and server side. This approach provides tremendous flexibility to a business in choosing its web server and application environment. Furthermore, it can change its own computing hardware or face changes in computing platforms of its users, without necessitating a redesign and implementation of its applications.[4]

CORBA and Internet Inter-ORB Protocol (IIOP)

CORBA is an open cross-platform communications architecture developed by the Object Management Group. OMG's charter includes establishment of industry guidelines and detailed object management specifications to provide a common framework for application development. CORBA has grown to be the de facto standard for flexible interoperability and heterogeneous application integration. CORBA objects may be implemented in any programming language that has a defined mapping with CORBA (including C, C++, Ada, Java, SmallTalk, and COBOL).

There are three important concepts in the CORBA approach: an Interface Definition Language (IDL), Object Request Broker (ORB), and the invocation interface. The development of a CORBA object begins with the declaration of its interface in an IDL. This defines an application programming interface (API) to the object, and IDL-specified methods can be written in any language supported within CORBA. The ORB is the middleware that enables objects to discover and communicate with remote objects. CORBA supports two mechanisms to discover and invoke remote objects. The static invocation interface is used when objects are predefined, and interface definition results in the creation of server skeletons and client stubs. Class definitions are declared in the interface repository, and runtime objects are registered in the implementation repository, thereby enabling objects to be called by other applications. The dynamic invocation interface is used to support discovery of objects in real time. When application components must be put together on demand, they discover objects at runtime by browsing the interface repository and use the interface information about the desired object to construct an invocation request. While dynamic invocation is more complex than static invocation, it provides greater flexibility.

The CORBA framework provides a complete set of services required in any distributed implementation by any large businesses—user interface, information management, systems management, and task management. There are several services to choose from (all based on the same specification), and together these services make up the foundation upon which future technologies will interoperate. The building blocks are there, so there is no need to spend unnecessary resources reinventing the wheel. By one estimate, as much as 30–70 percent of a traditional application's functionality is already enabled by CORBA services. Therefore, a CORBA implementation allows the business to focus on the domain or business logic necessary to integrate the applications and leaves the "basic building blocks" work to the vendor.[5]

XML and Metadata

While distributed object technologies facilitate an open, flexible, and scalable application architecture, there is one other aspect of open and flexible e-business applications—they need to communicate with each other and exchange transactional and other data that must be manipulated by other programs. While hypertext markup language (HTML) provides a simple language for exchange of information between heterogeneous machines in a distributed network, it supports only display for, and interpretation by, humans and is inadequate for the task of representing structured data for manipulation by machines. To provide an open and flexible data structure that can be understood by any application and systems within an enterprise or between different enterprises, XML (extensible markup language) is a standards-based enabling technology.

XML is a substantial subset of the standard generalized markup language (SGML), the worldwide standard meta-language for creating markup languages. Like SGML, XML is a meta-language, meaning that it is not a specific markup language; rather it is used to define particular markup languages such as HTML. XML permits information providers and application developers to design their own markup languages by creating markup tags specialized to their needs.

For example, while an HTML page encoding a product description may have tags that essentially say "put this name in boldface" and "put this number in italics," a corresponding XML document would say "the following string identifies the product's name" and "the following number is the product's price." The set of tags and the grammar for combining tags (i.e., the document type definition) are themselves defined and stored separately from their values and could be made accessible to the receiver of the information or to other participants in the exchange of such documents, thereby enabling a community to use a consistent set of tags and grammar and enabling document receivers to extricate the meaning of the document's contents for the purpose of further processing.

Creation of an XML-based markup language involves defining the tags (i.e., setting the vocabulary) and defining the grammar for combining the tags (i.e., creating a document type definition). XML documents can be manipulated by document parsers, either to validate or display the document or, more important, to perform any programmatic manipulation of the document data, based on an understanding of the document's grammar and meanings of the tags. XML parsers are often written in Java and can be obtained dynamically as the client machine comes across a new document type.[6]

While much is said about the ability of XML to encapsulate the meaning or semantics of a document, XML itself has little to offer in this regard. However, in conjunction with frameworks for metadata representation such as Resource Description Framework (RDF) and document standards and agreements in trading communities, XML provides a powerful means for exchanging structured data and documents without loss of meaning and for recovering the semantics of a document's contents to allow for machine processing of the contents. Such standards are rapidly being developed across a variety of communities. We discuss this issue in the next section.

Remain Open and Flexible with Online Communities

Many e-business solutions require the integration of an enterprise's information systems with those of its trading partners, customers, and financial institutions, among others, to develop so-called extraprises or "extended enterprises." Information system integration started with simple data exchanges between companies, typically using electronic data interchange (EDI) technology. Today, businesses are quickly becoming members of online communities sharing data through XML-based technologies. These new technologies are accelerating the development of new business models and collaborative solutions between these online communities beyond the usage of the electronic data exchanges. In this section we describe some of the technical challenges and available alternative solutions for implementing online community integration.

Technical Challenges
Companies preparing for online community integration face several key challenges:

- Scalability of collaborative solutions
- Support of multiple technologies
- Support of multiple collaborative business models
- Support of fast deployment cycles

As the need for online community integration increases, businesses must focus more on external rather than internal transactions. This shifts the complexity from a controlled and relatively simple environment to an uncontrolled and complex environment. The traditional days-long or weeks-long period for accomplishing transactions is no longer acceptable as businesses move toward real-time trade and data exchange. Businesses that were content with a streamlined internal procurement system enabled with workflow and approval systems now face the challenge of complete value chain integration—enabling vendor-managed catalog, fulfillment, real-time product availability check, and invoice and payment transaction. Businesses must develop the ability to work with the specific business process and data requirements of multiple trading exchanges. This forces companies to adopt more standard technologies and interfaces such as technologies built around XML (although you can choose from more than one kind of XML-based language).

What should a business do? Since we can't dictate the architectures of our customers or suppliers (except in rare cases), we must work with their existing technologies and business processes. If we knew the architecture, design standards, coding standards, and implementation processes of just one of our suppliers, we may be able to build an interface for this one supplier. But what about the other suppliers? An open and flexible solution requires businesses to be aware of technologies available in their communities—prebuilt components, services, infrastructure, and standards that help integrate the enterprise's business process, data, and communication with their online communities.

Online Trading Communities

There are many online trading communities and standards available today. Most of them are industry-specific, such as RosettaNet (an independent high-tech electronics data and process standardization effort). There are a few general ones such as BizTalk (Microsoft's XML data standardization efforts). The adoption of business process integration standards, such as RosettaNet or BizTalk, will help reduce the complexity of online trading community integration.

RosettaNet—Common E-Business Processes

RosettaNet is a trading community for the computer and electronics industries. It was established in May 1998, with IBM Corp. and Microsoft Corp. testing the first XML-based Partner Interface Processes (PIPs) in April 1999. The initial focus on electronic ordering, pricing, and adding products to catalogs had expanded by December 1999 to ten PIPs. These had been completed for basic supply chain functions to distribute product information, for purchase order management, for querying technical information, and for transferring shopping carts. RosettaNet now includes many organizations, such as CompUSA, Compaq, Ingram Micro, 3Com, Cisco Systems, Hewlett-Packard, Intel, SAP, Quantum, Federal Express, UPS, Arrow Electronics, Avnet, and Marshall Industries.

RosettaNet's mission is to harness the global and pervasive reach of the Internet by defining and leading the implementation of open and common electronic business processes between partners in the information technology supply chain. These processes are designed to align the electronic business interfaces between partners, ultimately resulting in measurable benefits for IT buyers and supply chain partners. RosettaNet specifies these open and common e-business processes as PIPs and their implementation guidelines. RosettaNet distributes these guidelines to partners in the supply chain so that they can configure their specific e-business processes to interoperate with those of their partners.

The RosettaNet Implementation Framework project was chartered to specify an open and common RosettaNet networked-application framework so that partners and RosettaNet solution providers can implement computer solutions that can collaboratively execute RosettaNet-compliant PIPs. The PIP specification model enables RosettaNet to specify partner-to-partner electronic business processes in terms of "actions," "transactions," and "execution processes." The implementation framework specification enables RosettaNet partners and solution providers to create networked applications that can execute these e-business processes by communicating according to strictly defined protocols. These protocols specify application message formats and message exchange sequences.

Figure 7-3 illustrates the conceptual RosettaNet business model.[7] The RosettaNet model is intended to enable supply chain business partners to execute interoperable e-business processes by continuously developing, maintaining, and distributing partner interface process implementation guidelines.

RosettaNet adopts existing e-business standards, guidelines, or specifications wherever possible and creates new e-business framework specifications where necessary. Typically these frameworks are generic and all-embracing in nature so that they can be used for all types of e-business applications. There are five conceptual parts to the RosettaNet business model:

1. *E-Business Framework Service.* RosettaNet's Partner Interface Process teams use these frameworks to create PIP guidelines (labeled "1" in Figure 7-3) that define how computer systems will cooperatively execute e-business processes in the supply chain. These guidelines narrow the general information frameworks into detailed specifications that must be embraced by all members who wish to conduct e-business with RosettaNet-compliant partners.

2. *Implementation Guidelines.* The implementation guidelines are provided to companies that wish to conduct e-business according to RosettaNet's specifications (labeled "2" in Figure 7-3).

FIGURE 7-3
RosettaNet Business Model

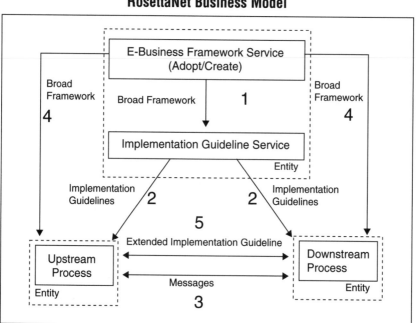

3. *Message Exchange.* Guidelines are used to validate the information exchanged between companies (labeled "3" in Figure 7-3). These guidelines can also be used to create the content that is exchanged and to support tools used to create and manage content in each company's internal system.

4. *Broad Framework.* RosettaNet intends to allow companies to extend the implementation guideline for their own individual needs. Companies can extend the implementation guideline according to the broad framework (labeled "4" in Figure 7-3). These extensions cannot override those specified by RosettaNet.

5. *Extended Implementation Guidelines.* The extended implementation guidelines are then exchanged between companies (labeled "5" in Figure 7-3). This allows companies to validate these message extensions during exchange.

A unique aspect of the RosettaNet e-business model is that all guidelines and translations are distributed as machine-readable documents. This allows companies to quickly configure their RosettaNet-compliant applications to execute and validate new or updated PIP specifications. A company that plans for integration with the high-tech electronics community that complies with RosettaNet can simply purchase middleware that provides RosettaNet interface readiness rather than try to build the process from scratch.

Microsoft—BizTalk

BizTalk from Microsoft provides more generic support for online trading. The BizTalk Framework is a set of guidelines on how to publish schemas in XML and how to use XML messages to easily integrate software across the communities. BizTalk defines XML tags (called Biz-Tags) for document handling and routing information. They define information similar to that used by a physical envelope for message delivery. This includes a <header>, with <delivery> tags defining the <message>, <to> and <from> address details and relevant processing applications, a <manifest> detailing for the receiving application information that is transmitted in the message, and then the document <body>, as shown in Figure 7-4.

The typical BizTalk message shows a platform-neutral XML message with delivery details defined by the BizTalk tags, as if in an envelope. BizTalk does not dictate any specific hardware, operating system, or language for message transmittal, receipt, or processing. The sending and receiving organizations can make these decisions independently of each other.

The actual documents to be delivered are contained in the <body> of the message. Clearly, in the example in Figure 7-4, these documents are one or more Purchase Orders. The XML tags that detail the content of these Purchase Orders are defined by the sending enterprise (customer. com, in this case) and must be understood by the receiving enterprise (supplier.com). The definition and interpretation of these XML tags must be agreed to by both enterprises. For example, in February 2000, General Motors, Ford, and DaimlerChrysler, strong competitors themselves, joined forces to create one of the world's largest trading communities to buy $240 billion per year from tens of thousands of suppliers. In this case, the relevant document XML tags will be defined by these large customers and must be understood by their many suppliers if they are to do business with them in the future. But in most cases, customers and suppliers that trade with each other in many industries must all agree on their own common XML tags.

OMG—Common Domain Interface

The Object Management Group's view of the key to an open and flexible solution for integration with online trading partners is building common domain interfaces. OMG believes that common, industrywide domain interfaces are the key to a flexible architecture. It is no surprise to find that not many of the existing internal interfaces are based on industry standards. In addition, we may agree that very few of the value

FIGURE 7-4
A Typical BizTalk Message

```
<?xml version = '1.0'?>
<biztalk_1 xmlns = "urn:schemas-biztalk-org/biztalk_1.xml">
  <header>
    <!—The leader defines details for the message envelope—>
    <delivery>
      <message>
        <messageID>12345678</messageID>
        <sent>2000-03-17T10:00:00 + 10:00</sent>
        <subject>Purchase Order</subject>
      </message>
      <to>
        <address>http://www.supplier.com/po.asp</address>
      <state>
        <referenceID>9876</referenceID>
        <handle>6</handle>
        <process>POProcess</process>
      </state>
      </to>
      <from>
        <address>mailto:receiving@customer.com</address>
        <state>
          <referenceID>9876</referenceID>
          <handle>6</handle>
          <process>RcvProcess</process>
        </state>
      </from>
    </delivery>
    <manifest>
      <document>
        <name>Supplier_PO_9876</name>
        <description>Supplier Purchase Order</description>
      </document>
    </manifest>
    <body>
    <!—The body contains tags for Purchase Order documents—>
      ... ... ...
      ... ... ...
      ... ... ...
    </body>
</biztalk_1>
```

chain interfaces are generic and agreed to by all of the suppliers. OMG's argument is that in most cases the custom interfaces are built to support a single supplier and wouldn't have reached consensus prior to implementing the interfaces. Probably the interfaces were added slowly over time, as business needs changed, rather than all at once. Business needs in the past didn't necessitate that entire value chains come together and define common interfaces. However, the value that can be gained today in defining and using common interfaces for the trading partners and suppliers will make integrating value chains a reality not just now, but into the future.

A generic online community integration model by OMG[8] is divided by suppliers, the company, and customers/stakeholders, as shown below in Figure 7-5. Companies use the CORBA architecture in conjunction with the open services to form their foundation. If a company needs to standardize the interface, the company then works with OMG on one or more Domain-focused task forces that are of interest to the company, either horizontally between functional areas (e.g., finance and manufacturing) or vertically from one end of the value chain to the other end. In Figure 7-5, the second column shows banking/financial services as a supplier to the company, while the company has a finance department internally and may have financial analysts or stockholders as its stakeholder(s).

The huge benefit for standard specifications comes from the Do-

FIGURE 7-5
OMG Generic Online Community Integration Model

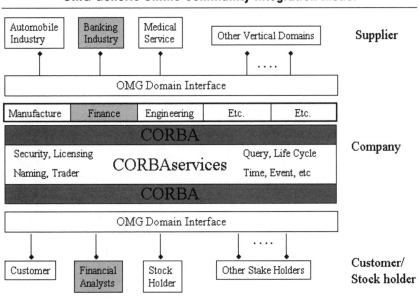

main Interfaces between the company and the suppliers and stakeholders as shown in Figure 7-5. Without these common interfaces defined, an exponential number of interfaces may result and make integration—between suppliers, the company, and stakeholders—economically or technically unfeasible.

We have introduced only some of the available online trading communities and standard services they provide. By adopting these standard interfaces and processes provided by the online trading communities and standards consortia, companies can reduce the integration complexity greatly and remain open for integrating with the future online communities.

Conclusion

Developing an open, flexible, and scalable e-business information system solution is no easy task. For a business interested in developing only simple, stand-alone solutions, it may not be worth the effort. But if you want to transition to a true e-business that fully exploits today's technological innovations, an internally focused development approach simply won't work. Unplanned use of innovative e-business technologies will simply help build more "legacy" faster. A good, long-term, outward-looking solution requires the business to:

■ Carefully study and choose technological, architectural, and communitywide solutions

■ Compose from building block components rather than start from scratch

■ Design according to industrywide standards rather than ad hoc formats

■ Create platform-neutral applications rather than those wedded to particular underlying technologies and platforms

By doing so, your business will promote the development of applications that are open, flexible, and able to accommodate unforeseen change.

Endnotes

1 John A. Zachman, *The Framework for Enterprise Architecture: Getting Beyond the "Legacy."*

2 Marc Cecere, Giga View, "Architecting Architecture," *CIO Magazine* (April 15, 1998). Available from: http://www.cio.com/archive/041598view.html (December 15, 2000).

3 For additional reading on distributed computing platforms, see D. Krieger and

R. M. Adler, "The Emergence of Distributed Computing Platforms," *IEEE Computer* Vol. 31, No. 3 (March 1998), pp. 43–51.

4 For additional reading on Java and JVM, see J. Gosling, "The Feel of Java," *IEEE Computer* Vol. 30, No. 6 (June 1997), pp. 53–57; and T. Downey and J. Meyer, *The Java Virtual Machine* (New York: McGraw Hill, 1996).

5 For additional reading on CORBA, see S. Baker, V. Cahill, and P. Nixon, "Bridging Boundaries: CORBA in Perspective," *IEEE Internet Computing* 1:6 (November–December 1997), pp. 52–57; R. Orfali, D. Harkey, and J. Edwards, *The Essential Distributed Objects Survival Guide* (New York: John Wiley & Sons, Inc., 1996); and J. Siegel, *CORBA Fundamentals and Programming* (New York: John Wiley & Sons, 1996).

6 For additional reading on XML, see D. Connolly, "XML: Principles, Tools, and Techniques," *World Wide Web Journal* Vol. 2, No. 4 (Fall 1997); S. Holzner, *XML Complete* (New York: McGraw-Hill, 1997); and R. Khare and A. Rifkin, "XML: A Door to Automated Web Applications," *IEEE Internet Computing* Vol. 1, No. 4 (July–August 1997), pp. 78–87.

7 RosettaNet, RosettaNet—Implementation Framework Specification, Version: 1.1.

8 Wayne Haughey, "OMG—Strategic Approach to Value Chain Integration" (October 18, 1999).

CHAPTER 8

Evaluations and Metrics for the E-World

Charles R. Rieger, IBM Global Services
Douglas S. Boothe, Xerox.com
Mary P. Donato, Xerox Corporation

In 2000, according to International Data Corporation, corporate spending on information technologies will be more than $1.1 trillion. This is simply spending for computer systems, networks, and telecommunications: those components that increasingly comprise the set of "e-technologies" necessary for a firm to conduct e-business over the Internet. It is upon these e-technology resources that firms are increasingly building the core capabilities of the firm and upon which they depend for their very survival. Charles Schwab, which has captured 24 percent of the transaction volume for stock trading in the United States,[1] would cease to be a powerhouse without the intricacies of its online systems. Similarly, Dell Computer's very business model, based on direct sales and build-to-order, would not exist without e- technologies that enable it to achieve speed and flexibility in an industry in which time is critical.[2]

But in today's fast-moving competitive environment, where stealth competitors can rise up almost overnight, how are senior executives to know whether their efforts with e-business are contributing to firm success? In 1997 and 1998, we witnessed dot-com companies that quickly put together Internet-based business models and achieved high levels of market capitalization almost overnight, only to be bought out by Fortune 1000 companies who didn't want to be locked out of e-business market segments. With the recent downturn in dot-com fortunes, these Fortune 1000 companies have been forced to reevaluate the wisdom of their investments. Look what happened to the Dutch grocer Royal Ahold when it bailed out Peapod, the online grocer, from almost certain bankruptcy.[3] On April 16, 2000 the company invested $73 million in cash in Peapod, set up a $20 million credit line, contributed fifty new "rapid pick centers" in Ahold's U.S. stores, and increased marketing on the East Coast, where Ahold's U.S. stores are based. Even with this significant infusion of cash and assistance, Peapod has continued to experience difficulty, with its stock trading at a third of what it was when Ahold made its investment ($2.75 in April 2000 compared with $0.88 in October 2000).

Part of the problem in discussing "e-valuation" and measurements involves the issue of new yardsticks by which e-business efforts can be understood. Eric Brynjolfsson, professor of economics at MIT, writes, "[L]iterature highlights how difficult and perhaps inappropriate it is to translate the benefits of information technology into quantifiable measures of output."[4] In other words, traditional metrics alone may not give the entire picture about the performance of e-business efforts.

This chapter offers a prism for company executives to view the value of their efforts in e-business and to help them in managing these strategic efforts. We suggest a framework within which e-business value can be understood, and then provide examples of how e-business value can be measured and managed. We realize that we cannot cover all possible measurements and metrics, nor do we suggest that metrics alone should be used for fully understanding e-business decisions. However, we do hope to cover the more salient points of e-business valuation and metrics.

The Spectrum of E-Business Value

In 1995, a *Computerworld* survey of CEOs and CFOs found that only 28 percent of respondents believed that IT could be a potential source of competitive advantage for their companies.[5] Just five years later, the opposite is the norm. Senior executives across all industries understand that competitive value can be received from their investments in information technologies, but struggle in recognizing the potential competitive value from e-business. In 1999, a cross-industry, worldwide survey of senior executives found that fully 33 percent of firms had yet to move beyond a simple website offering basic company information, and another 34 percent didn't even have a Web presence.[6]

The potential of e-business lies in its ability to transform the very foundation of a firm. Whether it is in reducing organizational costs, improving customer service, or tapping into new markets, the power of e-business is across the entire organization and across all organizational relationships. As such, the value that can be realized from e-business is not static, but is instead dynamic across a range of dimensions. Figure 8-1 lays the groundwork for the remainder of this chapter. It highlights the spectrum of value that can be realized from a firm's investments in e-business.

There are five different types of value that can be realized from a firm's investments in e-business. Each provides a different lens on the value prism, and each is realized in a different way.

1. *Efficiency.* This value is realized by a firm when e-technology capabilities are deployed to provide cost economies to operational processes. This may be in the form of reducing organizational costs or increasing economies of scale. For example, in the first quarter of 2000, IBM Corp. handled 22 million self-service transactions on IBM.com, resulting in more than $300 million in cost avoidance and productivity gains.[7] Through these web-based self-service inquiries, customers can get product information and installation and service information, download software updates and fixes, download "early release" or beta code, track the status of open problems, and communicate with IBM via the Web.

2. *Effectiveness.* This value is realized when e-technologies are leveraged to improve organizational operations. This type of value typically takes the form of improvements in organizational functioning, enhancements to core competencies, or even the creation of core competencies. For example, as a result of extensive business process reengineering and the integration of legacy systems with web applications, IBM's cycle time (defined as order entry to delivery) has been reduced from an average of 27–44 days to 2–23 days, depending on the product.[8]

3. *Reach Value.* This is the integration of e-technology capabilities to extend organizational boundaries. It may take the form of creating

FIGURE 8-1
E-Business Value Spectrum

E-Business Value				
Efficiency (Cost)	Effectiveness (Operations)	Reach (Boundaries)	Structure (Industry)	Opportunity (Markets)

SOURCE: Economist Intelligence Unit (EIU) and IBM Global Services, "Assessing the strategic value of information technology" (London: The Economist Intelligence Unit Limited, January 1999) and "E-business transformation" (London: The Economist Intelligence Unit Limited, March 2000).

customer loyalty, satisfaction, image, or mind share; creating linkages, leverage, or channel control over suppliers; or creating alliances, reducing cost of ownership, and enhancing marketplace perception through partnered relationships. For example, PartnerCommerce, IBM's web-based ordering tool for business partners, gives partners the ability to check on supply status, purchase products, and track orders on the Web.[9] PartnerCommerce also offers IBM's business partners the means to apply for and receive credit and financing online through IBM Global Financing.

4. *Structural Value.* A firm realizes this value when e-technology capabilities are used to influence the overall dynamics of a firm's industry. This takes the form of orchestrating industry forces, protecting or improving industry position, enabling new sources of revenue, or changing competitive dynamics. Home Depot is a clicks-and-mortar example of a firm that is intently focused on customer service and altering the structure of the do-it-yourself home improvement subindustry. The Home Depot, Inc. launched its online store, www.homedepot.com, to allow customers to choose from any of 40,000 products just as if they were walking down the aisle in their local Home Depot store. This approach to integrated commerce is an example of doing business on the customers' terms.[10] The site is electronically integrated with each local store's merchandising system. When a product is ordered, it can be picked up by the customer at the store, delivered to a job site or other location, or shipped by UPS. Professionals save time and money, and do-it-yourself customers find a depth of information on projects and products. By tightly leveraging physical assets with e-technology capabilities, the structural nature of this subindustry is being permanently changed.

5. *Opportunity Value.* This is the ability to use e-technology capabilities to create marketplace options that a firm may exercise at some future date. For example, a bookstore with stores located throughout the United States in major shopping malls may develop a website that provides a future option of linking a virtual transaction with the physical world. This option would offer customers the ability to order a book online while allowing customers to pick up those books at the shopping mall bookstore (instead of waiting two or three days for mail delivery). The bookstore may not currently offer this capability. However, if it were deemed a competitive advantage over other booksellers, it would have the option to exercise this capability.

Not all firms emphasize the same area of e-business value. However, there are three general "investment" patterns among firms where senior executives will focus their time, decision making, and dollars. These patterns are shown in Figure 8-2.

FIGURE 8-2
Firm E-Business Value Focus

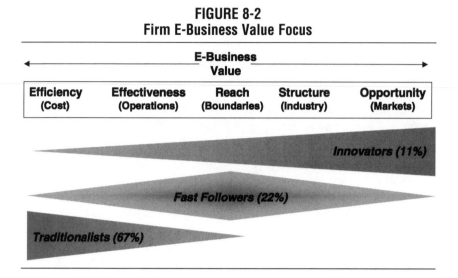

Innovators (11%)

Fast Followers (22%)

Traditionalists (67%)

Innovators are those firms that take e-technology capabilities, immediately integrate them into their business model, and aggressively move those capabilities into their marketplace. Dell Computer and E*TRADE are companies well known for this approach. Comprising about 11 percent of all firms,[11] innovators typically reshape the rules of play within their industry. They are driven by market valuations and increasing share price. Accordingly, their value focus is strongly oriented toward the opportunity end of the value spectrum. But that does not mean they ignore the other areas of value. Instead, they tend to realize value across the entire spectrum, never forgetting that in order to capitalize on opportunity value, they must also keep the basics of efficiency and effectiveness value in place.

Fast followers are those firms that tend to watch closely the strategies and adaptations of the innovators. Comprising about 23 percent of all firms,[12] they typically adopt the same e-technology capabilities as innovators, also working those capabilities into their business model, but about six to nine months after the innovators. Those capabilities are then brought to the marketplace on a massive scale, possibly to millions of consumers at a time. Their goal is to capture market share. The value focus of fast followers is on reach, but as with the innovators, they tend to realize value across the entire spectrum.

Traditionalists are those firms that really have yet to move on the possibilities and benefits that e-business offers. Comprising 67 percent of all companies,[13] these firms either have not done anything with e-business and e-technologies, or they may have taken the first basic step of creating a basic website with company information. They tend to hold on to traditional measures of success like market share or margins, even while the world around them is changing. The value focus of traditionalists is on efficiency and effectiveness. They may even begin to realize reach value, but almost never go beyond.

Measuring E-Business Value: Examples along the Value Spectrum

As we look at many of our marketplaces today, profit and market share are being driven more by how you sell than what you sell. The traditional model for many bricks-and-mortar companies has been the face-to-face sales force. In today's environment, we now see a more hybrid approach. There must be a balance between face-to-face, call/contact centers, agents, partners, and the Internet. The overall goal is to better serve the customer more profitably as costs are driven down. Having an effective hybrid go-to-market strategy in itself becomes a competitive advantage.

But how do you measure the effectiveness of your marketing tools that involve the Internet or intranet? We explore several examples.

Efficiency—Cisco Systems

Most of Cisco Systems' internal business is in the ether; that is, every process is automated and online.[14] This forces the organization to use the Internet for everything it does. Every employee is issued a desktop computer or laptop, never more than two years old. Cisco integrates the use of the Web into all that the organization undertakes. The Cisco Connection Online (CCO) is the strongest link between Cisco and its customers. On the same day a product debuts, all of its documentation, including marketing tools and operation manuals, is posted on CCO.

One of the areas customers have particularly liked is the Cisco Marketplace, an online catalog that not only can be used for purchasing equipment, but to compare and configure products online. The online configuration process is especially useful for resellers and those who install their own systems.

By all accounts, results have been excellent. In the past, one-third of all faxed orders contained errors that delayed processing. With CCO, customers find it difficult to make purchasing mistakes. More than 90 percent of Cisco's software upgrades have been delivered via the Internet—over 20,000 upgrades per week. Cisco has saved more than $500,000 per year in shipping charges alone. In 1999, CCO exceeded the $10 billion run rate, achieving the status of one of the top revenue-producing websites in the world. This website has saved Cisco over $250 million annually in IT services, which has allowed it to spend more in research and development than most of its direct competitors.

Effectiveness—Xerox Corporation's Eureka Solution

Eureka, a community-based knowledge-sharing solution for customer service engineers, has been cited as one of the world's best knowledge management (KM) solutions by at least a half-dozen organizations and publications. Why so much exposure? It represents the state of the art in KM solutions because it's part sociology, part work practice, and part technology. It uses information management technology to support the most efficient work practices possible among a community of people with a distinct culture and set of values and incentives. Most importantly, Eureka has proven its worth.

Xerox customer service engineers worldwide make more than a million visits to customer sites every month to service printers and copiers. Eureka started as a way to help them become more effective by capturing and sharing the knowledge they amass in their field experience. Much of this knowledge isn't contained in standard service manuals. It's usually gained by solving very difficult, complex, or rare problems, and it's often passed along informally through the telling of "war stories" in the tight community of customer service engineers.

Based on the collection and sharing of machine-repair war stories, Eureka gathers tips contributed by the service technicians themselves. Respected peers from within the community of engineers validate these tips. Once validated, they're put into a searchable database that's available to all customer service technicians through an Internet web browser.

Now in use by some 14,000 customer service engineers worldwide, Eureka has improved this community's ability to diagnose, solve, and prevent equipment problems. Results have included a 5 percent savings in parts costs and engineer time, and a corresponding 5 percent reduction in repair time when Eureka is used to diagnose a problem.

Eureka is being expanded to new Xerox communities including customer-support centers. By year-end 2000, Xerox expected to have 25,000 users in field service and call centers solving 250,000 customer problems and saving the company more than $10 million.

Reach—Xerox Corporation

In 1999, Xerox implemented a new Internet-based channel called Global TeleWeb. The purpose of this unique approach was to sell document solutions, copiers, printers, and fax machines to customers of all sizes through the Web. This online environment was very different from the traditional line of coverage. The face-to-face representative, called the virtual sales executive (VSE), built client relationships by consulting on the phone. Therefore, the correct development of web-based tools was critical.

Based on VSE feedback, there was a need to shorten the sales cycle at the point when the customer required a live demonstration of a product. Typically, the customer was brought into a local sales office and given the demonstration by a face-to-face sales representative. This added incremental days, and sometimes weeks, to the sales cycle of the VSE in addition to cost. Therefore, the Xerox TeleWeb channel focused on the creation of the "virtual demo."

The resulting virtual demo was a web-based tool that used Macromedia Flash technology to give customers an experience similar to a live, face-to-face demonstration. The customer can either open these virtual demos on Xerox's website or the demos can be sent electronically to the customer. Xerox estimates the virtual demo has reduced the number of days within the sales cycle, and the company is just beginning to put specific measurements in place to see exactly how much time can be saved. This example illustrates the effectiveness of combining a hybrid coverage approach with web-based tools to bring a firm's products closer to the buying decision maker.

Structural Value—Napster

Structural value is the value realized by a firm when e-technology capabilities are used to influence the overall dynamics of a firm's industry. It is the use of e-technologies in their most sophisticated of supporting roles, yet few firms have attempted to explore this area of value. Most innovation around industry structure has occurred by dot-com start-ups, with the likes of Napster.com or autobytel.com taking advantage of underserved needs of consumers within specific industries.

The music distribution industry is being revolutionized by an up-start technology called MP3 (short for MPEG-1 Layer 3). MP3 is a file format that stores CDs on a computer in one-tenth of the space of other formats, but the sound quality is near perfect. Napster.com addresses unmet consumer needs by providing a way for individual consumers to swap MP3 songs electronically. Songs can be easily searched for through the Napster website, downloaded from other Napster users anywhere on the Internet, stored on a Napster user's computer, or transferred to other MP3 playing devices. All of this occurs without the knowledge of the record company or (more important) without any sort of financial transaction having ever taken place.

This type of structural change has tremendous financial implications to the record industry. They have recently begun a series of lawsuits to stop Napster from allowing Napster users to swap music. In response, Napster is now in alliance with Bertlesmann, and is considering charging users a small monthly fee. However, the process of change has already begun. Regardless of the exact business model Napster settles on, the record industry will be changed.

These types of structural change usually have implications well beyond the industry experiencing the change. As new e-technology capability becomes available, firms will experiment with ways to derive value from that capability. Beyond Napster's centralized approach, peer-to-peer networking allows any computer on a network to directly query and interact with any other computer on the network. This capability offers the potential for buyers and sellers to easily conduct business electronically, without the need whatsoever of having to go through a middle-person to conduct the transaction. Thus, the Napster model, extended with peer-to-peer capabilities, could potentially impact every industry in existence today.

The key lesson is this: *Structural value will come from firms using e-technologies to meet unmet marketplace needs; in particular, unserved consumer needs.* The result will be the long-term alteration of the competitive dynamics within an industry. Michael Porter's five forces model (Figure 8-3) offers a framework for thinking about the measurement and metrics of competitive dynamics.

Firms will increasingly use e-technologies to focus on the needs of buyers by offering 24/7 services, high levels of interactivity, and increasing levels of information content, and by being respectful of the time and attention buyers give to sellers. Focusing on buyers will reshape the criteria on which firms compete within an industry, reducing entry by potential competitors, equalizing the power of suppliers, reducing the threat of substitute products, and in effect reducing inter-

FIGURE 8-3
The Five Forces Model

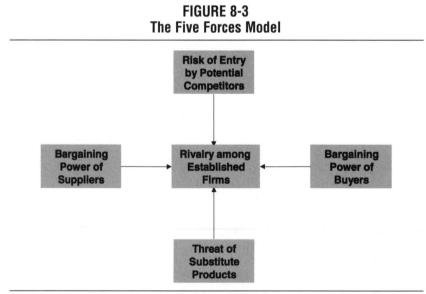

SOURCE: Michael E. Porter, *Competitive Advantage: Creating and Sustaining Superior Performance* (New York: The Free Press), 1985. Reprinted with permission.

industry rivalry as firms are able to further differentiate themselves from their competitors.

Metrics must focus on competitive dynamics, such as:

- **Potential Competitors.** These are firms that are not competing in an industry but have the potential to do so. Metrics focus on barriers to entry: brand loyalty, absolute cost advantages, economics of scale and scope, and nonreplicable products or services.

- **Power of Suppliers.** Suppliers have the ability to influence the price of a firm's product or service. Metrics focus on supplier strength: uniqueness of supplies, switching costs, degree of interconnectedness, and degree of mutual success.

- **Power of Buyers.** Buyers have the ability to drive down prices while commanding better levels of quality and service. Metrics focus on buyer strength: switching costs, degree of interconnectedness, ability to price-compare, and ability to group orders.

- **Substitute Products.** Products or services from competing firms may serve similar consumer needs. Metrics focus on product and service uniqueness: degree of information content, ability to personalize offerings, and linkage between the physical and virtual world.

- **Industry Rivalry.** Competitors are able to impact price. Metrics focus on industry conditions: number of direct competitors, industry structure (fragmented to consolidated), demand conditions, exit barriers, and level of coopetition.

Opportunity Value—First Data Corporation (FDC)

In an Economist Intelligence Unit (EIU) study, 60 percent of executives reported that one of their main drivers for adopting e-business was the "ability to capture new opportunities."[15] Opportunity value is the ability to use e-technology capabilities to create marketplace options that a firm may exercise at some future date. It is the option to use e-technologies to take advantage of entirely new opportunities to strengthen the firm's position within its marketplace. This might mean moving into markets that were previously out of reach, extending the company's range of products and services, working with suppliers in dramatically more efficient ways, or creating a new business model.

FDC is an example of a company taking advantage of the opportunity value of e-technology. The primary business of FDC is credit card processing. The company has worked diligently to develop web-based products and services and an e-technology infrastructure designed to carry them into the future. The company has recently taken advantage of its past efforts in order to capitalize on a totally new opportunity. FDC has leveraged its experiences as an e-business, and its extensive customer relationships, to embark on a completely new line of business. It now offers services to help small and midsize businesses build fully operational websites.

When it comes to measurements, nearly 44 percent of executives in the EIU survey planned to measure the value of their e-business investments in terms of the improved "ability to seize new growth or profit opportunities." In addition, 53 percent planned to measure revenues generated from new customers and markets, and 25 percent planned to measure the increase in share price and business valuation.

Managing E-Business Value

You cannot manage what you do not measure—that's a Management 101 classic statement. With respect to e-business and e-business investments, in many cases you have to define the metrics to be measured in order to validate the measurements and the return on e-business investment (ROeI). This is not a trivial task, as the new set of business capabilities enabled by the Internet have created an entirely new category of management measurement and analysis tools, benchmarks, and services—e-business metrics.

Aligning Measurements with Business Goals and Objectives

The purpose of any measurement program is to provide a set of highlights in understanding progress toward organizational results. E-business measurement programs are no different: Measures and metrics must support progress toward a firm's strategic objectives. Jack Welch of General Electric Company has expanded his view of the Internet opportunity from "Destroy-your-business.com" to "Grow-your-business.com" through smart e-business investments to generate sustainable competitive advantage.[16]

As described earlier, the potential value derived from a firm's investments in e-business can be aligned across the spectrum of efficiency, effectiveness, reach, structure, and opportunity (see Figure 8-1). The critical measurements for e-business investments are the same as those for other strategic organizational initiatives. Key questions to ask are:

- What impact do e-business initiatives have on the organization's profit and revenues?
- What are the effects of e-business initiatives on firm productivity, possibly through cost and time efficiencies?
- What are the effects of e-business initiatives upon shareholder value and business valuation?

Figure 8-4 provides an illustration to describe the value drivers between organizational objectives and e-business measurements.

Creating a Measurement Process to Identify and Capture E-Metrics

The measurement of e-business investments should be based on clearly defined business objectives, web tactics, and success criteria. Based on specific business objectives (e.g., generate 10 percent new orders via the Web), e-metrics need to be identified (e.g., shopping cart completion rate) and tracked via reporting and analysis tools. These initial sets of metrics should then be continuously refined and updated in order to:

- Validate the effectiveness of the e-metric
- Validate the effectiveness (ROeI) of the initiative
- Interpret the e-metric indicators such that future actions can be determined

Figure 8-5 provides an illustration of this measurement lifecycle approach.

Efficiency, Effectiveness, and Reach: The Xerox.com Example

In early 2000, the Xerox.com business team embarked on a site redesign and technology infrastructure upgrade activity designed to accomplish these specific business objectives:

- Build Xerox Corporation's online brand.
- Increase e-commerce revenues.
- Develop online customer relationships.

These strategic business objectives were aligned with the website redesign planning through a more defined set of web objectives and website tactics. Figure 8-6 captures this alignment.

Tracking E-Metrics

In addition to identifying the web objectives and tactics, Xerox also had to define the specific web tracking e-metrics to be able to validate progress toward these strategic objectives. These tracking metrics included the following:

Build Brand

- **Summary.** Refers to the number of visits, number of qualified visits, and the number or percent of new visitors.

FIGURE 8-4

Value Drivers between Organizational Objectives and E-Business Measurement

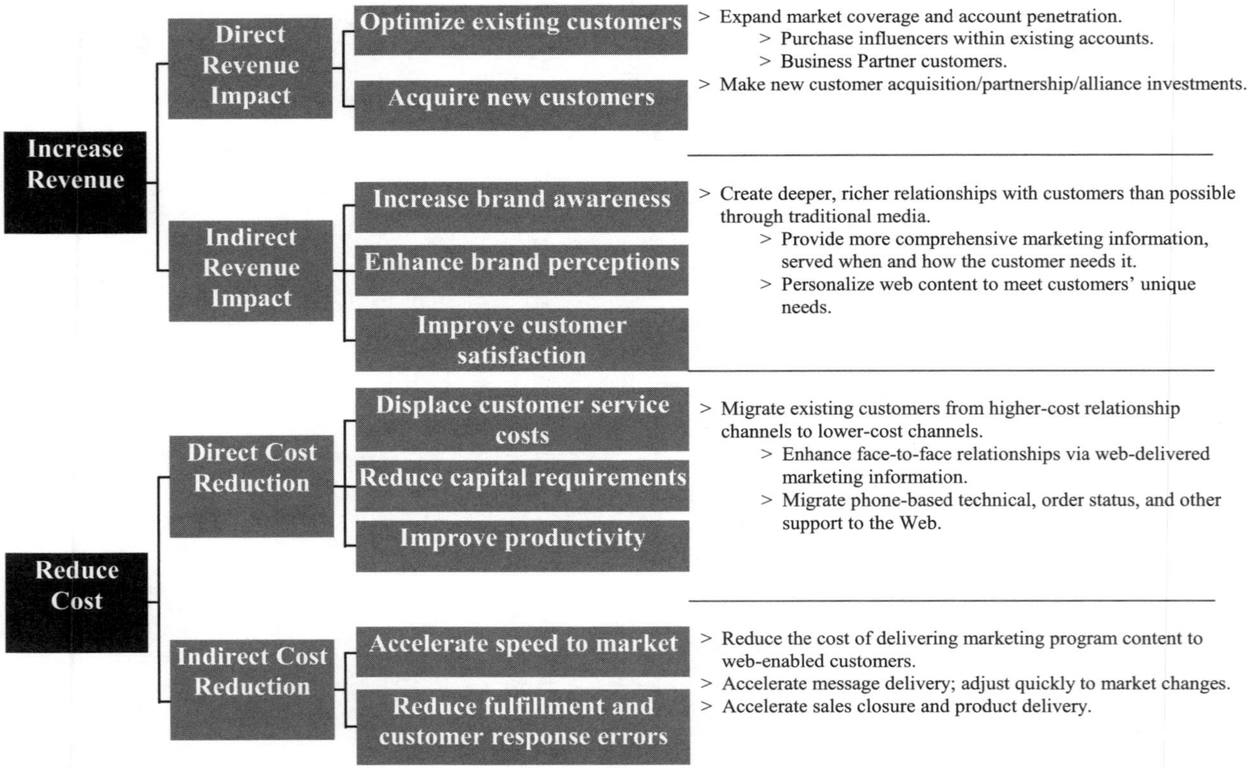

SOURCE: Xerox Corporation, xerox.com, April 2000.

FIGURE 8-5

Efficiency, Effectiveness, and Reach: The Xerox.com Example

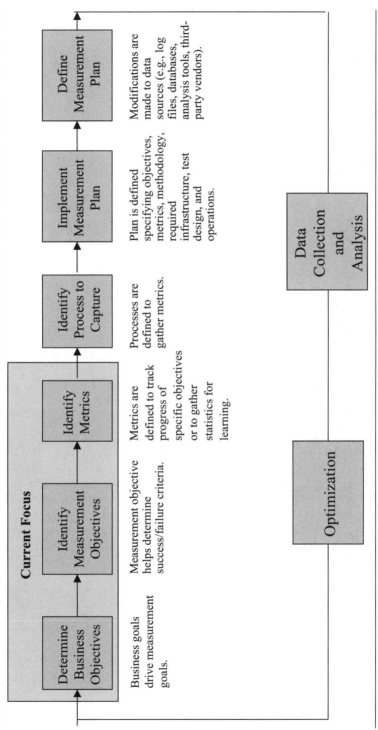

Source: Xerox Corporation, xerox.com, April 2000.

FIGURE 8-6
Xerox.com Redesign Metrics Summary

Strategic Business Objective	3.0 Web Objectives	3.0 Website Tactics
Build Brand	• Transform Xerox.com into a globally dynamic, interactive, and customer-focused site aligned by customer segments/communities.	• Develop new global, intuitive site navigation based on customer needs. • Provide cohesiveness across U.S. and international content to support business strategies and customer needs worldwide. • Enhance product information and functionality, including product selector to assist in identifying best product for customer needs. • Establish value-based customer relationship via strong online care and knowledge capabilities.
Increase Revenue	• Delight customers and make a positive financial impact for Xerox by developing a suite of post-sale applications and services valuable to each customer segment/community.	• Redesign for easier, more innovative e-commerce capabilities coupled with improved stability. • Provide cross-sell and upsell opportunities. • Facilitate an improved learning and shopping experience for customers via Customer Segments and more effective marketing/sales programs. • Implement U.S. contract customer extranets. • Redesign and remarket existing Supplies Catalog, Competitive Compatible Supplies Library, and Supplies Manager.
Develop Customer Relationships	• Leverage the platform to expand the value, relevance, and use of Xerox products, services, support, and solutions offerings.	• Enable various levels of registration. • Launch initial "My Xerox" personalization functionality to facilitate managing relationship with Xerox. • Facilitate an improved learning and shopping experience for customers via easy access to product information and simplified comparisons. • Provide seamless integration with key partners to support solutions strategy, including direct access to partner services and sites. • Implement new Subscription Manager for personal e-mail reminders for tools and applications.

SOURCE: Xerox Corporation, xerox.com, April 2000.

■ **Site Stickiness.** This industry term is used to describe the value and depth of the web experience as a measure of the average number of page requests/visits and average visit duration. The higher the "stickiness," the greater the number of pages reviewed and the longer the visit duration. Site stickiness needs to be balanced with site design to enable "frictionless" navigation to critical content.

■ **Search Functionality.** Refers to the number or percent of total searches; number or percent of successful, top-searched keywords/phrases; number or percent of small searches; and the frequency of top-searched keywords.

■ **Distribution of Visits/Page Requests.** This is the number or percent of visits and page requests to URL categories, including by international site, by product family, and/or by segment.

■ **Product Functionality.** Refers to the number or percent of visits using product selectors; number or percent of e-care product registrations; and top products registered. Here, e-care is described as customer-centric applications that enable support and self-service via the Internet. Examples include Xerox printer driver downloads, FAQs, order status and histories, and equipment tips.

Increase Revenue
■ **Summary.** This metric looks at the conversion rate, or the number of orders relative to the number of visits and/or number of purchases.
■ **Order Demand.** This is a measure of the number/dollar amount of orders and the number or percent/dollars of orders by product and/or by product family.
■ **Average Order Value.** This is the average transaction value (in dollars) per order received.
■ **Supplies and Subscription Manager.** Refers to the number or percent of visits registered; top supply items registered; average clickthrough rates for e-mails; and the conversion rate number or percent.
■ **Shopping Cart.** Refers to cart abandonment rate; number of expired carts; top products inserted/deleted from cart; top product families; and/or top supply items.
■ **E-Billing.** Refers to the number or percent of e-billing submissions and the average number of visits before purchase.
■ **Extranets.** Refers to the number or percent of successful logins and the number or percent/dollars of extranet revenue quotes/purchases.

Develop Customer Relationships
■ **Summary.** This is the number or percent of repeat visits and/or repeat visitors.
■ **Basic Registration.** Refers to the number or percent of basic registrants; the login rate; the number or percent of updates; number

visits/times before extended registration; and number of repeat visits after extended registration.

- **Product Drivers/Updates.** Refers to the number or percent of successful downloads; number of submitted feedback forms; number or percent of virtual demos; and the number of TeleWeb "call me" leads.

Diagnostic E-Metrics

In addition to tracking metrics, the Xerox team also developed a set of diagnostic metrics that were used to assess and refine the customer experience through the site. The diagnostic metrics included:

- Exit Rates
- Pathing (source and next click)
- Yield Loss
- Demographics (registrants)
- User Feedback/Online Surveying

In general, diagnostic metrics can provide benchmark standards and insight into opportunities for improving the site's performance for meeting strategic objectives. However, two additional diagnostic metrics proved especially useful: URL/site content and user segmentation categorization. By categorizing the site content along the various stages of the Xerox.com online customer relationship and buying cycle, the team was able to closely monitor and track user effectiveness and value. For example, the Xerox.com team used the following categorization for content/URLs:

- Traffic Generation (offsite)
- Awareness/Learning/Shopping
- Consideration
- Purchase/Lead Generation
- Service/Support
- Value Add/Loyalty

By measuring both the tracking and diagnostic metrics by these content subcategories, the team was able to respond faster and more discreetly to refine and improve the site capabilities and experience.

In a similar manner, by segmenting customer visits, you can determine when different patterns of behavior emerge. These user segments include:

- Purchasers
- Nonpurchasers

- New Purchasers
- Basic/Extended Registrants
- Traffic Source
- Customer Segment/Community
- Geographic/Territory
- Purchase Type (e.g., lease, purchase order, credit card, replenishment)
- Extranet/Global Partners

Reporting—The Xerox.com "Dashboard" Example

As part of tracking the performance of the Xerox.com website against its business objectives, a high-level "strategic dashboard" was created. The dashboard was designed to be able to quickly capture the e-metrics, serving as a communications vehicle for understanding performance against strategic objectives and ROeI.

The elements of the dashboard included site traffic, page views, e-commerce revenues, customer e-care, and site operating performance. Consistent with the measurement objectives for the team, the specific e-metrics were as follows:

- **Site Traffic** (i.e., total number of unique and repeat visitors per week; percent repeat visitors; and the percent internal vs. external visitors)
- **Page Views** (i.e., total number of page views; number of page views per visitor; and the average time per visit)
- **E-Commerce Revenues** (i.e., total per week, by equipment and by supplies)
- **E-Care** (i.e., total number of downloads from the site, via FAQ or FTP, per week)
- **WebMaster Mail** (i.e., total number of mail per day and per week; the percent response rate per day; other issues/trends)
- **Operating Performance** (i.e., weekly average error pages; the percent errors per total page views)

The e-metrics were chosen because they were able to directly reflect business objectives (or the closest proxy) while also being understandable for the team and executives. The dashboard is updated weekly and reviewed during regular operations review meetings and management communiqués.

Utilizing the dashboard as a starting point, the Xerox.com team is able to analyze data to understand the drivers and trends of the metrics. For example, if a certain metric spikes up or down, a hypothesis is tested as to what may have caused the movement. This is consistent with the diagnostic phase of e-metrics development outlined previously. By maintaining the fact base behind the dashboard, Xerox is able to more directly align the cause and effect of market conditions, company news, specific promotional actions, and the impact of new customer applications or functions. This diagnostic ability also allows Xerox to continually refine measurement objectives and ROeI for future initiatives.

The next step in Xerox's e-metrics development cycle will be the ability to leverage the fact base (i.e., dashboard results, customer traffic logs) to actually predict (or drive) the customer behavior on the site. Figure 8-7 offers a framework for developing e-metrics that evolve from measuring, to diagnostics, to predicting.

E-Metrics: Summary of Evolution and Methods

As the previous examples highlight, e-business measurements and metrics are a vital element in the achievement of corporate strategies. They help quantify and qualify the alignment of e-business initiatives to business objectives. Failure to identify the measurements and success metrics before implementation eliminates a tight connection between the business objective, the tracking and diagnostic metrics, the ability to course-correct/refine, and ultimately to identify ROeI for the initiative.

With the proper set of e-metrics (both tracking and diagnostic), firms can demonstrate the impact of e-business investments on strategic business objectives. Furthermore, firms can begin to develop the necessary expertise and competency in measuring and diagnosing the activity of e-business investments. As e-metric competencies develop, firms may also be able to more directly predict, drive, or even shape the online behavior of customers.

The space of evaluation and metrics continues to evolve and expand with the capabilities and opportunities of the Internet. Large cor-

FIGURE 8-7
E-Metrics: Summary of Evolution and Methods

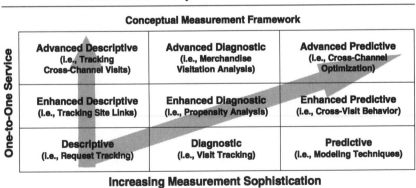

Conceptual Measurement Framework

One-to-One Service	Advanced Descriptive (I.e., Tracking Cross-Channel Visits)	Advanced Diagnostic (I.e., Merchandise Visitation Analysis)	Advanced Predictive (I.e., Cross-Channel Optimization)
	Enhanced Descriptive (I.e., Tracking Site Links)	Enhanced Diagnostic (I.e., Propensity Analysis)	Enhanced Predictive (I.e., Cross-Visit Behavior)
	Descriptive (I.e., Request Tracking)	Diagnostic (I.e., Visit Tracking)	Predictive (I.e., Modeling Techniques)

Increasing Measurement Sophistication

porations and small businesses increasingly recognize the power of this medium: to drive revenues, sustain customer relationships, improve efficiencies, and reduce operating expenses. The Internet also provides profound structural and value-creation opportunities.

As firms embark on their e-business initiatives, they must carefully identify the connection between business objectives, web objectives, and the specific e-metrics to test and validate the anticipated ROeI. These capabilities need to be invested in and developed. Given the pace of change in this space, many current investments are based on high-level benchmarking and strategic direction. E-measurement and metric capabilities provide both the rationale for investments and, more important, the fact base to validate success and opportunities for improvements in this rapidly changing environment.

Endnotes

1 "The Impact of E-Business on the Insurance Industry: Pressure to Adapt—Chance to Reinvent," Zurich: The Swiss Reinsurance Company, Economic Research and Consulting, Sigma #5, 2000.

2 Kenneth L. Kraemer, Jason Dedrick, and Sandra Yamashiro, "Refining and Extending the Business Model with Information Technology: Dell Computer Corporation," Center for Research on Information Technology and Organizations (CRITO) Graduate School of Management and Department of Information and Computer Science, University of California, Irvine (May 19, 1999).

3 Carole Winkler, "E-Grocery Stocks Not Delivering," *The Industry Standard,* www.TheStandard.com/newsletters/ (April 25, 2000).

4 Eric Brynjolfsson and Shunkyu Yang, "Information Technology and Productivity: A Review of the Literature," *Advances in Computers* Vol. 43 (Academic Press, February 1996), pp. 179–214.

5 "Special Supplement: Survey of Senior Executives," *Computerworld* (June 12, 1995).

6 Economist Intelligence Unit (EIU) and IBM Global Services, "E-business transformation" (London: The Economist Intelligence Unit Limited, March 2000), p. 14.

7 IBM Corp., "E-business Talking Points," 2000.

8 Ibid.

9 Ibid.

10 Ibid.

11 EIU and IBM Global Services, "E-business transformation."

12 Ibid.

13 Ibid.

14 D. Bunnell and A. Brate. *Making the Cisco Connection—The Story behind the Real Internet Superpower.* New York: Wiley and Sons, 2000.

15 EIU and IBM Global Services, "E-business transformation." p. 20.

16 *Fortune Magazine,* www.fortune.com (May 1, 2000).

CHAPTER 9

Competencies and Capabilities: Staffing the E-Business

Thomas Summerlin, Unisys Corporation
Albert A. Vicere, The Smeal College of Business Administration,
The Pennsylvania State University

The e-business economy has at least one distinctive characteristic that greatly affects any individual who hopes to successfully navigate its complexities: *velocity*. There have been several revolutions that changed the complexion of the American workplace, but never one that has involved this rate of speed. Throughout history, and even during the industrial revolution, there existed a far wider time frame between massive waves of change. But today is different. We are challenged with a workforce that must decide on careers that may not exist in a few months, or, even more significantly, have yet to be defined and come to fruition.

The employee of today must have exuberance while striving to compete in an arena where reassembling knowledge in newfound ways will spell the difference between independence and a long string of jobs, not careers, in search of the perfect play. In fact, the notion of a career has, in the face of extraordinary levels of freewheeling money and never-ending organizational realignment, been retired from view. We are within a new paradigm, one in which Alan Greenspan readily admits he has no clue of how to behave. The old saying, "Money does not cure greed," has reached a new level in a society where money is so free that it is only used as a numerical value counter to success. There once was a view that with the use of chips in gambling a person would be far less hesitant to bet. There now doesn't seem to be a need to replace currency with anything at all. Currency is the denominator for success; without it you are nothing, and with it you are still less than the person next door with more.

Where does that leave us? We have one group of people participating in the new e-world—the new economy—another group trying and wishing to participate, a group getting dragged along by it, a group fighting it, and a group left behind, either by choice, capacity, or situation. This is no different from the reaction to previous economic revolutions, but this time the costs and opportunities have far greater divergence. An idea brought about by "thinking differently" may bring great wealth with little or no investment. We are in the era of the "deferred life," as is pointed out in the book *The Monk and the Riddle: Education of a Silicon Valley Entrepreneur,* by Randy Komisar. This is the idea of working hard, cashing out, and then finding a satisfying life. Yet, for some, "cashing in" is the satisfying life. Jim Clark, the legendary Silicon Valley entrepreneur of Sun Microsystems and Netscape fame, says if you're not in it for the money you're not really in it. Does this change the profile of the e-business staffer? Are there skills outside of the norm necessary to succeed? And how is success measured? What is the physiological profile of this e-business brain trust?

What Stays the Same

Whether in this life or another, there are a number of propositions that will not change. These propositions are constants that characterize any talent pool and its chances for success. Number one in this equation is that no matter how many stories are told of the young, uneducated person launching a successful e-business or dot-com business, that is not the norm. The successes in e-business and dot-com are bred, for the most part, from educated, trained, and focused people, more often than not what may be referred to as "geeks." A few of these geeks, like Bill Gates, although perhaps not college graduates, make great decisions and great managers. Even though the Internet has delivered the availability to new markets, new channels, unheard-of cost savings (to buyers, sellers, and producers), and knowledge sharing, the basic principle still stands: To succeed you must work hard, train hard, and at the end of the day deliver value to someone, somewhere.

The desire to innovate, whether independently or within an organization, is what determines success in the new economy. Companies like General Electric and Intel Corp. spend millions of dollars and work very hard to maintain an environment where creativity cannot only survive but also flourish. Successful companies invest in philosophical and motivational techniques to encourage and promote innovation and "thinking outside of the box." Some companies, such as Cisco Systems, innovate by making change the rule of the day and e-volutionizing their structure every six months. Oracle Corp. has long touted its management capability to out-motivate employees, a rather draconian management style of growing jobs away from their managers and sales away from their salespeople.

This shift in workplace values is not, contrary to some views, an about-face or radical change. But the creation of cyberspace provided the opportunity to many who would otherwise never participate in the economy to flourish. The person who would never consider being in an office environment or collaborating with others on projects is now fully availed of technology that allows unparalleled, nonintrusive communication and knowledge sharing. The individual has not changed; a new path of communication and collaboration has merely opened their minds to other people and their ideas. "Know thyself" can now better be stated as "be thyself," and only those with well-identified expertise will avoid the vulnerability to substitution by others who know themselves even better.

People, no matter where they are, still care deeply about their environment, their families and friends, and their privacy. All of these issues are contributing significantly to the evolution of the cyberenvironment. Physical attributes surrounding individuals in the evolving e-business space require inordinate measures to secure essential privacy and security. The castles of old are being replaced with firewalls and screens of many variations to ensure continuity for the individual. Society won't be the protector because everything will live in cyberspace. An individual must ensure his or her own sanctity and protection from outside threats, of which there can be many. E-business lends itself to an environment of relentless force, creating and destroying wealth and knowledge with no pity. It is the ultimate expression of Joseph Schumpeter's description of capitalism as "creative destruction." As a practitioner, the e-business participant must learn to live by these rules.

Shaping Forces: What Doesn't Stay the Same

The Internet and the move to e-business are the shaping forces that have created a tidal wave of change, opportunity, threats, and challenges. From the beginning of the industrial revolution through the 1990s, there were four significant technological shaping forces: industrialization, transportation, communications, and computerization. Each of these forces had such profound influence that they changed not only business, but also society. All four of these preceding technological advances are now being eclipsed by the creation of cyberspace. The world is evolving toward a global community of people, business, and information living dynamically on a network backbone that transcends all boundaries. The Internet has created a virtual superhighway, even more a community, linked by mouse clicks, not miles; by seconds, not hours.

The ability to virtually link any groups, businesses, or individuals anywhere in the world has spurred the delivery of all information in digitized form. Substance is in content, permission, and relevance, not necessarily in any physical form. In the old economy, one had the time to think. Now the pressure is "to do." When people learned to speak they began to expand and deliver knowledge. Now knowledge is everywhere, and trying to find it, understand it, disseminate it, and learn from it in a hurry is the issue of the day. It isn't that knowledge doesn't exist; it's how to find and use knowledge with a measure of relevance.

Are we to become slaves to the search, are the new e-business people going to be masters of sorting, or are they to be innovators and experimenters? Where is the value going to be found among the working people of the next fifty years? Are information gathers going to be the underclasses of the early 2000s? What are the profiles of the valuable technologists and businesspeople of the new millennium? There is no doubt that the transcending nature of the cyberworld has brought diversity to new levels. Globalization issues will greatly affect the e-business world, the only business world that will exist in the coming years.

In a world filled with strategic transformations, a fundamental set of changes in the way we do business, and a realization that it isn't e-business that is going to kill you but the new business model that it spawns, what can someone do to prepare? To be an e-business person, relationships need to be established, as they always have been, one-to-one and one-to-many. Yet, in these relationships, diversification around competencies, not tasks and work products, determines survival and success. Redefining value chains involves individuals in the same manner. Careers, as they exist, are short-circuited regularly by individuals with different talents and views.

The successful individuals in the new economy must create ever-expanding value chains of their own. Individuals are evolving to be information sources, brokers, creators, and innovators. With new business models sprouting up everywhere, individuals have to manage not only their position but also their knowledge base and capabilities quotient. A real-time, 24/7/365 customer view is the norm, as is becoming a change agent and change manager. Without a traditional old-style, command-and-control, hierarchical organization to direct and inform them, individuals become responsible for their own growth and change. The e-business person focused on delivering real value added for the company and the customer, whether evolutionary or revolutionary, will succeed.

Contrasting Profiles

To delineate the comparative differences between the traditional recruit and someone who is likely to be successful in an e-business environment, we have constructed a lists of contrasts. These contrasts are further illustrated in Figures 9-1 and 9-2. In a highly competitive global arena with extraordinary velocity, companies benefit most from highly efficient and effective structures and processes that are steeped in employee knowledge and commitment. Yet people can also be the number one obstacle to change. So the culture created by an organization as it adapts to the e-world is critical to its success. There are only two rules at this point: If you can't change you will perish, and if you change slowly you will perish. A fast mistake can more easily be rectified, and certainly at a lower cost, than a slowly delivered correct response. You might even say, "Death to the slow, wealth to the deliberately courageous."

The Profile of the Effective E-Business Person

What kind of people are we looking to bring into the e-business? An individual who can flourish and build the appropriate e-culture has the following characteristics:

- Possesses a broad and deep understanding of the business the company is in from a skills perspective, not a product or deliverables perspective
- Demonstrates an ability to understand the landscape and think strategically in finding new ways to attract and transact business
- Takes risk, with a view to value
- Demonstrates customer focus unequaled in the company
- Is humble and tough
- Is a great and frequent communicator
- Focuses on doing what he or she does best and leaves the rest to others
- Is never discouraged
- Is never close-minded
- Is informed and learns on own time
- Looks for success, not career steps
- Controls self, influences others
- Knows his or her value proposition
- Knows failures, accepts failures, gets over them
- Never fails to be creative and innovative
- Doesn't "marry" his or her own ideas
- Understands and communicates how to become the customer's first choice
- Understands and communicates how to be own best competitor

FIGURE 9-1

Profile of Someone Likely to Be Successful in an E-Business Environment

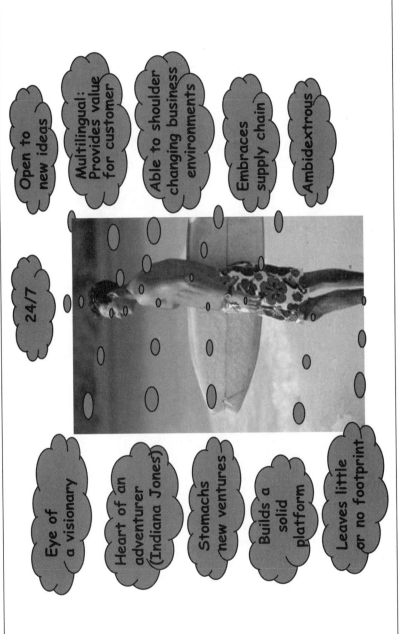

Open to new ideas

Multilingual: Provides value for customer

Able to shoulder changing business environments

Embraces supply chain

Ambidextrous

24/7

Eye of a visionary

Heart of an adventurer (Indiana Jones)

Stomachs new ventures

Builds a solid platform

Leaves little or no footprint

FIGURE 9-2
Profile of the Traditional Business Recruit

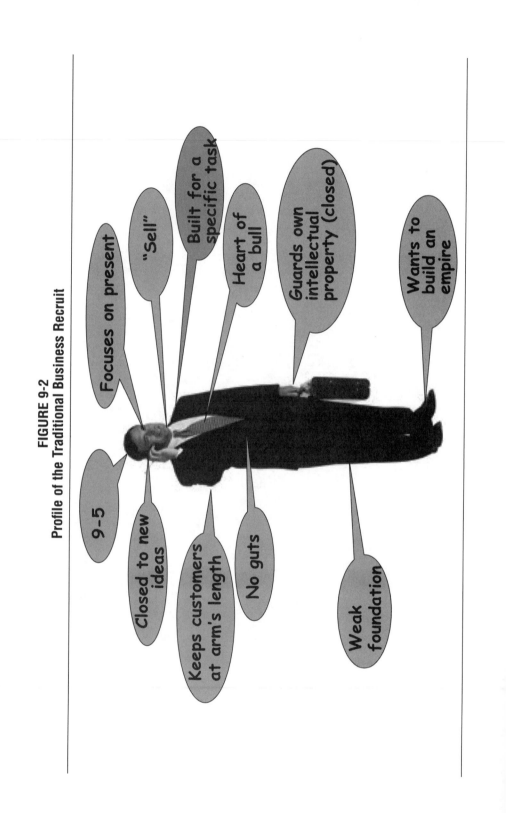

■ Is technology aware and literate
■ Evangelizes

The Profile of an Ineffective E-Business Person

What kind of people are unlikely to flourish in the new economy? An individual with the following characteristics is likely to undermine the development of an effective e-business culture:

■ Demonstrates a broad and deep understanding of the company's deliverables to excess
■ Demonstrates a broad and deep understanding of the competition's products and deliverables to excess (this, combined with the previous characteristic, can lead to a closed mind)
■ Avoids risk, with a view toward promotion and self-preservation
■ Shows an unquestioned customer requirement focus (i.e., communicates what the customer asks for without review, comment, or perception)
■ Is self-promoting and generally nonconfrontational
■ Communicates inconsistent and unrewarding messages
■ Tries to do, or tell others how to do, nearly everything
■ Is often discouraged
■ Is often closed to ideas
■ Is uninformed, accepting information through innuendo and hearsay; always wants to attend classes, functions, and shows
■ Looks for the next retirement as an opportunity to move up
■ Influences no one and seldom controls self
■ Knows only sales quotas and billable hours
■ Never sees failure, therefore never accepts it and never has to get over it
■ Never fails to be negative and is a naysayer to new initiatives and solutions.
■ Always married to personal ideas and never lets go of them
■ Is unwilling to challenge conventional wisdom
■ Is technology dependent
■ Internalizes

Obviously, the successful e-business person can be a young high-flier who has an innovative idea to lead him or her to great wealth; a graduate of an MBA program who now is more likely to be looking for an opportunity in the Russell 5000 than the Fortune 500; or a middle-aged executive with endless streams of enthusiasm to compete and direct in a high-velocity business environment. When asked where the best e-business executives come from, one of the top recruitment firms in the nation specified the sales and marketing side of an organization rather than the traditional technically minded person. The reason pointed to most often is the continually repeated axiom that e-business is *not* about technology, especially since virtually any technology needed can be bought from someone, but it is about customer experience. Who better to define customer experience than a sales/marketing executive? E-business is all about getting closer to the customer; it is not about delivering technology. On the other hand, adapting this set of rules from Gary Hamel works very well to understand how individuals can re-create themselves as e-business people:[1]

■ **Set unreasonable expectations.** If you can think of expanding your business by 100 percent, then you will naturally have to come up with innovative solutions to get there. Not only do you create an environment for yourself, but an opportunity for your company.

■ **Stretch business definitions.** Think of the competencies in your company and yourself—not what you produce, but what you have skills in—and then apply them.

■ **Create a cause.** Transcend purpose, display courage, do the unexpected.

■ **Listen to new voices.** You are not alone unless you choose to be; use numbers and minds to your advantage.

■ **Lead a program for visionaries; design a template for ideas.** A forum for depositing and exchanging information that is yours to foster will drive you in new directions.

■ **Make sure you deliver value.** Don't drive ideas for ideas' sake; rather, understand the benefit and value of every idea and know where the returns are.

■ **Find and hire talent.** Smart and talented people can accomplish almost anything. Make it a crusade to find and hire anyone who can help move you forward.

■ **Work where the price of failure isn't death.** Choose your ground. Some environments don't understand failure. If you know you can fail you will take more risks.

■ **Find, support, and position innovation.** Even what happens by mistake needs a home. If it's yours, so much the better; if it isn't, do it anyway.

■ **Get paid for what you do.** Communicate your successes and those of others. Deliver value, get paid well.

Technologists in E-Business

What about the development of technology experts in the new economy? Figures 9-3 and 9-4 are skills matrices used in Unisys as we search

FIGURE 9-3
Technical Infrastructure Discipline View

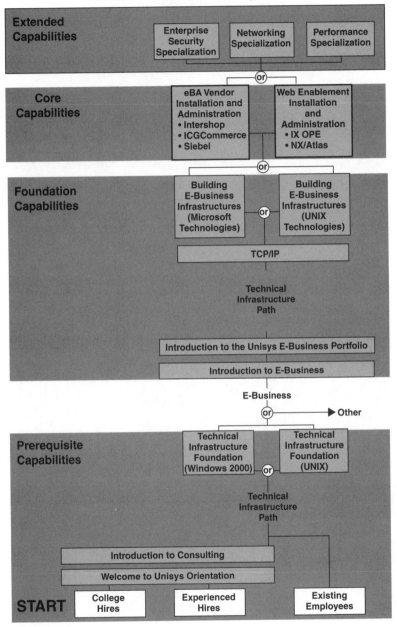

FIGURE 9-4
Software Development View

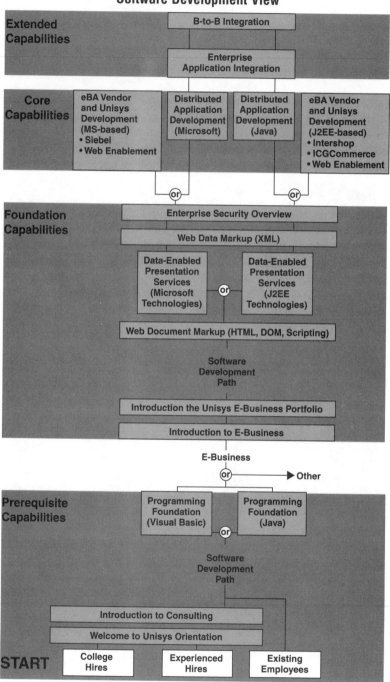

for and develop technology delivery people in the e-business environment. Of key importance here is that there are two tracks to each matrix. The world is presently divided into the Microsoft world and the so-called open world. The liabilities and risks associated with not supporting either of the technology infrastructures have mandated a dual skills matrix. The architects and business analysts in the e-business world are not concerned about which of the architectures are used. Whether an individual works in the technical development or software side of the business, we believe that success is rooted in fully developed sets of capabilities that range from those that are prerequisite and fundamental to success, to those that are core to effectiveness, to those that move into the realm of leading edge. It is imperative for an organization to ensure that all of its e-business people follow a path of capability building that tracks these matrices.

Although there is the recurring theme that technology is not the issue in e-business, there is a need for the e-business person to understand the integration and deployment issues surrounding a defined e-business initiative. Without some level of appreciation for the available technologies and the challenges of integration, the e-business executive can be too easily caught short. An e-business team member with specific technology assessment skills is often a prerequisite to overcome the substantial internal and external hurdles of transforming a traditional bricks-and-mortar company into a true e-business delivering both increased value to its customers and cost savings and efficiencies to the company.

Leaders in E-Business

Many of the characteristics we described as essential for success in e-business (see Figure 9-1) are magnified for the role of the e-business leader.

Leadership in the e-world is different. It involves the ability to get results and at the same time build commitment and enthusiasm among highly mobile knowledge workers. Today's college graduates expect to work for seven or eight companies, they expect to become financially independent, and they expect to have an impact on a business. And they need leadership more than ever. It isn't the pure play dot-coms that will rule the world in the future. Nor is it the old economy dinosaurs that hope to avoid extinction (they won't). Rather, it's the companies that blend the best of the old and the new that hold forth the greatest potential. Effective leaders in this evolutionary revolution must play four key roles:

1. *Boundaryless Thinker.* Leaders in the new economy need to think outside of the box and help their organization to do the same.

That means they can't be bogged down in traditional orthodoxies. They must be open to new ideas. They must help their organization and the people within it to know themselves—their strengths, competencies, and limitations. And they must help their organization and those within it to recognize the strengths and capabilities of potential partners who possess complementary capabilities and knowledge.

2. *Network Builder.* Leaders who think in a boundaryless manner are more likely to have a relationship mind-set, one focused on helping the people around them to connect together to share ideas, information, and knowledge. Knowledge management starts with good people who enjoy the challenge and stimulation of interacting with other good people. When these people are linked together in a knowledge-sharing network, the potential is incredible.

3. *Diplomat.* To facilitate the development of those networks, new economy leaders must have the ability not only to bring the constituencies together, but also to help them see the benefits of the linkage—how by working together they can achieve more than they ever could on their own.

4. *Interpreter.* To fulfill the previous role, leaders must have the ability to interpret the nature of business opportunities to the network. They must be able to interpret the partners to each other and to coach, facilitate, and provide feedback to an organization that is no longer a collection of lines and boxes, but a living, growing, expanding ecosystem.

The Human Resources Management Challenge

The e-business superhero responsible for moving an organization forward may not exist today. The skill sets may not become evident because of longevity, corporate infrastructure, or poor personnel management, among other reasons. However, considering that a company's move to become an e-business will be the single greatest challenge of the next decade, the individual must be found. What can an organization do to ensure it that it is able to recruit and retain the right people with the right skills? The following discussion presents a series of suggestions and challenges to organizations from the standpoint of human resources management in the e-business world.

Selection

At the heart of the new economy are shifts in employee skill sets and values that are part of a potential skill-related generation gap. As a result, companies are spending huge amounts of money and time to develop competency models and skill assessments to ensure that they are hiring and retaining the right people with the right skill sets. But skill sets for which era?

To be sure, competencies such as interpersonal effectiveness, personal drive, and a results orientation are necessary in any era. But what about the e-skills discussed earlier in this chapter? What about the ability to establish and work in networks? What about the need for risk taking in a world that demands the reconfiguration of business models? What about the ability to communicate with, coach, and mentor employees? Most companies are struggling to address these critical needs, often armed with old economy tools and mind-sets.

This challenge is complicated by what may be the most critical issue in the recruitment and retention of key talent for e-business: the "brand character" of the recruiting organization. People with the talent and the drive to succeed in the new economy are searching for great jobs in great companies—jobs where they can make an impact, where their skills and knowledge will be put to the test in organizations that are seen as leaders, as benchmarks of effectiveness driven by leading-edge thinking.

It is imperative, then, for companies to pay as much attention to creating their brand image as an employer as compared to creating their image as a leading provider of products and services. Talent recruitment is a seller's market today, and organizations must aggressively pursue the prize. The people an organization recruits—and keep in mind that these are the people who ultimately will own the company's core competencies and hold together its critical business relationships—must feel compelled to join the company and stay with it. That means that the company must have a strong brand image as a great place to work and as a great developer of people.

Development

Highly motivated, knowledge-based workers want to be challenged not just by their work, but also by the opportunity to continually learn new skills. They want feedback and lots of it. They want leaders who teach them, work with them, and help them to grow. They want access to the latest thinking and the latest tools that will enable them to put that thinking to the test. They want to be assigned to visible projects where they can demonstrate their mettle. And above all, they want to feel they are part of an organization that respects them for the new knowledge and ideas that they bring to the business.

These desires seem simple enough, yet in many ways they fly in the face of traditional views of career development in organizations. In the old economy model, people put in their time, paid their dues, kept their eye on the ball, and gradually advanced until they finally achieved their day in the sun. That pattern has no relevance in the e-business world. Challenging assignments, effective leadership, and ample feedback are essential in today's organization, as are opportunities to advance knowledge and skills through targeted, purposeful education and training experiences. These experiences should be designed as much for the networking opportunities they provide as for the information they impart. New economy workers are looking for great jobs in great companies. Highly networked environments contribute to the development of both. Training and development must move beyond the classroom and into the workplace, where real-time assignments and relevant, effective coaching help knowledge workers grow and succeed in a challenging, real-time, exciting environment where information is shared and expertise valued.

Appraisal

The demand for ample, well-developed, and well-delivered feedback among new economy workers has already been discussed. The annual appraisal, coupled with a pat on the back, is not enough in today's environment. Skilled knowledge workers want and deserve more input and more honest appraisals of their work. And they want it packaged with a good helping of recommendations for improvement/advancement delivered by a respected boss and mentors. That means that companies need to train current leaders to deliver feedback and assist in development planning. It means that notions of leader-led development, championed by authors such as Noel Tichy, are essential to the development of a strong culture and a vibrant work environment. It means that great companies will create great jobs that are coordinated by effective leaders—leaders who are skilled in the art of communicating and educated in the science of human development.

To a very large extent, that means that incumbent leaders need to learn to operate in new ways. They need to learn not only "e" skills, but also the essence of leading in a relationship-driven world. The most critical relationships for a new economy company (at least at this point in time) involve relationships with the people inside the company who are helping it to make the shift to the new economy world; therefore helping incumbent leaders master the requirement for teaching, coaching, mentoring, and communicating may well be the most critical challenge facing companies today.

Rewards

In return for their willingness to accept a great engagement from a great company, in addition to a great boss and a highly networked group of colleagues, what else do new economy employees want? They want to be paid fairly for what they do, and that means that they want a piece of the action. True enough, the bloom on the rose of stock options is wilting in the face of the declining stock market, but never doubt that equity in some form has become the currency of the realm in the new economy. Shareholder value appeals only to shareholders. If a company wishes to deliver on that mantra, it had better be sure that employees have a vested interest in creating that value. This, too, flies in the face of old economy structures where equity fell into the hands of only the elite few at the top. Companies that continue to subscribe to that notion will find themselves rapidly moving to the outside ranks of great companies, at least in the minds of talented new economy workers. And those new economy workers are the lifeblood of a company's future.

Of course, there is the slacker theory. The one that says that new economy workers want a cushy life and don't want to work hard. That's bunk. With careful observation, you can learn the secret. They can and do work very hard. It's just that it's more on their own terms. They want a great job *and* a life, and they are finding that with the help of e-connections and more flexible work arrangements they can have both. The companies that are learning to take advantage of flexible work arrangements through utilization of telecommuting and related technologies are reaping the benefits.

How Do We Get There?

For any organization, adapting to the e-business economy is both incredibly simple and enormously complex. It is simple in that it is only a matter of great companies structuring great work experiences for technologically savvy people in feedback-rich environments presided over by skilled leaders. It is enormously complex in that it requires redefining the organization to be a great company that provides great work experiences for technologically savvy people in feedback-rich environments presided over by great leaders. For many, the magnitude of that challenge seems immense. But there are some things that can be done to prepare an organization to meet the challenge. The following are some suggestions:

■ **Build your company brand.** Building brand requires that a company tell its story: how it provides challenging work assignments, how great things can be achieved by good people, how effective feedback and relevant rewards are the norm, how the organization is teeming with effective and technologically savvy people, with leaders who are committed to developing talent. All of these elements are part of a great company brand. An organization must start by making talent management a top priority. But the words must be backed up with action. Leaders, especially those who must unlearn old economy business practices in order to learn new ones, must be held accountable for becoming the leaders in the relationship-oriented new economy milieu.

■ **Create a challenging work environment.** Dare to be creative when structuring the work environment. Use project and task force assignments to keep the workplace enriched and vibrant. Make sure project team members get the feedback they desire and the development plans they need to move ahead. Be open to moving people across business units and functions, and even across joint venture and alliance partners. Remember, once knowledge workers leave the organizational family, they are a lost resource. Keep them challenged and networked, and keep telling them how they're doing and how they can do even better.

■ **Train leaders to lead.** This may be the most difficult hurdle to clear. In the old economy, leaders were often, in reality, auditors. They watched over things, approved things, and kept things running smoothly. Today, that's not enough. They must facilitate, interpret, coach, teach, mentor, and develop. They can't do those things unless they are taught how to do them, and they won't do them until they are held accountable for delivering on the demand. Leadership development, in this sense, may be the biggest challenge facing organizations over the next few years, and processes for leadership development must be rooted in helping the organization master the shift from the old control-oriented management philosophies of the industrial age to the new relationship philosophies of the information age. No company will continue to grow and succeed until it addresses this challenge.

■ **Facilitate networks.** A new economy organization is made up of talented people who work together, who share resources and information, and who are committed to both personal and organizational success. Interestingly, General Electric, an old economy company that seems to understand the need to shift to the new world, is not only one of the highest performing companies, but is also one of the most development-oriented and best-led companies in the world. GE executives say that the key to the company's success is understanding the three critical resources of an organization: money, people, and information. If you allocate and reallocate resources toward exciting opportunities, if you seek out the best minds in the organization regardless of where they reside, if you put those minds to work on challenging opportunities, and if you share the knowledge they possess and help create across the organization, then you will prosper.

■ **Make shareholder value real.** Yes, new economy workers want great jobs in a great company. They want to be challenged, pushed, developed, and rewarded. They don't want someone else to be rewarded, so don't tell them about shareholder value creation unless you make them shareholders. Only then will they grasp the impact of the value their contributions create, and only then will the company reap the rewards of both their knowledge and their commitment.

■ **Think "tools and flexibility."** A significant number of new economy workers grew up in the e-world where they have become familiar with e-mail, cell phones, chat rooms, software, and flexible hours. Account for that when you are creating assignments and work environments. Also, keep in mind that if the incumbent leaders in a company are uncomfortable with technology, software, and flexible hours, then the inconsistencies in word and deed will stick out like a sore thumb to the e-business talent the company is so desperately pursuing. Both sides need to make an effort is true, but in this instance, perhaps some reverse mentoring is in order. Maybe we can find ways to enable the new economy workers to teach the old dogs a few new tricks.

■ **Be real.** This last point is a very basic one. The new economy requires that companies rethink and refocus their operational systems to accommodate new business models and new-thinking workers. It also requires that organizations redefine the requirements of leadership and, further, that they hold leaders accountable for redefining themselves in the mold of the e-business world. That means informing, training, coaching, prodding, and in every way helping leaders to learn the new skills and adopt the new mind-sets. But it also means holding them accountable for personal and organizational change.

Conclusion

The emergence of the new economy and the shift to e-business are, indeed, revolutionary developments. The rules for success in business are changing, as are the characteristics and capabilities of effective leaders, practitioners, and workers. By thinking about these changes, and by measuring yourself and your organization against emerging models of effectiveness, you are off and running to the exciting new e-world.

Endnotes

1 Gary Hamel, *Leading the Revolution* (Boston: Harvard Business School Press, 2000).

Linking Business Imperatives to Human Capital Strategies: The Case of Encyclopedia Britannica

John W. Boudreau, Center for Advanced Human Resource Studies, ILR School, Cornell University

Benjamin B. Dunford, ILR School, Cornell University

Peter M. Ramstad, Personnel Decisions International

Most writing about e-business strategy and models provides little specific guidance to develop human capital strategies tied to competitive shifts, while the writing on e-HR focuses mainly on specific labor market developments or specific human resources (HR) techniques that are affected by new technology such as delivering training on the Web.

Thus, it is important to develop strategic analysis that provides a rich and actionable logic linking human capital to the significant shifts in the business landscape. There is a need for rich strategy diagnosis—seamlessly linked to implications for organizational talent. This has been variously described as a need to develop richer and more detailed descriptions of strategy and its implications for human capital,[1] as well as the need to look inside the "black box" linking HR practices to organizational success.[2] In this chapter we describe an approach to strategic analysis that identifies the links between strategic success and human capital, articulating the key strategic elements and then translating them clearly into implications for human capital and human resources management.

Specifically applied to e-commerce, such an analysis would begin to answer questions such as: "What human capital response is most appropriate when technology fundamentally shifts the relationship between our firm and our suppliers?" and "What is the appropriate human resources strategy to optimize the value of a sales force when our customers receive more information through the Web?"

We will use the HC BRidge™ framework (Figure 10-1)[3] to understand these links. This framework uses three main "anchor points" as the elements that bridge decisions about human capital investments with strategic organizational success. "Impact" identifies the core elements of strategic success, including changing industry and economic factors, and refines those broad business elements to identify how particular human capital (talent pools) affect strategic success. "Effectiveness" identifies how HR practices affect talent pools by supporting employees' aligned actions. "Efficiency" identifies how HR resources are deployed to produce the HR practices. This chapter will apply Figure 10-1 to illustrate how organizations can identify the talent implications of changes in the competitive environment due to digitalization and e-commerce.

In this chapter we illustrate how this model can be applied, using a case study of Encyclopedia Britannica (see sidebar) originally described by Evans and Wurster.[4] The Britannica example has implications for the methods that other organizations use to translate their e-business challenges into human capital implications. Our goal is to help organi-

FIGURE 10-1
HC BRidge™ Framework

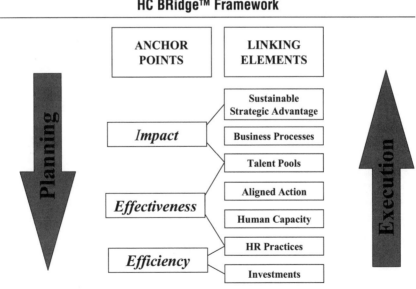

zation and human resources leaders not only understand some of the strategic challenges created by the emergence of electronic commerce, but to show how strategic analysis tools can help HR executives who must translate the strategic changes into specific implications for their key talent.

THE ENCYCLOPEDIA BRITANNICA CASE STUDY[5]

Encyclopedia Britannica, founded in 1768 in Edinburgh, Scotland, was the world's first compendium of knowledge. As Britannica grew, it built a reputation for having solid, authoritative, and comprehensive content. Britannica maintained its position as a content leader by continually revising and adding innovative features to its content, such as an atlas and a yearbook. Britannica's initial market was with institutions such as libraries. While this was a slow-growth market, it provided a reliable source of income that allowed Britannica to build its financial foundation. However, the key to Britannica's market success was recognizing and extending the market to homes.

Britannica created an aggressive and direct sales force that targeted middle-income families by going door-to-door. At its peak in 1989, Britannica's worldwide sales force numbered 7,500 and was the envy of nearly every sales-oriented industry. Britannica's executives realized that middle-income parents had intensely strong desires to provide their children with educational opportunities. The sales force learned that they could convince parents to purchase the $1,500 to $2,500 encyclopedia as a means of improving their children's education. A fundamental value proposition for Britannica was alleviating parents' guilt, and the in-home sales experience made that guilt even more tangible and provided the product to assuage it. Market research demonstrated that the encyclopedias were actually opened less than once a year, on average, after the initial excitement of the purchase wore off. Britannica maintained its position as the industry's dominant firm. By 1990, sales reached a peak of $650 million.

Britannica's decline began with the CD-ROM. The CD made a natural replacement for the bound encyclopedia, because it was able to store large quantities of easily searchable information (text, sound, video, and photos). In the mid-1990s competitors such as Funk and Wagnall's (later renamed as Encarta when it was acquired by Microsoft Corp.) and Grolier (formerly Encyclopedia Americana) devoted themselves entirely to CD-ROM production and stopped printing bound editions. Encarta and Grolier quickly gained market share by distributing free versions of their products with new home computers. Britannica failed to see that parents would buy a personal computer for their children (with its free CD-ROM-based encyclopedia) in favor of purchasing a bound product for roughly the same amount of money (about $2,000).

Britannica developed its own CD-ROM in 1995, but it was too expensive (originally priced at $800), and its initial version was text only because Britannica's vast and rich content was too large to fit onto a single CD. Consumers opted for the cheaper, more interactive multimedia products offered by Encarta and Grolier. By 1995, Britannica's future looked bleak. Sales of print-bound encyclopedias had plummeted 80 percent from the 1990 peak, and company revenues dropped to $400 million. Consequently, Britannica was sold in 1996 to Swiss financier Jacob Safra (an avid reader of Britannica since childhood) for half of its book value.

Lessons from this era of Britannica's experience show that the "richness" of the sales experience (a vast in-home personal sales force) made sense when expanding into a new market (in this case, moving from institutions to homes). However, "reach" and convenience can become more important when selling into an already-developed market (such as CDs bundled with personal computers). The "richness" of Britannica's vast and unique content also became a liability because even CDs couldn't hold the content. Since 1996, Safra has made sweeping changes to Britannica's strategy in an attempt to save it from sure failure. Safra began by eliminating Britannica's once-dominant sales force. In addition, he has broadened Britannica's fundamental value proposition in a crowded industry dominated by computer- and Internet-related product and strategies. Britannica now defines itself as the preeminent information community on the Web.

The core of Britannica's new value proposition is its new website, Britannica.-com, which offers a wide range of products and services, from news (e.g., sports scores, stock quotes) to filtered search capabilities (edited by their expert staff) to e-mail accounts, all free of charge. "This is not an encyclopedia online," explained one marketing executive, "but a community of intellectually curious people."[6] The Internet now makes it possible for Britannica to deliver its vast content very efficiently. The new value proposition is that this unique content, and the information-based meeting place where it resides, will attract a critical mass of repeat customers who use the site as their home base for information. With a critical mass or "community" of loyal users, Britannica can then attract advertising revenue and more effectively sell specialty educational products (such as the $2,500 Encyclopedia of Art) offered online. Ironically, Britannica's offer of free content is now distinctive. As recently as 1998, users paid an $80 yearly subscription rate.[7] Currently, Britannica offers both the free online access, AND a fee-based enhanced Web site that costs $50 per month, compared to other fee-based online encyclopedias that range from $49.95 to $395 (including Encarta, Americana, Grolier, and World Book) and free sites (for example, Funk & Wagnalls).[8] What was once a source of price premium has now become the vehicle to attract customers in a crowded web space.

Britannica's recent efforts to increase its web presence appear to be paying off. *USA Today* reports that home user traffic has increased more than 75 percent since January 2000 when the Super Bowl ad aired.[9] Over a three-month period, the number of unique users to the website has jumped from 594,468 to 1,003,216. Britannica has also introduced a free software application called "Britannica Traveler" that allows Palm handheld computer users wireless access to its website. Using the latest global positioning technology, the new Britannica software can be programmed to automatically send users information relevant to wherever they are located. For example, visitors to San Francisco could be sent articles about its history and landmarks as well as information about local restaurants or entertainment. This not only provides Britannica with additional e-business partnerships, but more important, increases traffic on its website, and is another example of Britannica's effort to reach its goal of becoming the preeminent online information community. Britannica's emerging information community business model creates value by acting as an information agent to consumers. Revenues are thus generated by creating a critical mass of regular users who make direct purchases from the Britannica marketplace and attract advertising revenues.

A Framework for Understanding the Human Capital Lessons

Britannica's strategic response to the advancement of information technology provides an instructive business case study, with lessons for other companies striving to redesign their businesses to meet technology challenges. It is interesting that while the marketing and technological aspects of the Britannica case are well known, the human element remains unexamined. Of course, we know that the traditional sales force has been removed, but other, more subtle human capital lessons can be learned.

However, examining the lessons for human capital requires a framework that can look beneath the strategy and business elements of the case. It requires a mechanism to translate the strategic shifts into implications for talent, and then into implications for human resources management. Here, we use the HC BRidge framework to analyze the Britannica case and to derive strategic talent and human capital implications.

Identifying "strategic impact" is often the most difficult yet the most critical task in applying the model. Moreover, many of the unique elements of human capital strategy in the Internet era require a detailed understanding of the impact elements.

As shown in Figure 10-2, the "strategic impact" is expanded into ten detailed elements:

- Industry
- Industry context
- Points of differentiation
- Strategic intent
- Strategic resources
- Value chain/business processes
- Business algebra
- Constraints

FIGURE 10-2
Detailed Elements of Strategic Input Linking to Talent

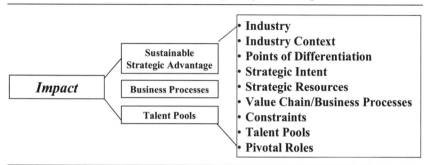

- Talent pools
- Pivotal roles

By isolating the elements of impact, it is possible to analyze strategy and competitive advantage so that they link clearly to implications for organizational talent.

Industry and Industry Context

Industry describes the markets in which the organization competes to create value—now and in the foreseeable future. It includes the list of key competitors, defined as those organizations whose actions should spur a competitive response.[10] For example, if increases or decreases in the prices of a potential competitor would cause an organization to adjust its prices, then those competitors should be included in the "industry" element. The same analogy would hold true in the areas of supplier relationships, regulatory activities, or customer impressions. The result of an industry analysis is a list of competitors or future competitors.

The importance of industry analysis is underscored by the concept of "strategic groups." Strategic groups have been defined as a set of firms within an industry sharing similar strategies or mobility barriers.[11] Proponents of strategic groups argue that they are helpful in explaining variance in firm performance between firms within an industry and enhance understanding of the nature of competition in a firm's environment.[12] Recent work suggests that the analysis of strategic groups as a heuristic tool for managers has become increasingly useful in an era of expanding industry boundaries through strategic alliances and partnerships.[13]

In addition, one of the most distinctive characteristics of the Internet era is the speed at which the composition of industries can change. Advancements in information technology can create rivals out of previously unrelated firms. The application of the competitor definition is seen in Figure 10-3. When printed reference materials defined the industry, the sole competitors were other makers of encyclopedias. However, with the development of the CD-ROM and later the Internet, the competitive landscape changed dramatically. For example, Britannica's new strategic direction places them in direct competition with a host of companies representing an array of previously unrelated industries. As an information community that also sells retail products, Britannica now competes with the likes of Yahoo.com, CNN.com, Amazon.com, and many others. By defining competitors systematically and broadly, whole new competitive arenas are identified.

In the same way, industry analysis can be applied to any organization to make more specific the implications of emerging e-commerce challenges. Broad strategic patterns such as the rise of infomediaries, disintermediation, hypermediation, the virtual value chain, and the network economy are useful frameworks. By specifying how they change the competitor space, we begin to better understand their implications.

Industry context describes the forces that impact the industry.[14] These forces can include the industry's size and growth rate (including the life cycle stage and the "value migration" pattern); factors affecting industry profitability (e.g., competitors, suppliers, buyers, new entrants, and substitutes), as noted by Porter;[15] government regulation; and turbulence (including hypercompetition or technology development). Industry context defines the factors that determine the amount of available "rents" or profits for the players in that industry. Size and growth rate affect the absolute amount of rents; the Porter dimensions affect the amount of "excess rents" likely to be available due to imperfect competition; and regulation and turbulence reflect the riskiness of the stream of rents. Thus, industry context identifies common challenges and opportunities facing all of the industry competitors. For example, identifying that the industry will become increasingly regulated suggests developing resources such as strong relationships with regula-

FIGURE 10-3
Britannica's Industry, Then and Now

Print-Only Era (circa 1980)	Internet Era (circa 2000)	
Competitors	**Competitors**	
• Compton's	• Compton's	• CNN.com
• Americana (Now Grolier)	• Grolier	• USAToday.com
• Funk and Wagnall's (Now Encarta)	• Microsoft Encarta	• Yahoo.com
• World Book	• IBM/World Book	• Altavista.com
	• Encyclopedia.com	• MSN.com
		• Amazon.com
		• eToys.com

tory agencies. Identifying that an industry is entering a period of more rapid growth suggests that the emphasis may shift from gaining market share from competitors to increasing sales from emerging customer segments. Before we can understand how an individual organization will choose to compete, we must understand the profit potential of the industry.

Figure 10-4 depicts a strategic context analysis that may have occurred circa 1983, as the emergence of the PC was apparent, but before technology had actually changed the industry. In a nonelectronic world, encyclopedia makers had significant bargaining power over content suppliers and over in-home buyers, because printed versions were the only form for the information. New entry into the printed reference industry was limited due to the need to build up production, content, sales, brands, and distribution. Moreover, Britannica had developed a reputation and relationship with libraries and other institutions. While this market was very small, it provided a reliable source of revenue to cover the fixed costs of content development and production. Libraries, once sold, ordered encyclopedias regularly, paid the asking price, and placed standing orders. In fact, the two-year cycle of encyclopedia production was in part due to the two-year purchase cycle of libraries. This

FIGURE 10-4
Britannica's Industry Context, Then and Now

Print-Only Era (circa 1980)	Internet Era (circa 2000)
Bargaining Power of Suppliers Suppliers: • Manufacturers of book printing materials • Content suppliers	**Bargaining Power of Suppliers** Suppliers: • Content suppliers (e.g., AP wire) • Manufacturers of print and CD-ROM materials • Toy and educational product manufacturers
Bargaining Power of Buyers Buyer reach: • Door-to-door • Schools	**Bargaining Power of Buyers** Buyer reach: • Online sales • Bricks-and-mortar retail • Some schools
Threat of Potential New Entrants Threats: • Companies that could match Britannica's value proposition but do so more cheaply and more conveniently (e.g., Grolier and Encarta)	**Threat of Potential New Entrants** Threats: • Companies that can copy and/or expand Britannica's new value proposition as a reference information community (e.g., Yahoo or some variant).
Threat of Substitutes Threats: • Technologies: CD-ROM, PC, Internet	**Threat of Substitutes** Threats: • Technologies that increase the ease of information flow. But which information and which technologies?

reliable revenue base was one factor that made it feasible for Britannica to consider investing in an in-home sales force to expand the market.

Technology also transformed the size and growth rate of the industry. In the print-only era, the market for encyclopedias was small and static. The expense of producing and purchasing the print volumes kept the market small. In the CD era, however, rivals such as Encarta and Grolier exploded the market for encyclopedias by distributing their products free with new PCs. Very quickly, millions of consumers had cheap and easy access to rich information content, and the market was instantly transformed from small and stable to rapidly growing. Admittedly, hindsight is easier than foresight, but the case does illustrate the potential value of a structured and logical approach to strategic context analysis. As e-business technology emerged, this analysis may also have helped to anticipate the emergence of competition from search engines, news services, retail educational products, and even makers of other education-related products (such as PCs, as discussed previously). Thus, identifying the industry context takes the competitor list and specifies the implications for how competition will be defined in the industry. The next step is to determine how the organization will define itself within that competitive space.

Dimensions of Differentiation and Strategic Intent

Dimensions of differentiation, the third element of strategic impact, builds a map showing the dimensions on which industry competitors distinguish or differentiate themselves to gain economic value.[16] Traditionally, these dimensions focus on customer relationships, such as price, service, product customization, and innovative features.[17] However, competitors can also create sustainable competitive advantage in production, resource acquisition, distribution, and support functions, such as patents, relationships with regulatory agencies, or organizational features (e.g., Dell's "Be Direct" model). These dimensions may be "invisible" to ultimate customers,[18] but they are often key to competitive advantage now and in the future. This is why identifying buyers, suppliers, and substitutes is so important in defining the strategic context. The differentiation dimensions provide the "map"of possible competitive positions. Each current and potential competitor can be placed on the map according to its position on the key dimensions.

With regard to e-commerce, defining the dimensions or points of differentiation is particularly important and is a key source of insights regarding the competitive space. For example, the emergence of online providers of information about automobile features, availability, and pricing options made *the information itself* an element of the competitive space. Previously, such information was necessarily connected to the manufacturer or the dealer. Now, the timeliness, detail, and comprehensiveness of such information is an element defining competition in this industry. Similarly, while personal health advice was not traditionally considered an element of competition between pharmaceutical companies because the necessary information and expertise resided with physicians in their offices, consumers increasingly look to the Web for health-related information, making it a new arena for competition.

Strategic intent defines the organization's target position on the map.[19] For each dimension of differentiation, it shows how different or similar the organization strives to be, compared to competitors. Deciding the organization's intended position on each dimension articulates strategic intent at a detailed level. The term *strategic intent* has been used to describe a "sustained obsession with winning at all levels of the organization" even when the firm's strategic goals transcended its current resources and capabilities.[20] As such, strategic intent not only articulates a desired leadership position within an industry, but also defines a set of measures to assess the firm's strategic progress. Here, we take a more specific use of the term, emphasizing that an organization may choose to position itself differently on different strategic dimensions, rather than win on all dimensions.

The Britannica case illustrates how information technology can change the dimensions of differentiation within an industry. Figure 10-5 contrasts selected elements of the differentiation and strategic intent "map" that may have been constructed for the encyclopedia industry in the 1980s to the emerging map with the advent of the Internet. Before the emergence of electronic technology, the differentiation map was fairly simple. Companies differentiated themselves on the bases of price, content quality, and alternative products. Britannica differentiated itself as a high margin leader on the basis of its premium content and packaging leadership. Britannica leveraged its history of having world-class contributors to generate a strong content reputation. Second, Britannica sought out and obtained the powerful endorsement of libraries and schools, which provided an even greater boost to its reputation as a content leader. A key source of Britannica's profit was packaging options (e.g., premium leather bindings) that carried very high profit margins. In fact, selling these additional options was both a reason for the in-home sales force and a requirement to cover the high cost of the sales force. In contrast, Funk and Wagnall's differentiated itself as a discount product, available in grocery stores. Others, such as Compton's and World Book, made their mark by serving the middle of the price and content market and also by targeting schools as a primary customer. They did not employ the in-home sales force.

Figure 10-5 also depicts elements of the industry's current differentiation map. There is much greater parity among competitors. All have a web-based encyclopedia, and most offer an array of alternative products (e.g., retail books, toys, and educational services) that are sold

FIGURE 10-5
Differentiation Map of the Encyclopedia Industry, Then and Now

The Print-Only Era (circa 1980)

	Britannica	*Compton's*	*Funk and Wagnall's*	*World Book*	*The New Book of Knowledge (Grolier)*
Retail Price (1984)	$1,500	$599	$144.99	$499	$398
# of Volumes	32	26	29	22	21
Primary Distribution Channels	Door-to-door, bookstores, and libraries	Bookstores	Grocery stores	Schools	Preschools and mail order
Content Quality	• World-class expert content providers • Reputation • Endorsement from libraries	• Average content • Little library representation	• Average content • "Grocery store" image not high in reputation	• Average content • Strong reputation with schools	• Average content. • Little library representation
Additional Products and Options	Premium packaging (e.g., leather bindings)	Webster's Dictionary	None	World Book Atlas, Medical Journal, and Dictionary	None

The Internet Era (circa 2000)

	Britannica	*Compton's*	*Encarta*	*World Book*	*Grolier*	*Encyclopedia.com*
Product Channels	CD-ROM, Web, Print	CD-ROM, Print, Web	CD-ROM, Web	CD-ROM, Web, Print	CD-ROM	Web
# of Base Articles	72,000	40,000	42,000	21,000	37,000	14,000
Retail Price	CD: $69 Web: Free Print: $1,250	CD: $14.95 Print: $599	CD: $100 Web: $49/year	CD: $89.95 Web: 49.94/year Print: N/A	CD: $49.95	Free (Revenues through advertising)
Other Products	Web: News services, feature articles, search engine, e-mail, educational toys, navigation software	Web: E-games, virtual tours, books, personal improvement products	Web: E-games, web-based lesson plan archives, various CD products	Literacy programs and products, electronic learning aid toys	Retail children's books, reading clubs, educational CDs	None

SOURCE: *The New York Times* (December 23, 1984). Bookshelf: Section 7, p. 20. Other sources: www.britannica.com, www.comptons.com, www.msn.encarta.com., www.encyclopedia.com, www.grolier.com., www.worldbook.com.

online. Thus, competitive advantage is more difficult to create through the sales experience and through optional product features. Unlike the earlier era, in which Britannica was virtually the only competitor reaching into the home with a direct sales force, in the Internet era everyone can reach directly into any home with a web connection. "Presence" in the customer space is no longer differentiated through the sales force. So, what is Britannica's "strategic intent" in the Internet era?

Britannica is now trying to create a first-mover advantage through an "information community" business model, offering its premium content to consumers for free and generating revenue by attracting a critical mass of repeat visitors to entice advertisers. The information community model requires that users make the Britannica their primary source for news, stock quotes, and quality reference information, even e-mail. Now, Britannica's differentiation depends on two key factors. First, it must maintain the high standard of quality and authoritative content associated with its long-standing reputation. Second, it must ensure that users have a unique and satisfying experience when they access the site. In other words, premium content is not enough to attract a base of repeat users if the experience on the Web is poor. To accomplish the first-mover advantage and obtain the critical mass, Britannica must ensure that user experiences are uniquely compelling.

It is interesting to note that Britannica's large number of base articles (72,000) hints at a potentially valuable differentiator—the ability to offer users a uniquely *authoritative* experience. In the print era, this authoritative distinction led to endorsements by libraries and added to the compelling message of the in-home sales force, but it was seldom experienced by actual customers (since the encyclopedia was seldom opened after it was sold). Now, it may emerge as a strategic resource for a very different reason. To understand that, however, requires that we move to the next level of specificity in the strategic diagnosis and identify strategic resources and market power.

Strategic Resources and Market Power

Strategic resources and market power define the factors necessary to achieve the strategic intent and protect it from imitators.[21] *Strategic resources* are the valued organizational elements that make the biggest difference in achieving, sustaining, and protecting strategic intent.[22] Traditional examples include physical assets (e.g., locations, raw materials, plant/equipment), exclusive rights (e.g., patents, leases on raw materials), brands, core competencies, and data. The Internet has created a whole new array of strategic resources. For example, having a unique and recognizable URL, having a large customer base that has "bookmarked" your site, and having top web development talent are all strategic resources that never existed before the emergence of the

Internet. *Market power* is the organization's ability to extract value from others in the market (e.g., buyers and suppliers). For example, market power with buyers can be used to charge higher prices and to hold or increase market share, while market power with suppliers can be used to lower costs or obtain exclusive rights to key inputs.[23]

While firms should be aware of their existing resources and market power when formulating their intent, it can be dangerous to base strategic plans strictly on existing resources to the exclusion of the industry context. Resources that are sources of sustainable advantage in one setting, due to their rareness or difficulty to imitate,[24] can become liabilities if clung to in the face of fundamental changes. For example, Britannica's decline illustrates that its key resource in the print era—superior content and sales force—could not prevail over competitors who adapted to changes in technology that altered the value of key resources.

There has been significant debate regarding whether strategic advantage is best created through an external perspective—adapting the organization's internal resources to address shifts in the industry's competitive environment, versus an internal perspective—building hard-to-copy internal strategic resources and finding competitive environments that capitalize on them. Many writers now acknowledge that both perspectives are necessary, and that integration is the key.[25] As we see here, the HC BRidge™ framework reflects an integrated view. Elements of external competitiveness are used to identify how internal resources can offer unique and hard-to-imitate advantages. This integration is particularly valuable in understanding the strategic human capital implications of the Britannica case.

Figure 10-6 illustrates the analysis of three strategic resources in the Britannica case. Traditional resources may be valuable only if translated to fit the electronic content acquisition and distribution channel. It is ironic that, despite technological advancement and strategic transformation, one of Britannica's current key resources is also one of its oldest: its content and brand recognition. Although Britannica has quickly transformed itself into a web-based information community, nothing prevents rivals from imitating the company. What rivals cannot imitate, however, is Britannica's content tradition and famous brand. It is especially notable that the trusted brand name and content leadership (in terms of authority and uniqueness of experience) has the potential to create not only a critical mass of users, but also a *differentiated user community* that rivals will be unable to duplicate. Users who choose Britannica's website for the authoritative content are likely to represent a desirable demographic group for advertisers and are likely to respond more predictably to product offerings. The power of the authoritative content is now that it attracts only those web users who value high-end and education-oriented experiences and products. This potential

FIGURE 10-6
Strategic Resources and Market Power in the Britannica Case

Resource	Market Power Created	Britannica's Unique Position	Competitors' Position	Future Value and Sustainability
Exclusive and Extensive Unique Content	• Unique information thwarts substitution and content infrastructure creation. • Allows price and market share maintenance.	• Well-established through exclusive, long-term relationships with in-house and outside content suppliers. • Historically oriented toward two-year revision cycle.	• Possess few in-house content suppliers—competitors rely on cheap and ready access to Web-based sources. • Pure content providers (CNN) are quicker in updating information. • Technology providers (Microsoft) can compete on content to threaten market share.	• Easily duplicated • Britannica's uniqueness is less valued by customers in Internet era.
Brand Recognition	• Unique customer trust creates awareness and habitual purchase decisions. • Product awareness creates market share and allows price maintenance.	• High customer brand trust is limited to printed product. • Brand attributes are oriented toward a printed and bound product, and not well-transferred to electronic products/channels.	• Competitors are inferior in quality, but superior in price and accessibility. • Short-term difficulty in matching Britannica's brand image, but competitors can emphasize other product features in the e-market.	• Brand can retain its value in trust and quality if translated into key features of the e-market. • Potentially sustainable if successful as a trusted adviser in the e-information arena. • High potential for building a trusted community of users around a known brand and shared experience with print product.
Knowledge of Customer Buying Patterns	• Anticipating customer desires creates market share and price premium. • Customer information allows market innovation that new entrants cannot duplicate.	• Long-term understanding is built through intimate, in-home customer contact. • Sales force understands buying decisions and selling processes. • Focus is on printed product and door-to-door selling.	• Search engines and software makers do not have expertise in encyclopedia and information sales. • Both types of future competitors will amass information electronically that could eventually match this resource.	• Sustainable only if quickly applied to the electronic information area. • Significant risk of loss through attrition of sales force to competitors.

additional resource could potentially be as powerful as Britannica's massive sales force once was.

The value of integrating the external (industry-based) and internal (resource-based) strategic perspectives is clearly illustrated. Resource-based analysis would suggest that Britannica's traditionally authoritative content satisfied the "VRIO" requirements of sustainable strategic advantage.[26] It was valuable, rare, and hard to imitate, and Britannica was organized to exploit it. In the Internet era, authoritative content still satisfied the first three requirements (VRI), but the Internet requires organizing (O) differently to exploit the resource.

Business Algebra

Business algebra refers to the mathematical logic that shows how the organization creates value and generates profits and cash flow. This logic often draws on accounting data, but is not simply the accounting statements. Rather, business algebra expresses the logic of value creation for the particular business in mathematical form. For Britannica, a component of the business algebra related to sales volume is shown in Figure 10-7. Sales volume is seen to be a function of *market size* (the number of potential buyers) and *market share* (the percent of buyers choosing Britannica), which in turn is a function of *product line density* (the number of different products offered), *product presence* (the likelihood that buyers will encounter the product), and *close rate* (the probability that buyers choose the product when they encounter it). Business algebra provides explicit indicators of strategic success, enabling quantitative diagnosis. For example, Britannica's leaders might use the logic of Figure 10-7 to ask whether falling sales volume is due primarily to a shortage of products, lack of presence, or a poor close rate. The power of business algebra is best seen when we combine it with the value chain and constraint analysis.

FIGURE 10-7
Business Algebra for Sales Volume

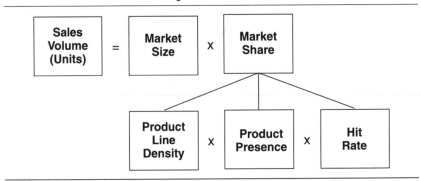

Value Chain and Constraint Analysis

Value chains are the processes that create and exploit strategic resources and market power. Physical value chains, for example, often reflect a sequence of acquiring materials, services, or components, then the transformation of those components into products or services, followed by outbound movement of finished products, then sales and customer management, then order-to-payment processes. Porter proposed that in most industries, firm-level value chains consist of five key activities—inbound logistics, operations, outbound logistics, marketing/ sales, and service—plus the four support activities of technology development, procurement, human resource management, and corporate infrastructure.[27] Describing value chains helps us see precisely what "happens" to create or exploit strategic resources and market power. Value chain elements not only change with e-business technology, but they can also be "reconstructed" when information is combined across several value-chain elements.[28] For example, information from service encounters and marketing/sales may be combined to better predict customer needs and identify customer segments where high-margin service will be possible after the sale and where additional sales can be made through the service encounter.

Constraints are bottlenecks in the value chain.[29] They are important because relieving bottlenecks not only enhances value at the bottleneck, but allows other processes to create more value because they are no longer limited by the constraint. For example, if an organization with limited distribution adds distribution channels, it creates more valuable distribution, but it also allows the organization to exploit existing production and sales resources more fully because there is sufficient distribution capacity to accommodate them. Augmenting sales and production capacity makes little sense until the distribution constraint is addressed. Thus, understanding constraints is one key to focusing on the most critical internal processes and avoiding potentially wasteful attention to important but less critical processes.

Figure 10-8 depicts Britannica's basic value chain. The first element involves collecting, editing, and organizing the content of reference information. In the second stage, the content is designed, and the presentation approach is determined (e.g., printed, pressed onto a CD-ROM, or organized into a web page). The third stage involves the sales process (e.g., in-home sales in the print era and web-based sales in the Internet era). Next, the production and delivery of the product is either physical (i.e., via ground transportation in the printed product) or virtual (i.e., year-round maintenance of a network server on the Web). Finally, the user has a distinct experience, including the impressions and feelings the user has toward the product and related support services for getting the most from the product.

FIGURE 10-8
Britannica's Value Chain

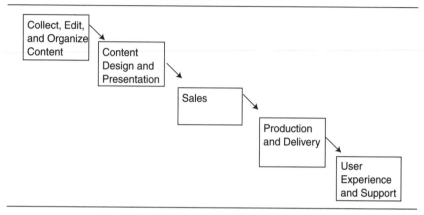

As we have noted, in the print era the user experience after the sale was not critical to success because the volumes were rarely opened after the sale. Still, content was important because Britannica sold the product to the much smaller institutional market, which in turn created Britannica's reputation as a content leader and generated the basic financial returns to cover the fixed costs. The in-home selling experience did create a unique value point, but the content and experience were not closely tied. In the new "community of users" model, the experience and content are much more closely tied. Britannica's content gets customers to the website, but they will return based on their entire web experience: the accessibility of the content, the ability of the editors to steer the user toward the most useful websites, and the presence of useful products and features that the user did not expect. It is this unique product experience that is instrumental in building the critical mass of customers—the community of users that can give Britannica a competitive advantage over rivals who also offer web-based information. Content and experience were largely distinct in the print era, but they are now inextricably linked.

This realization flows from the systematic analysis of Britannica's strategy through the earlier elements of the model in Figure 10-2. Moreover, understanding this value chain link has significant implications for talent planning and analysis, as shown in Figure 10-1.

Now let's combine the "constraints" analysis with business algebra. Recall that one of Britannica's dimensions of differentiation was the sales margin the company could generate from premium packaging options. One of the reasons that Britannica was able to succeed on these high margins was because of its ability to expand the market for print encyclopedias. In the print era, a primary constraint was the size of the market, which was limited to institutions (see Figure 10-9).

FIGURE 10-9
Constraints in the Print Era

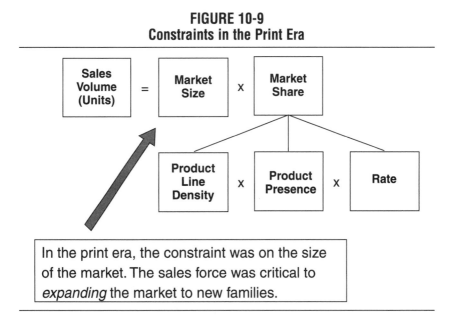

In the print era, the constraint was on the size of the market. The sales force was critical to *expanding* the market to new families.

Britannica successfully addressed this constraint with its massive sales force that expanded the market door-by-door, family-by-family. When less expensive, more accessible CD products made by competitors were packaged with the distribution of new PCs, millions of consumers had access to this information, and Britannica's edge in artificially expanding the market became obsolete. In an immense and quickly expanding market, the constraint was no longer the size of the market, but rather market share. Encarta and Grolier created an edge through alliances with PC distributors and quickly overtook the lion's share of the market.

In the Internet era, Britannica faced the technological transformation by embracing the "online community" business model. As a result, Britannica's primary constraint shifted again (see Figure 10-10). Market share is still more important than market expansion, but now the specific constraint is product presence rather than close rates. For the information community to succeed, Britannica must now expand its presence among consumers. A marketing executive at Britannica recently noted, "We are entering a new stage of our evolution into an Internet and news media company, and our new model requires that we raise our profile among consumers in a significant way."[30] It is ironic that despite all of the transformation of the value chain due to information technology, Britannica's key constraint is still centered on sales.

The nature of the market power created by sales and marketing in the Internet era is now clearer, because we can link it to the competitive

FIGURE 10-10
Constraints in the Internet Era

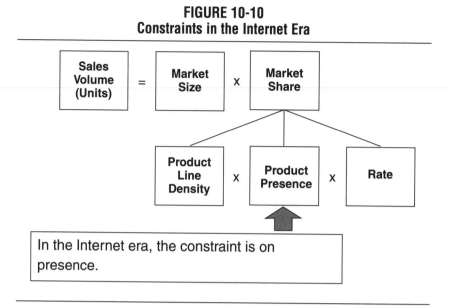

In the Internet era, the constraint is on presence.

analysis and to the interaction of marketing and sales with the other key value chain processes using business algebra. Specifying the value chains and constraints thus calls into sharp focus the need to clearly define the nature of the talent required to create, enlarge, and support those business processes. It allows us to identify key talent pools and their specific actions necessary to carry out the new strategy.[31] We now describe how talent links to the strategic analysis in e-business.

Talent Implications of Constraints

Talent implications link the analysis of constraints to human capital by identifying the specific human capital with the greatest potential to relieve the key constraints.[32] Thus, through talent implications, we create the tangible link from strategic success to human capital. Moreover, because the implications are built on the foundation of constraint and resource analysis, they are seamlessly linked to the broad strategic imperatives. *Talent pools* are thus the linchpin in the impact model—the element that provides the bridge between strategy and people.

Pivotal roles describe the specific elements of talent that combine to create the talent pools. Roles can be pivotal through their effect on critical constraints. Roles can also become pivotal if they are clearly linked to critical resources or when differences in performance in those roles have a large effect on key resources or constraints. Job descriptions are helpful but not usually identical to pivotal roles. For example, a role in drug development is managing subjects for clinical trials. This role is a combination of elements of the jobs of clinical subject recruiters, schedulers, data managers, and clinical experiment designers.[33] Translating strategic resources and constraints into talent and role implications reveals the key human capital areas that will have the most impact on strategy.

In the past, Britannica's key talent pool was the sales force because of the market constraint driving the need to expand the market into homes. The sales force was extremely expensive to support, but worth the investment because it was so successful in bringing new families into the market. The high margins gained from the premium packaging allowed Britannica to support the massive sales force. However, in the era of the Internet, Britannica's primary constraint has shifted. The path to increased market share is centered around increasing product presence rather than increasing hit rates.

Britannica's new critical talent pools must center around those involved in designing, refining, and promoting the new information community. Of course, important talent pools will be website designers, information specialists, and market researchers. However, the strategic analysis reveals that the talent implications go well beyond simply eliminating in-home sales representatives and replacing them with web designers and programmers. The competition to create an information community still revolves around delivering an experience that is uniquely informative. It seems likely that many of the same capabilities that made the Britannica content unique in the past will remain important. Talent pools that identify and deliver uniquely informative web content are just as important as in the past when unique content motivated libraries to purchase the product. In fact, Web customers experience this content firsthand.

The elimination of the in-home sales role does not eliminate the need for customer-savvy talent pools. Britannica's "community of users" strategy requires that it differentiate itself to attract precisely the education-oriented customers who might have purchased a print encyclopedia in earlier times. In fact, the Britannica website still features high-end bound collections, such as a $2,500 "Encyclopedia of Art." The expertise of the in-home sales force and their intimate customer knowledge may well be valuable in creating a unique and user-driven community.

Our analysis shows vividly that the Internet era places even greater strategic value on cross-collaboration among various talent pools. The users of the Britannica website experience the content firsthand in ways that traditional users could not. The experience must integrate with the content, and vice versa. Web designers, information specialists, and market researchers must draw on one another's knowledge and expertise. This is a good example of the pivotal role concept in action. Roles become pivotal when differences in their performance make very large differences in key resources or business processes. Roles go beyond jobs, to specify the combined work of different talent pools. With Britannica's new Internet focus, a pivotal role is understanding what consumers want from the information community (e.g., what search engine improvements or which supplementary products are in demand) and then quickly designing ways to maximize "stickiness." Stickiness, in the world of electronic commerce, is how well a site holds its visitors, brings them back, and becomes one of their favorites.[34] This "role" depends on the *combination* of expertise from those in jobs with customer contact, market analysis, and product design.

For HR and business leaders concerned with managing talent, the implications are now much clearer. For example, enhancing these pivotal roles requires creating opportunities for customer contact experts, technology designers, and content experts to work more closely together than in the traditional print product. By linking the talent analysis to the earlier elements of industry, processes, strategic resources, value chains, and talent, richer human capital implications can be identified. We move well beyond the idea of reducing the sales force to adding web designers. In fact, our earlier analysis suggests that it may be possible, perhaps even critical, to capture the intellectual capital of the former sales force by creating new capabilities, opportunities, and motivation systems to bring that knowledge to bear on the new electronic community. The next step, then, is to specify precisely what it is that these talent pools would *do* in their pivotal roles.

Aligned Actions

Aligned actions are observable human behaviors that support key talent.[35] By translating talent pools and pivotal roles into aligned actions, human resources and business leaders specify what it is they are looking for and "how we'll know it when we see it." Specifying aligned actions is essential for building "line of sight" among employees and their managers by specifying how individual behaviors relate to the strategic objectives of the organization.[36] Figure 10-11 and Figure 10-12

FIGURE 10-11
The Print Era: Talent Pools and Aligned Actions at Britannica

Strategic Advantage	Library-endorsed content	Expanded market of in-home users
Talent Pools and Pivotal Roles	• Authoritative writers • Strong, trusted relationships with libraries	In-home sales experience providers
Aligned Actions	• Find and develop unique authoritative content • Sell to libraries	• Sell the upgrades • Sell the in-home idea • Trade on "educational guilt"

show the contrast between the talent pools and aligned actions in the print and Internet era at Britannica.

Aligned actions were always important. For example, even in the "print" days it was strategically important for Britannica's sales force to focus on the fundamental value proposition of alleviating parental guilt. The Internet vividly reveals the value of collaboration across pivotal roles. For example, web designers can maximize their strategic impact by collaborating with information specialists to design optimal marketing strategies. The need for collaboration across the value chain was always important, but it is even more imperative in the increasingly competitive Internet era.

Creating "presence" in an Internet market is very different from the traditional role of selling a physical product, or even from determining what to put on a CD. In the present era, not only must the sales force understand and build stickiness and presence, but they must bring key market information to the design team to help them constantly understand customer changes. Not only must the design team be very good at technical innovations that support a "community," they must also be good at translating those technical possibilities into language that allows the sales and marketing talent to understand their implications and communicate them to customers. The traditional strengths of each group must be integrated.

Moreover, traditional sales actions may have new counterparts in the Internet era, where customer interactions often occur by phone or e-mail. Amazon.com reportedly has hundreds of "blurbs" that represent scripts for responding to customer complaints (such as the late arrival of an order). These blurbs are carefully written to appropriately convey Amazon.com's core customer messages.[37] At Britannica, this may suggest a role for former in-home sales representatives. Experi-

FIGURE 10-12
The Internet Era: Talent Pools and Aligned Actions at Britannica

Strategic Advantage	Professionally endorsed content	Web-based content experience
Talent Pools and Pivotal Roles	• Authoritative writers • Creative information locators	• "Discerning customer" marketers • Designers of information communities
Aligned Actions	• Find and develop unique authoritative content • Alleviate "information overload" • Develop content to fit the "community of users" marketing concepts	• Build community-enhancing features • Make the experience match the content uniqueness • Respond to visitor questions consistent with the Britannica "brand"

enced in-home representatives undoubtedly learned effective phrases or selling points in dealing with customers. Thus, former top salespersons may become top "blurb" writers in the Internet era. Once again, the integration of the internal and external strategy perspectives reveals how a resource (sales talent) can best generate competitive advantage when the competitive context changes.

Human Capacity, HR Practices, and HR Investments

The bottom three elements of the HC BRidge™ framework (Figure 10-1) further links *human capacity* (i.e., the potential to carry out aligned actions) to *HR practices* (i.e., the array of HR programs that serve to nurture and create the necessary capacity), and finally to *HR investments* (i.e., the resource deployments designed to put in place the HR practices).[38] Figure 10-13 shows how the human capacity and HR elements at Britannica flow from the aligned actions, using two of the key talent pools discussed—in-home sales for the "print" era and information-community designers for the "Internet" era.

Human capacity consists of the following three factors: capability, opportunity, and motivation (COM). Balance across these three elements is essential to achieving aligned actions, although capability (i.e., skills, competencies, and abilities) frequently receives the most attention. Figure 10-13 shows that in the print era, the human capacity was driven not only by appropriate compensation and selection, but also by the insight of placing sales professionals in the homes most likely to respond to the Britannica value proposition. Decades of successful in-home selling set Britannica apart in its ability to target appropriate households, and thus to provide the sales force with unique opportunities to excel. In the Internet era, for "community designers," the matrix reveals an array of HR practices and investments that go well beyond the typical qualifications in technical web skills or programming. Rather, at Britannica, the unique strategic value proposition requires web designers with a strong connection to building an educational community. That includes the motivation to promote the Britannica "brand" of online knowledge and the ability and opportunity to work closely with content finders and designers. Capability, opportunity, and motivation to *collaborate* are much more important now than in the print era and, as we'll show, possibly more important at Britannica than at other Internet companies.

A similar distinction emerges comparing the HR practices and investments in Figure 10-13. In the print era, the key practices involved standard sales support functions, with a significant unique element to promote in-home sales and investments in excellent samples of high-end products. Compensation systems based on a straight sales commission were effective in motivating the sales force to extend the market

FIGURE 10-13
Effectiveness and Efficiency Elements in the
HR BRidge™ Framework at Britannica

	Print Era (circa 1980)	Internet Era (circa 2000)
Talent Pools	In-Home Sales Experience Providers	Designers of the Information Community Experience
Aligned Actions	• Sell the upgrades • Sell the in-home idea • Trade on "educational guilt"	• Build community-enhancing features • Design experience to match the content • Respond to visitor questions consistent with the Britannica "brand"
Human Capacity	Capability • Knowledge of door-to-door sales techniques • Extroverted personality • Ability to accept rejection Opportunity • Place the direct sales force in middle-class neighborhoods where Britannica sells the best—avoid areas where Britannica's value proposition doesn't work Motivation • Passion for door-to-door sales • Perceive a strong link between performance and pay • Pride in being a part of the Britannica brand	Capability • Market research skills, understanding what is valuable • Knowledge of what features cause "stickiness" behaviors in users Opportunity • Frequent chances for designers and content finders to share knowledge • Frequent chances for designers to work directly with user groups • Eliminate structural barriers to collaboration Motivation • Enjoyment of web design/ e-commerce • Desire to be on cutting edge of the industry • Pride in being a part of the Britannica "community"
HR Practices	• Train on the "guilt alleviation" value proposition • Provide updates on new product upgrade features • Pay emphasizing sales commission, especially on high-margin features • Select for door-to-door experience	• Provide recognition awards based on ranking of features by key community members • Redesign the organizational structure to create cross-functional teams with content developers • Recruit from pools of specialized "information" talent, such as libraries, museums, and schools • Select based on experience using high-end educational websites
HR Investments	• Obtain time from top sales managers to design and run classes on the "message" • Budget for recruiting from leading in-home sales organizations • Provide budget for high-end samples for all salespeople • Hold highly public sales conferences to recognize sales leaders	• Budget for recruitment ads in outlets for professional librarians • Increase pay allocation, to attract and retain the "best and brightest" in the information world • Increase professional travel allocation to allow designers to attend professional information specialist events

into homes, alleviating a key constraint in the print business process. In contrast, the Internet era requires a significantly different business model with processes that are constrained in different ways.

This analysis reveals implications well beyond the popular general notions of changes in labor markets (e.g., the e-lance economy or talent wars or virtual teams). These developments may provide important ways to accomplish the strategic human capital goals, such as by forming virtual teams of designers and content developers. However, unique strategic human capital advantage emerges from the specific human capital processes that link to the rich strategic analysis. By understanding the key strategic resources and process constraints, it is possible for HR leaders to be discerning adopters and responders to these developments. It is critical that HR leaders understand where to fight the "talent war," where the "e-lance" economy provides the greatest benefit and threat, and when and where investments in "virtual teams" will pay off the most. Business algebra (Figure 10-7) provides ways to measure these payoffs so that they logically link to strategic goals.

Ideally, HR investments translate the decisions about HR practices into specific resource deployments.[39] These resources certainly include money, so HR budgets are important; but an even more important resource is the time commitment required of key constituents (e.g., trainees and managers who do the training, the cross-functional team members, among others). Such resource commitments and requests are more seamlessly and logically linked to the strategic imperatives of the business.

In the print era, Britannica likely tolerated the fact that its sales compensation and support system was higher than competitors. It was obvious that the in-home sales force was allowing Britannica to strategically expand the market to areas where competitors could not go. In the same way, the analysis of the Internet era shows that Britannica's "community" designers must possess unique human capacities well beyond those of more typical web designers, and thus must be supported by different HR practices and investments. Britannica will likely gain an advantage through its practice of selecting web/product designers from unconventional talent pools that may have unique insight into how to "sell" informative content. For example, Britannica may recruit and select from libraries, museums, and schools. Compensation systems at Britannica are likely to set higher base salary levels because of the need for web community designers who can and will work more closely with content developers than at other Internet companies. Incentives built on positive feedback from users who best fit the target community profile make sense now. Thus, in terms of HR investments, Britannica may actually appear expensive when simple benchmark comparisons are made. Cost-per-hire and pay-per-designer may well be higher for Britannica, but they are well worth the investment because of the increased collaboration and integration with content that results.

Conclusions and Take-Aways for Managers

The Britannica case study presented here shows how a rich and logical strategic analysis can link strategic impact to talent, providing important insights as organizations anticipate challenges and opportunities in e-business. The importance of the "linking elements" between strategic changes and HR practices is clear.

"One Best Way" in the Internet Era?

The debate rages on regarding whether a particular set of HR practices is best for many situations.[40] The temptation to search for "magic bullets" is certainly no less apparent in the Internet era. As we have noted, there are already signs of emerging general prescriptions about the future of work (e.g., teams, free-lance deals, outsourced HR, individualized incentives). However, the logic and theory of sustainable strategic advantage suggests the importance of uniqueness and the ability to protect those things that differentiate a business to achieving long-run success. We continue to believe that there will be opportunities to capitalize on differentiated human capital strategies. However, identifying and executing those strategies requires the kind of rich and logical strategic links depicted throughout this chapter. There is no free lunch, and uniqueness comes through hard analytical rigor.

The Britannica case study illustrates this vividly for the Internet era. It is certainly important to engage the talent war for web design, but the analysis reveals the importance of authoritative content in the Internet era. This reveals talent pools (e.g., library professionals) that may be relatively untapped in the rush to attract more typical web design professionals. Moreover, the example has revealed the value of drawing on traditional strengths (e.g., the knowledge of the in-home sales force for writing "blurbs" or the value of traditional content experts in creating the web "community").

Implications for Benchmarking

The value of uniqueness, richly integrated with strategy, has implications for benchmarking. HR practices need to "fit" the strategy, but more important they must fit an entire array of linking elements (e.g., key constraints, talent pools, pivotal roles, and aligned actions). Best practice and benchmarking approaches to HR management become more difficult in the new economy, precisely because of the exploding variety of ways to create value. Moreover, new practices can be shared and adopted at a much faster rate due to technological communication and diffusion. The Britannica story illustrates that new business models transform entire industries, making competitors out of previously unrelated businesses and industries. Critical constraints and key talent pools change rapidly both between and within organizations, making unique, strategic alignment crucial for survival in the new economy. Benchmarking will not go away in the new economy. In many ways, it becomes easier due to greater access to information and greater cross-pollination as professionals move between organizations. However, the depth of strategic analysis necessary to benchmark effectively will increase.

General Talent Implications of E-Business

Within the caveats about overgeneralizing, it seems likely that changes from technology will make certain talent pools increasingly critical across a wide variety of industries. Certainly as Internet-related firms continue to thrive and bricks-and-mortar firms launch web initiatives, it is clear that talent pools surrounding the technological support (e.g., programmers) become strategically important. One particular talent pool becomes especially important across all industries that are related to the development and establishment of communication protocols, standards, and procedures.[41] Often the primary constraint to mass communication (or "reach") is not technology, but a lack of communication standards that link different types of systems together.[42] For example, electronic data interchange (EDI) systems have been in place for more than twenty years but have been limited in their influence because they could only be used by firms that had the same proprietary software. The success of the Internet has been largely due to the fact that it established protocols or standards by which all different types of systems could communicate with each other. Standards may take the form of routinized processes such as those in operating rooms that allow doctors, nurses, and technicians who have never seen each other to work together efficiently. For Britannica, for example, talent pools with a facility regarding emerging standards for finding content on the Internet may be a key resource for the future. This is one reason for the importance of tapping library professionals, where existing knowledge of these standards resides.

Information technology is likely to lead to a decrease in the importance of the typical managerial role as network organizations become more and more common. With the emergence of freelance (or e-lance) workers and temporary, self-managed work teams and virtual teams, managers are not needed for daily tasks; however, top leadership becomes increasingly important in terms of determining a firm's strategy (as technology changes the industry context) and creating a firm's culture that is supportive of that strategy. Thus, talent pools that involve strategic leadership are important across all industries. For Britannica, such leadership would be particularly key in facilitating collaboration between content developers and content deliverers. Developmental experiences that take these technical experts and develop their ability to lead and facilitate teams are likely to be valuable across a wide variety of future strategic possibilities.

The Importance of Context and Logic

The Britannica story clearly demonstrates that disruptive technologies such as the Internet can change not only individual businesses (affecting their business model, strategy, and value chain), but also entire industries. In particular, the Internet generates entirely new ways of creating value, opening the door for an unprecedented array of potential substitutes and new entrants. Responding quickly to such changes creates a paradox. On the one hand, it can appear to make deep strategic analysis impossible because changes simply occur too quickly to be analyzed. However, abdicating the responsibility to understand strategic context and innovate in richly differentiated ways is likely to be counterproductive, especially with regard to human capital. Scarce and important resources require rich strategic responses. The paradox is that the rich logic provided by detailed strategic frameworks such as the HC BRidge framework illustrated here may actually increase the speed of response. The logic can be applied repeatedly, even if the information and conclusions change. Over time, organizations that develop shared logical frameworks can move more quickly and decisively precisely because they have no need to reinvent their strategic language and logical linkages. The strategies, processes, pivotal roles, and HR practices may change continually, but the logic of the links may provide the kind of "standards" for human capital strategy that have allowed the Internet to flourish and evolve so quickly.

Endnotes

1 C. Chadwick and P. Cappelli, "Alternatives to Generic Strategy Typologies in Strategic Human Resource Management," in D. Lewin, O. Mitchell, and P. Sherer, eds., *Research Frontiers in Industrial Relations and Human Resources* (Madison, WI: Industrial Relations Research Association), pp. 165–192.

2 J. W. Boudreau and P. M. Ramstad, "Counting What Counts: HC BRidge™ as a Guide to Strategic Human Resource Measurement" (Unpublished manuscript, 2000).

3 Ibid.

4 P. Evans and T. S. Wurster, *Blown to Bits: How the Economics of Information Transforms Strategy* (Boston: Harvard Business School Press, 1999), pp. 69–97.

5 This case study was developed from the following sources: Evans and Wurster, *Blown to Bits,* op. cit.; R. A. Melcher, "Dusting off the Britannica," *Business-Week* (October 20, 1997), p. 143, available from www.businessweek.com/1997/42/b3549124.htm; "Encyclopedia Britannica launches largest ad campaign in its history, *Business Wire* (www.businesswire.com), June 16, 1999; "Door Closing on an Era Pounding Pavement Accounts for Fewer Sales as Changes in Technology Hold," *Columbus Dispatch* (December 19,1999), p. 1G; L. Corman, "Why Britannica Got Rid of Its Reps," *Sales and Marketing Management* Vol. 148, No. 9 (September 1996), pp. 82–84; G. Farrell, "Bailing Out from the Super Bowl Ad Binge," *USA Today* (April 25, 2000), p. 01B; and P. Jasco, "Multimedia Strategies in Online Encyclopedias," *Information Today,* Vol.15, No. 5 (May, 1998), pp. 40–43.

6 J. Useem, "Withering Britannica Bets It All on the Web," *Fortune* (November 22, 1999), pp. 344–348.

7 Peter Jasco, "Multimedia Strategies in Online Encyclopedias," *Information Today* (May 1998), Vol. 15-5, p. 40.

8 *Booklist* (September 15, 2000).

9 P.W. Tam, "One for the History Books," *Wall Street Journal* (December 11, 2000), p. R32.

10 P. Ramstad and J. Boudreau, "HC Bridge™ Framework Core Impact Elements" (Unpublished manuscript, 2000).

11 M. Porter, *Competitive Advantage: Creating and Sustaining Superior Performance* (New York: Free Press, 1985).

12 See J. McGee and H. Thomas, "Strategic Groups: Theory, Research and Taxonomy," *Strategic Management Journal* Vol. 7 (March/April 1986), pp. 141–160; and M. Peteraf and M. Shanley, "Getting to Know You: A Theory of Strategic Group Identity," *Strategic Management Journal* Vol. 18 (Summer 1997), pp. 165–186.

13 M. Gordon and G. Milne, "Selecting the Dimensions that Define Strategic Groups: A Novel Market-Driven Approach," *Journal of Managerial Issues* Vol. 21 (Summer 1999), pp. 213–233.

14 Ramstad and Boudreau, "HC BRidge™ Framework Core Impact Elements."

15 Porter, *Competitive Advantage,* op. cit.

16 Ramstad and Boudreau, "HC Bridge™ Framework Core Impact Elements."

17 M. Treacy and F. Wiersema, *The Discipline of Market Leaders* (Reading, MA: Addison-Wesley Publishing Company, Inc, 1997).

18 S. Chatterjee, "Delivered Desired Outcomes Efficiently: The Creative Key to Competitive Strategy," *California Management Review* Vol. 40, No. 2 (Winter 1998), pp. 78–96.

19 Ramstad and Boudreau, "HC Bridge™ Framework Core Impact Elements" (2000).

20 G. Hamel and C. Prahalad, "Strategic Intent," *Harvard Business Review* Vol. 67 (May-June 1989), pp. 63–76.

21 Ramstad and Boudreau, "HC Bridge™ Framework Core Impact Elements."

22 For a review of the resource-based view of organizations, see J. Barney, "Firm Resources and Sustained Competitive Advantage," *Journal of Management* Vol. 17 (March 1991), pp. 99–120; and B. Wernerfelt, "A Resource Based View of the Firm," *Strategic Management Journal* Vol. 5 (April/June 1984), pp. 171–180.

23 Ibid.

24 J. Barney and P. M. Wright, "On Becoming a Strategic Partner: The Role of Human Resources in Gaining Competitive Advantage," *Human Resource Management* Vol. 37, No. 1 (Spring 1998), pp. 31–46.

25 A. Marsden, "Strategic Management: Which Way to Competitive Advantage?" *Management Accounting* (January 1998), pp. 32–37. Also see Teece, Pisano, and Shuen, "Dynamic Capabilities and Strategic Management," *Strategic Management Journal* Vol. 18 (1997), pp. 509–533.

26 Barney, "Firm Resources and Sustained Competitive Advantage," op. cit.

27 Porter, op. cit.

28 Paul Timmers, "Business Models for Electronic Markets," in *Electronic Markets* Vol. 8, No. 2 (July 1998). Available from http://www.electronicmarkets.org/netacademy/publications.nsf/all_pk/949 (Accessed June, 2000).

29 Boudreau and Ramstad, "HC BRidge"; and Ramstad and Boudreau, "Deep Impact for e-Business."

30 "Encyclopedia Britannica Launches Largest Ad Campaign in Its History," *Business Wire* (online), June 16, 1999.

31 Boudreau and Ramstad, "HC BRidge."

32 Ibid.

33 Ibid.

34 E. Masie, "Creating stickier online learning sites, classrooms," *Computer Reseller News* (July 7, 1999), p. 56.

35 Boudreau and Ramstad, "HC BRidge."

36 Ibid. and W. R. Boswell, "Aligning Employees with the Organization's Strategic Objectives: Out of 'Line of Sight,' Out of Mind." Unpublished dissertation, Cornell University (2000).

37 "At Your Service," *The Wall Street Journal* (April 17, 2000), p. R12.

38 Boudreau and Ramstad, "HC BRidge."

39 Ibid.

40 For example, see: J. B. Arthur, "Effects of human resource systems on manufacturing performance and turnover," *Academy of Management Journal* Vol. 37 (June 1994), pp. 670–687; L. Baird and I. Meshoulam, "Managing two fits of strategic human resource management," *Academy of Management Review* Vol. 13 (January 1988), pp. 116–128; M. A. Huselid, "The impact of human resource management practices on turnover, productivity, and corporate financial performance," *Academy of Management Journal* Vol. 38 (June 1995), pp. 635–672; J. P. MacDuffie and J. Krafcik, "Integrating technology and human resources for high performance manufacturing: Evidence from the international auto industry," in T. Kochan and M. Useem, eds., *Transforming Organizations* (New York: Oxford University Press, 1992), pp. 209–226; and J. Pfeffer, *The Human Equation: Building Profits by Putting People First* (Boston: Harvard Business School Press, 1998).

41 T. W. Malone and R. J. Laubacher, "The Dawn of the E-Lance Economy," *Harvard Business Review* Vol. 76 (September–October 1998), pp.144–153.

42 Evans and Wurster, op. cit.

11

Personalization in the New Digital Environment

Venkatesh Shankar, Robert H. Smith School of Business, University of Maryland

Picture the following day in your (Jane or Joe) life in the not-too-distant future:

6.00 A.M.	You wake up to a proactive alarm message from MyYahoo.com delivered through a screen in front of a bed, which greets you with "Good morning Jane/Joe. Today's weather is. . . . Your appointments are . . . and events to watch in today's stock market are. . . ."
7.00 A.M.	As you get ready to go to work, you are greeted with "This hour's top news" on your watch or personal digital assistant.
8.00 A.M.	As you get into your car to go to work, the car displays a summary of today's traffic conditions on your route and automatically selects the fastest route to your workplace through an intelligent global positioning system navigator. In case you will be late to any meeting, it communicates with your scheduler and proactively sends e-mail and voice-mail messages about the delay to the person you were scheduled to meet.

9.00 A.M.	In the office PC that is seamlessly networked with your watch, cell phone PDA, and laptop, an automatic refill order is made for supplies that are running low (e.g., printer paper, toner).
10.00 A.M.	An intelligent online agent, or bot, displays and prints out competitive research reports that you had ordered previously.
11.00 A.M.	Your favorite airline has proactively sent you e-mails with special fares to the destinations to which you travel frequently. It reminds you of your frequent flier status and offers some holiday suggestions for the bonus miles that you already have in your account.
12.00 NOON	Your PDA shows today's special menus that conform to your tastes in the restaurants nearby. When you select one, it reserves a table and a parking spot in the restaurant for you.
1.00 P.M.	Your phone-cum-PDA alerts you that your stocks have hit your predetermined buy/sell prices. It also shows you a graphic of the stock's daily, monthly, and hourly trends so that you can better time your buy/sell decision.
2.00 P.M.	An e-mail from Amazon.com tells you that the latest Tom Clancy novel is available with one click on a hyperlink to be shipped overnight. It also shares with you the current outcome of a Stephen King e-book novel to which you had suggested an ending. In this new novel, Stephen King is collaborating with readers to write the complete novel after introducing the framework and cast of characters.
3.00 P.M.	An alert from www.planetall.com says your grandfather's birthday is next week. It provides some gift choices and also makes available a shop bot—MySimon.com. Once you click on a gift, it scours the Net to find the best price and fastest shipping time.
4.00 P.M.	You get a reminder about redoing your garden. You surf Garden Escape (www.garden.com), check out landscaping options, choose plants for the season, and create your own garden.
5.00 P.M.	You get a prompt when the mortgage rate you have prespecified gets nearer. A mortgage recalculator calculates your revised options. An agent shows the time trend of mortgage rates and gives some

	possible scenarios for future movement of mortgage rates.
6.00 P.M.	Your kids have been asking for a new pet in your home. You log on to eBay. For your predetermined pet profile, it shows all possible pets and available prices. You decide on one of the pets after showing the pictures to your kids.
7.00 P.M.	You log on to ImagineRadio.com, a web audio feed programmed with your favorite types of music and artists, that offers the latest music that fits your taste. You choose to retain it or skip it in your data warehouse.

Welcome to the world of web-based personalization. Personalization in the online context can be defined as the set of actions that tailors a company's website to a particular user or group of users. It is the web equivalent of the concept of the shopkeeper from *Little House on the Prairie*—the nineteenth-century country store owner who knew each steady customer's preferences and needs and offered different products and services to each. For example, in a personalized music website, a person who has indicated interest in classical music might be presented with an offer for Mozart, whereas someone who likes Christina Aguilera's music will be asked to try 'N Sync.

Personalization is growing rapidly. According to the Gartner Group, matching direct or inferred reader requests through content personalization will be the most dramatic development in the Internet through 2002, and will help differentiate the Web as a new medium.

Thinking Strategically about Personalization

The goal of personalization is to create *customized value*, not customer value. Customer value is about delivering value to a general customer. Customized value is about creating and delivering value solutions for each customer or customer group. The Internet has accelerated the creation of customized value through personalization.

There are different degrees of personalization: personalization of information, product, service, and relationship. Although companies have been trying to customize their offerings with limited success before the advent of the Internet, the Web has spawned new technologies that now allow companies to be able to do true personalization. The Web is a great vehicle for companies to offer these different degrees of personalization. Personalization on the Web is closely tied to e-CRM (customer relationship management).

The Web has brought about a revolution in the delivery of personalized information to customers. The concept of MyX.com that is available in many business-to-consumer (B-to-C) websites exemplifies personalization of information. With regard to personalization of products, compared to the offline environment, products can be more easily personalized in the online environment. For example, it is extremely difficult for a shopper in a grocery store to group a bunch of items according to her or his criteria and choose from them. The same task can be done much more easily on the Internet. Furthermore, the interactivity of the Web also helps customers better know their preferences that help them get their desired information and products—creating a more personalized offering. The Web also enables a company to offer tailored customer service in the form of billing, account management, and related features. Finally, the Web has the potential to create unique lasting relationships with customers and partners.

The Internet has the ability to transform many experience goods into search goods.[1] Search goods are those that can be easily evaluated before purchase and consumption. Dockers pants and Dell computers are examples of search goods. Experience goods are those whose quality and performance are hard to judge. Services such as dental care, hair care, and accounting services are examples of experience goods. The Internet helps reduce uncertainty about experience goods and move them toward search goods. For example, Valuestar.com is a service that provides approval stamps for hard-to-evaluate services such as auto repair, home contracting, and medical care. Similarly, Redherring.com provides ratings of new IPOs in terms Red Hot, Hot, Mild, and Cool. The transformation from search to experience goods can be personalized by incorporating individual needs gleaned from the Internet. Firms can profit from personalization only if they make consumers benefit from this capability.

Personalization is different from customization. It can be viewed as a step beyond customization. Customization is about giving what a consumer has explicitly asked for. Personalization is about predicting and anticipating consumer needs and providing value-added services. Customization can happen based on information provided by the customers. Personalization can be done based on customer purchase history or clickstream data. As an example of personalization, American Airlines uses information collected from its 40 million AAdvantage members as well as profile and clickstream data to tailor its offers.

When should a company undertake personalization initiatives? Personalization efforts are appropriate when a company's customer needs are differentiated and the lifetime value (LTV) of customers is widely distributed, as shown in Figure 11-1. When the needs are undifferentiated and the distribution of LTV is similar, mass marketing is practiced. If the needs are differentiated but the distribution of LTV is similar, niche marketing is the right strategy. When customer needs are undif-

FIGURE 11-1
Personalized Marketing

Distribution of Lifetime Value (LTV)	Customer Needs	
	Undifferentiated	*Differentiated*
Similar	Mass marketing	Niche marketing
Different	Frequency marketing	Personalized marketing

Source: Adapted from D. Peppers and M. Rogers, *One-to-One Future* (New York: Doubleday, 1993).

ferentiated but there is wide variability in the lifetime value, frequency marketing or loyalty programs are appropriate. If customer needs are differentiated and the distribution of LTV is different, personalized marketing is the best approach.

Personalization is evolving based on progress in two dimensions, namely, content and product, as shown in Figure 11-2. When a company offers all of its customers the same product and almost the same web content, we have a case of mass marketing. From mass marketing, personalization is moving to high product or high content personalization. Many companies differentiate product, but still deliver the same content on the Web to all their customers, thus practicing *differentiated marketing*. If product remains the same, but the content is personalized to reflect differences in preferences for information among customers, then the company is engaged in *personalized marketing*. However, successful companies will be those that move to high personalization in both content and product, a differentiated, personalized marketing approach.

To Personalize or Not

The decision to personalize and the type of personalization to use depend on three main factors: variance in customer lifetime values, differences in customer needs, and complexity of product attributes. Depending on the combination of these factors, there may be five decisions:

1. *No personalization.* When both needs and lifetime values are not very different across customers, there is no need for personalization. This is true for commodity goods. Mass marketing is more appropriate than personalization for these products.

2. *Endorsement personalization.* This approach is appropriate when customer lifetime values are very different, the product attributes are complex, but customer needs do not vary significantly. In this approach, products and preferred providers are recommended to a user based on endorsements from a reference group or rating organization, reviews by past users or third parties, and awards from independent organizations. Amazon.com's Reading Group Guides is an example of this approach.

3. *Rules-based personalization.* When customer lifetime value varies significantly across customers and when product attributes are not complex, a rules-based personalization approach is appropriate. In this approach, the company uses business rules to deliver products, promotions, and information based on a user's profile, dividing users into segments based on these rules. Because rules-based prediction relies on past behavior, it works

FIGURE 11-2
Evolution of Personalization

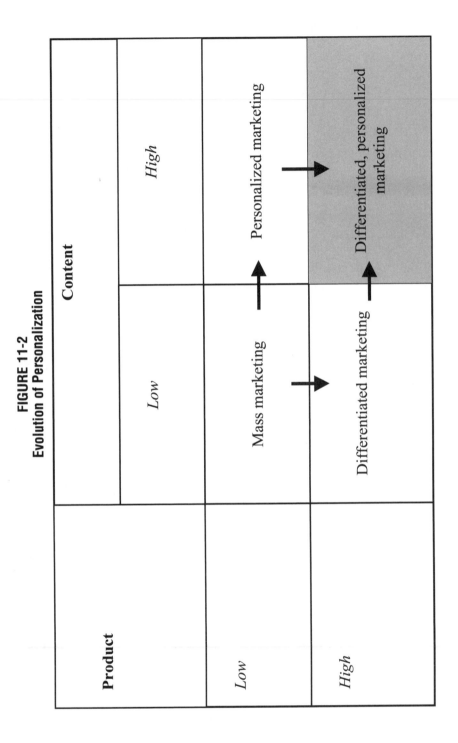

best when product attributes are not complex. This approach keeps marketing simple and allows personalization to be transparent. Kodak Picture Center (www.kodak.com) is an example of a rules-based personalization system that allows members to store, retrieve, manage, edit, and share pictures over the Internet. According to member attributes, it creates rules for management of this network.

4. *Computer-assisted self-explication (CASE) personalization.* This approach is relevant when lifetime values are very different across customers, customer needs are heterogeneous, but product attributes are not very complex. In this approach, the visitor answers questions regarding their preferences, and the system sifts through a large database of possible choices to offer the visitor a few highly ranked alternatives. This approach offers a structured system that allows customers to find their preferred product or service. Personalogic (www.personalogic.com), a division of America Online (AOL), uses this approach to help visitors make decisions on cars, colleges, pets, travel, and the like. It also quotes prices and offers ratings on products based on customer answers and connects them to AOL-related services for purchases. Since customers differ in their preferences, the system depends on active dialog and interaction with the customers to offer maximum value to them.

5. *Collaborative filtering personalization.* This method is followed in situations marked by high variances in customer lifetime value, customer needs, and complex product attributes. In this method, a user's behavior is tracked over time, and product recommendations are offered to that user based on comparisons with those that follow similar usage behavior. Amazon.com uses this approach extensively to recommend new books or CDs to its visiting customers (e.g., "Customers who bought this CD also bought . . .").

A schematic representing the decision process to personalize and the type of personalization appears in Figure 11-3. The use of these personalization approaches by Amazon.com is shown in Figure 11-4. Amazon.com uses endorsement and collaborative filtering approaches in more than one feature.

Consumer Personalization

Personalization has been most common in the business-to-consumer space. Today, you can order personalized books, videos, music, and food items from any number of sites. Some examples:

FIGURE 11-3
Deciding Whether and How to Use Personalization

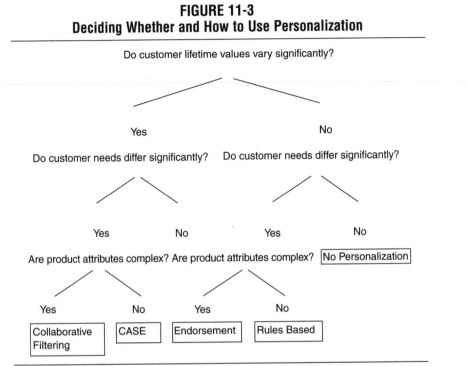

Do customer lifetime values vary significantly?

Yes — Do customer needs differ significantly?
No — Do customer needs differ significantly?

Yes — Are product attributes complex?
No — Are product attributes complex?
Yes — Are product attributes complex?
No — No Personalization

Yes — Collaborative Filtering
No — CASE
Yes — Endorsement
No — Rules Based

SOURCE: Adapted from W. Hanson, *Principles of Internet Marketing* (Cincinnati: South-Western College Publishing, 2000), p. 215.

FIGURE 11-4
Personalization at Amazon.com

Personalization Types	Personalization Features
Endorsement	Reading Group Guides, Gift Matcher, Award Winners
Endorsement, Collaborative Filtering	Customer Buzz, "If You Like This Author. . . ."
CASE	Mood Matcher
Collaborative Filtering (preferences)	Book Matcher
Collaborative Filtering (preferences plus history)	Instant Recommendations

SOURCE: Adapted from W. Hanson, *Principles of Internet Marketing* (Cincinnati: South-Western College Publishing, 2000), p. 218.

■ BooksForMe.com creates books with heroes whose names are the same as those of children reading the stories. Parents must provide the child's name, date of birth, town, and other details related to the story.

■ Artists at KidCartoons.com, operated by K Design, a computer graphics company in Brentwood, New York, create comic-book covers, books, and videos based on a child's photograph.

■ Edier Developer (www.edier.com/special/occasion/multimedia .htm) creates CD-ROM albums that includes pictures, videos, and music customized to the individual.

■ Musicmaker.com offers suggestions for song combinations for making custom CD mixes in various genres—from alternative to jazz to hip-hop to classical to Latin. You can pick your tunes and songs, organize them in a CD and order the CD, or download the collection of songs. At another site, www.giftsongs.com, the company uses information that the customer provides to create personalized songs for special people and events. You receive a digitally mastered personalized song on either a compact disc or a cassette and a custom printed lyric sheet.

■ American Greetings allows you to pick a card of your type, type in your personalized message, and provide an address for them to mail it. Members of AmericanGreetings.com can get custom-made greetings, interact with a greeting adviser, and choose from a variety of options. PhotoLoft.com can do the same for pictures.

There are different types of personalization software, including cookies (i.e., bits of code that reside in a user's web browser memory that tell a website who the person visiting the site is), checkbox personalization, collaborative filtering, content-based filtering, and rule-based systems. These software types, together with their functions and notable vendors, are listed in Figure 11-5.

There are several examples of successful personalization. They include Dow Jones Interactive, The Estee Lauder Companies, Netmarket.-com, Hallmark Cards,[2] and Yahoo!

Dow Jones and Lexis-Nexis have created a personalization section enhancing their "Custom Clips" option into a user-defined home page (www.djinteractive.com). "Custom Clips" allows users to select preformatted industry, company, investing, and news searches, or develop their own custom Boolean searches of 40,000 articles per day for relevant news. Searches are created and updated throughout the day and delivered by e-mail. The service is powered by Verity Inc.'s (www.verity. com) Profiler engine.

Estee Lauder (www.clinique.com) uses its site to do online skin typing. Customers answer eight questions about their skin type (e.g., color, oiliness) that determine which products they should use. These

FIGURE 11-5
Personalization Software

Type	What It Does	Vendors
Cookies	Web browser tag on a website identifies the user.	My Yahoo! pages
Check-box personalization	User-controlled process in which user checks interest on a checklist for the site to present the right information.	Site specific
Collaborative filtering	Identifies common patterns between purchase behavior of one with another.	Net Perceptions Firefly
Content-based filtering system	Identifies common patterns between contents of one database with another.	Webwatcher
Rules-based system	Uses business rules to deliver certain types of information based on user profile, dividing into groups.	Broadvision

SOURCE: Adapted from T. Quellette, "Web Personalization," *ComputerWorld* (December 20, 1999).

answers are matched with a product database, and suitable products are identified and recommended to customers. Through this process, Estee Lauder has acquired many new consumers. Twenty-nine percent of Clinique's registered users had never used, or had stopped using, the company's products.

Netmarket.com has more than 2.5 million sessions per month. It has a simple gift finder that asks customers to choose a gift category and price range and retrieves a handful of suggestions from Netmarket's massive database. If customers can't find what they are looking for, they can send messages to a Personal Shopper or Ask the Expert and are put in touch with a live human being for further help.

Hallmark Cards (www.hallmark.com) is the largest U.S. greeting card maker. Its personalization highlight is the online Reminder Service. By selecting dates with a Microsoft Active Server Page–based calendar, users can enter important dates. When users return to the site and choose a gift to send—a bouquet or a box of chocolates—they can pick the recipient's address from a drop-down menu of those in their personal address book, which resides on the company's servers.

Yahoo! has had a long personalization journey.[3] Personalization initiatives started in Yahoo! as far back as 1996 with its My Yahoo! feature.

The company today has three personalization initiatives: My Yahoo!, Yahoo! Companion, and Inside Yahoo! Search. In each of these initiatives, personalization occurs within modules. Both content and layout are personalized. Yahoo's experience offers important insights. They include:

- Most users take what is given to them and never customize.
- The default page (i.e., nonpersonalized page) needs the most design efforts.
- All users should be addressed in personalization.
- Power users do complex things, so personalize their sites to a greater degree.

Personalized digital delivery is another major step in music personalization. New York based Digital-on-Demand and its subsidiary Red-Dot-Net of California offer a virtual inventory system comprising a complete end-to-end solution for the networked transmission of fully encrypted digital files, both audio and video, to proprietary remote manufacturing stations. A number of retailers including Kmart, Target, and Musicland are working with RedDot-Net.

A key difference between personalization offline and online is transparency and visibility. An airline passenger who is a frequent flier is called to board the aircraft ahead of nonmembers, those with platinum status get priority over gold status customers, and so on. The preferential treatment is transparent to all customers. In the online world, through dynamic pages, a customer's MyAirline.com can be personalized without other customers viewing it. By making all special offers through this personalized location, the potential resentment from other customers can be surmounted.

Good personalization involves correct targeting. For example, the promotions to someone flying business class and a college student may be totally different. The business-class consumer will get information on upgrades whereas the college student will be shown inexpensive vacation packages. Such one-to-one marketing has long been touted as the Holy Grail of marketing on the Web, but very few companies have taken advantage of the potential, mainly because technologies are still in their infancy.

Business Personalization

In the business-to-business (B-to-B) context, personalization takes the form of customized business webs. Customized webs are designed to attract new customers and partners, improve customer retention, and achieve faster sales conversion. For example, a business website might display product availability, price changes, unique price configurations, upgrade information, and logistics and shipping processes. The site may support its customers with customized sites with account management, order status, problem resolution status, billing, and other customized reports. In short, the business site creates customized extranets for every customer or partner.

An example of a company doing business personalization is AIG, an insurance company. AIG is in the process of implementing customized business webs that link the company to its dealers and agents. By integrating AIG's back-office systems with its dealers and agents via a customized extranet, AIG expects to reduce the time for quotes from weeks to just hours and close sales faster.

Bowstreet is a company that provides web services solutions for businesses to build scalable business-to-business customized websites. With such a solution, companies can automate their business process for personalization. For example, Bowstreet can help a bank to personalize content for its gold-, silver-, and bronze-level customers. It links front- and back-end systems. It uses directory services and extensible markup language (XML) to enable data interchange between disparate platforms, across organizational boundaries, and without proprietary middleware. Dynamic customization is made possible by merging metadata templates based on XML with profile information stored in directories. This approach reduces the cost and time involved in deployment.

Personalization and Privacy

Personalization is raising customer expectations and also privacy issues. First, consumers are concerned about misuse of their personal information. A recent survey found that 70 percent of online users find online solicitations a hindrance rather than a help.[4]

Second, there could be potential backlash from those customers who perceive that they do not receive special treatment. Companies have to strike a balance between total personalization and respect for privacy. They have to be sensitive and realistic about personalization. Consider the case of DoubleClick, Inc. By integrating consumer information collected offline by Abacus Direct with its web profiles, DoubleClick has created a matched online profile identified by the person. This has resulted in the Federal Trade Commission (FTC) investigating DoubleClick over privacy aspects.

Another issue that may raise significant privacy concerns is "creeping personalization." In creeping personalization, individual user preferences and usage patterns are silently tracked without user initiation. Although such an approach can potentially help websites anticipate customer needs and tailor their offerings better, consumers can become increasingly uneasy of such "eavesdropping" moves.

In certain industries, personalization can be both a boon and a bane. For example, banks and financial services walk a tightrope with respect to personalization. Customers are wary of giving financial information lest their financial situationl become an open book to the Internet universe. Therefore, profiling should be permission-based. People should opt-in rather than be forced-in.

Personalization and Profitability

Profitability is a key question for companies making investments in personalization. There is not much information on the return on investment (ROI) of many personalization initiatives. Among the few published reports, a study of Excite.com has shown that users who personalized their site (MyExcite.com) returned to Excite.com five times more often than those who used a standard site. Estimates by Jupiter Communications suggest that the return on personalization initiatives can start to appear within one year, with an ROI that may reach up to 300 percent.

Some may question the wisdom of personalization from a profitability standpoint. For example, one might question why Garden.com, despite being a great example of personalization, is not a hot company on Wall Street? There are several possible reasons. Gardening is a focal activity in many people's lives. Those who use the Internet may not realize that they can use the Net to create their own gardens. Not many of them are knowledgeable enough to make choices in their garden creation. They may not like to spend time creating their gardens, but may prefer to outsource it to an expert. They may not find the cost/benefits acceptable.

Despite all of these questions, one thing is becoming increasingly clear. Personalization on the Web has changed the landscape in which all companies interact with their customers. It is unclear if companies can continue their profitability without significant personalization efforts on the Internet.

Organizing for Personalization

Although companies tout the praises of personalization and one-to-one marketing, a recent study spanning more than 300 companies in industries such as automobiles, energy, financial services, high technology, and travel reveals that the business models and the organization structures of many of these companies are very distant from their customers in today's rapidly changing digital environment.[5] In reality, many of these companies are in a product trap—that is, they are organized primarily around products, not customers. They have product managers driving strategies and sales executives implementing the product strategies. They talk about customer value, not customized value.

The Internet has enabled new companies without the bricks-and-mortar companies' baggage of being organized around products. As such, these companies can create fresh and flexible organizations with the customer as the center of their business universe and personalization efforts. Some of these dot-com companies may no longer be the darlings of Wall Street, but they have created an environment in which the bricks-and-mortar companies have been forced to rethink their enterprises.

With their customer-centric e-business model, dot-com companies almost interact one-to-one with customers (through e-CRM programs), create vibrant customer communities (through e-chat groups), and even collaborate with customers in product design and customization (through collaboration tools). These nimble firms have created new customer experiences and customized value, forcing many bricks-and-mortar companies to reshape themselves as hybrid clicks-and-mortar organizations.

In response to the dot-com challenge, most bricks-and-mortar companies that were interviewed in the study viewed e-business centered on customers as their top priority and saw it as potentially radically changing their business models. However, these firms spend much less on e-business initiatives and assess their e-business capabilities to be inadequate. Some believe that the Internet is another medium of communication or channel, but many view end-to-end web-based integration of business processes focused on customized value as very important. Yet they have done little to prepare themselves to personalize continually in the digital environment.

Many of the e-initiatives of bricks-and-mortar companies are directed at cost control (e.g., procurement). Unfortunately, competitors quickly catch up on cost-control mechanisms offered by the Internet. Sustainable long-term leadership can only be built through a revenue-enhancing digital strategy that allows the enterprise to be continually personalized. Bricks-and-mortar companies are on a continuum with respect to personalization initiatives. Although a majority of the firms score very low on personalization, some are further along this continuum than others. For example:

■ **Ford Motor Company.** In the auto industry, Ford has teamed up with portals to identify customer preferences. Through BuyerConnection and CarPoint, Ford offers customers a wide selection of cars. It has also web-enabled the auto loan process and is working on new cars with digital dashboards that provide Internet access and global positioning system (GPS) services. These personalization e-initiatives have led to the creation of a customer solution–based organization structure that is expected to result in a 15 percent improvement in profits.

■ **Enron Corp.** In the energy industry, Enron has re-architected the firm to be a one-stop energy shop for electricity, gas, and telecom bandwidth. EnronOnline, a global e-marketplace for wholesale energy and other commodities, enables participants to view prices and transact real-time with Enron over the Internet, free of commission. It did more than $80 billion worth of transactions in the first ten months after its launch, accounting for more than half of the company's transactions. It is personalized in that it offers more than 800 customer-structured solutions, such as an option to buy gas in December and sell electricity in March.

■ **Charles Schwab.** In the financial services industry, Charles Schwab has built and aligned itself around customer needs. Schwab treats the Internet, phone, and bricks-and-mortar entities as multiple touchpoints with the customer. The business processes are architected around these multiple touchpoints to deliver highest customized value. Today, Charles Schwab boasts of a market capitalization of $43 billion on a revenue base of $5.3 billion with a price-earnings (P/E) multiple of 57. In contrast, the established "blue-chip" in the space, Merrill Lynch, whose revenue base is seven times that of Schwab, has a market capitalization of $49 billion with a P/E ratio of 16. These figures reflect the market's perception of the future of a customer-centric e-business model.

Personalization Plan

What can bricks-and-mortar companies do to accelerate personalization as they evolve into hybrid clicks-and-mortar organizations? We recommend a personalization plan comprising the following critical steps.

1. **Perform a personalization scope and competence study.** A firm should identify and assess its "personalization-ability" of activities and business processes. How much of the organization is centered around customer solutions vis-à-vis products? What is the criticality of these activities for a favorable competitive position? What is the extent to which they are web-enabled? What are the current customer outcomes and the problems encountered in implementation?

2. **Set personalization goals and measures.** Formulate or revise personalization goals and set clear customer-related personalization performance measures. To do this, a company should benchmark its activities with respect to its competitors, similar firms, and those that are best-in-class. Look for metrics in the revenue growth areas.

3. **Do a personalization benchmarking analysis.** In this phase, the company determines the gap or difference between the identified cus-

tomer solution–based personalization model and its current product-based business model. It should identify the e-business applications that need substantial improvement and prioritize its efforts.

4. Formulate personalization strategy, initiatives, and implementation plan. The company must come up with a sound revised personalization strategy based on the gap analysis. This strategy should lead to a prioritized set of e-initiatives, each with a well-coordinated action plan.

5. Establish personalization partnership initiatives. Companies should form strategic alliances with technology firms for personalization and customer relationship initiatives or with service providers for offering customized bundles.

6. Design and monitor a personalization scorecard. All personalization initiatives and action plans need to be tracked on a personalization scorecard. Adequate intermediate metrics (both qualitative and quantitative) should be in place. Speed of implementation and response to competitive actions are key, so aggressive timelines should be followed.

7. Revise organization structure to support personalization. Create an organizational culture where all employees' activities are linked to delivering customized value. Such a culture should embrace change and speed, and hire and reward fast-acting and growth-oriented employees. It should create a new venture mind-set, consistent with the revised e-business strategy and implementation plan.

How should companies approach personalization initiatives? The key is to be flexible so that personalization initiatives can be continually improved. The trick is to balance personalization with scale advantages and privacy issues. To do so, companies need to think and act like a consumer. For example:

■ Consumers are tired of giving profile and registration information to multiple sites. They will have to be convinced that it is worth their time and loss of privacy before they give any more profiling information. Personalization should be about letting the customer get the most out of the Web, rather than the Web getting all it can out of the customer.

■ Consumers will only pay a reasonable premium for personalization, so build a realistic revenue model.

■ Consumers will not like all content, items, and products to be personalized all the time.

- Customers can give fake responses just to move forward in registration; therefore, making registration a prerequisite can backfire.

With these things in mind, companies may want to adopt the following personalization guidelines:

- Build customer trust before building customer profiles.
- Put customers in control of their personalization.
- Personalization efforts should be perceived as a value-add, not an intrusion into privacy.
- Multiple touchpoint personalization works the best. Any personalization approach needs integration of multiple touchpoints such as the Internet, call center, and bricks-and-mortar locations.
- When implementing a personalization initiative, start simple and go the whole hog. Be prepared for a nine- to twelve-month building effort.

Future of Personalization

What is the next frontier in personalization? Customer value bundles will perhaps emerge as the next-generation personalization initiative. In this initiative, personalization will transcend product boundaries. It will involve customer value bundles around an activity. Consumers think in terms of activity, not products. For example, a consumer thinks in terms of personal financial management, not about bonds, loans, and stocks separately (see Figure 11-6). To exploit such consumer thinking, an online brokerage such as Charles Schwab might personalize its site for individual customers by offering personalized financial management value bundles. Such a bundle will include a personalized online brokerage service, banking service, tax planning service, retirement planning service, home finance service, estate planning service, and so on. Such an initiative will mean that Schwab will partner with several different companies to offer different personalized bundle options. Extended further, this initiative might result in the formation of a constellation business model involving Schwab and partner companies and even cross-company end-to-end electronic integration.

Already, there are some signs of the formation of these value bundles. A bookseller such as BarnesandNoble.com hooks up through reciprocal agreements with Petsmart.com, 1-800-Flowers.com, Vitamin Shoppe.com, and Jcrew.com for no-fee cross-promotions. Those who use the link get a discount on the new merchandise. The partners exchange no money or customer data. Using personalization, Barnes & Noble could present a special VitaminShoppe link—say, new age music CDs—to customers buying health and fitness books.

FIGURE 11-6
Customer Value Bundle Personalization

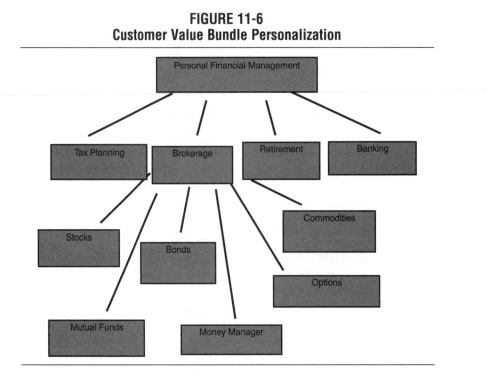

Price personalization may soon become a dominant personalization theme. MyPrice is more valuable than MyContent. Already, we see web catalogs being challenged by auctions, spot markets, exchanges, and dynamic pricing engines. MyPersonalPrice will be calculated from demographics, purchase history, time of shopping, likelihood to buy, likelihood of accepting cross-sell, total order price, and availability of inventory.

Intelligence and analytics will likely be the next killer application involving personalization. In web analysis, companies like Accrue, Webtrends, Visual Insights, Personify, Epiphany, Datasage, Responsys-.com, Netgenesis, and Microstrategy are well positioned. These companies offer e-CRM software. In the intelligence and analytics space, eBizResearch is likely to benefit significantly from next-generation personalization initiatives. eBizResearch, Inc. offers sophisticated online analytic intelligence tools in an application service provider (ASP) model that enable businesses to better personalize their content, product, service, and relationship.

Many pure content personalization sites will not survive. Everyone talks about how cool some of these content personalization sites are. The critical question is how much will each consumer pay for content customization? If consumers will not pay adequately for such customization, then the business models of these firms are fragile, and they will not survive.

The high-tech and high-touch theme will continue to dominate. Although personalization technology is getting smarter, it is only as good as the smart humans behind it. Therefore, human touch will always be a constant feature of ultimate personalization.

Penetration of personalization will critically depend on broadband network penetration and performance. Although customers may be delighted at the idea of personalization, they cannot afford to wait indefinitely to input their preferences and get responses, so high-speed data communication is crucial to growth in personalization.

Wireless or mobile commerce (m-commerce) developments will also be a major force in the growth of personalization. Proactive messaging through wireless devices is a key activity related to personalization, and its growth depends on widespread use of wireless technology. The Bluetooth initiative involving wireless networking of all Internet appliances promises to significantly boost personalization initiatives.

Amid such a fast-changing future scenario, successful companies should see the forest ahead of the trees with respect to personalization. They need to realize that the Web is not just a new medium or channel, but a transformation vehicle to create personalization around customers' multiple touchpoints and to continuously grow customized value.

Endnotes

1 W. Hanson, *Principles of Internet Marketing* (Cincinnati: South-Western College Publishing, 2000), pp. 184–220.

2 Christopher Lindquist, "Personalization," *Computerworld* (March 22,1999), pp. 72–74.

3 U. Manber, A. Patel, and J. Robinson, "Experience Personalization on Yahoo," *Communications of the ACM* Vol. 43, No. 5 (August 2000), pp. 35–39.

4 Available from www.personalization.com.

5 Venkatesh Shankar, *Customer-centric E-Business* (College Park, MD: Smith School of Business, University of Maryland, 2000).

CHAPTER 12

Collaborative Commerce: The Agile Virtual Enterprise Model

William M. Adams, G5 Technologies, Inc.

Raymond M. Wallace, G5 Technologies, Inc; College of Business and Economics, Lehigh University

Arpan Sengupta, College of Business and Economics, Lehigh University

Companies around the world are struggling to develop an Internet strategy that provides revenue growth without compromising their autonomy as independent corporations. Organizations must be able to foresee, adapt, and respond to change using new, innovative tactical initiatives to achieve strategic objectives. One of these strategies is the ability of companies to simultaneously work collaboratively and independently with new customers and emerging markets. The Agile Virtual Enterprise model, a theory of collaborative commerce, is a proven method of economic growth based on collaboration in the new economy.

Internet Strategies

There are four categories of commerce transacted over the Internet:

- **Consumer-to-Consumer (C-to-C).** Examples of C-to-C commerce are trading forums such as eBay.com.
- **Consumer-to-Business (C-to-B).** Commerce in the C-to-B model would include buyer-biased sites such as Priceline.com.
- **Business-to-Consumer (B-to-C).** B-to-C companies would include seller-biased companies such as Amazon.com.

■ **Business-to-Business (B-to-B).** The industry is currently stalled on implementing B-to-B strategies in the form of simultaneous buyer- and seller-biased e-marketplaces. There is a high level of uncertainty regarding the best choices among new B2B models, the technologies to support the models, and the right partnerships inside the model. Bad decisions can be deadly.

Recent articles have outlined the flaws in current B2B exchanges, trends in B2B, and the emergence of new models. A good example is "Beyond the Exchange: The Future of B2B," by Richard Wise and David Morrison, *Harvard Business Review*, November–December 2000. The authors attempt to create a road map for the future of how B2B commerce will evolve on the Internet.

In all the current uncertainty and among all the choices, successful new business models must stand out with clearly discriminate attributes. These models must have the following characteristics:

■ Benefits to both buyers and sellers
■ Be able to handle very complex products
■ Be flexible in terms of revenue sources
■ Be easily adapted by companies who are in various states of readiness

The B-to-B market is nascent and potentially quite large. Some estimates size the market at more than $7 trillion by 2004 (Gardner Group). We view the development of the B-to-B model as depicted in Figure 12-1. There is a strong relationship between the power of enabling information technologies, including the Internet, and the resultant speed, connectivity, and service to the customer. There are multiple regimes of maturity, or evolution, in how companies can harness this power to increase sales and profitability.

At first, companies use the Internet for simple product awareness and projection. Passive websites provide the potential customer with basic product information.

In the *real-time transactional phase*, companies choose to use the Internet for more commerce-critical transactions. Here is where we find e-markets where buyers can create auctions and, in limited cases, sellers gain value by direct sales and by swapping assets. There is widespread agreement that current B2B exchange-based models are flawed. The reasons vary but the essence of the argument is that current models are one-sided. The "pundits" are currently predicting that future exchanges will drive more intimacy between the buyer and the seller, i.e., more collaboration.

The *total integration phase* of B-to-B development will be based on sound new business models that will simultaneously generate value to

FIGURE 12-1
Designing Internet Strategies

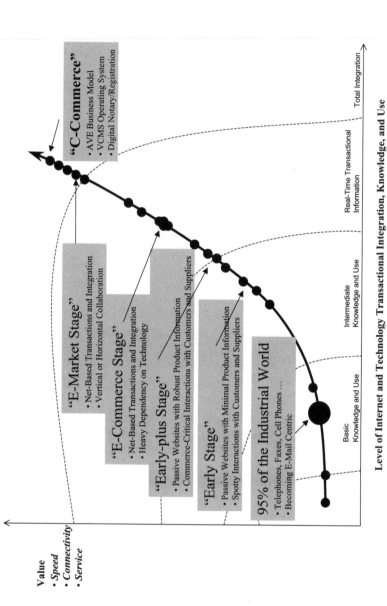

Value
• *Speed*
• *Connectivity*
• *Service*

"C-Commerce"
• AVE Business Model
• VCMS Operating System
• Digital Notary/Registration

"E-Market Stage"
• Net-Based Transactions and Integration
• Vertical or Horizontal Collaboration

"E-Commerce Stage"
• Net-Based Transactions and Integration
• Heavy Dependency on Technology

"Early-plus Stage"
• Passive Websites with Robust Product Information
• Commerce-Critical Interactions with Customers and Suppliers

"Early Stage"
• Passive Websites with Minimal Product Information
• Spotty Interactions with Customers and Suppliers

95% of the Industrial World
• Telephones, Faxes, Cell Phones …
• Becoming E-Mail Centric

Basic Knowledge and Use | Intermediate Knowledge and Use | Real-Time Transactional Information | Total Integration

Level of Internet and Technology Transactional Integration, Knowledge, and Use

the customer and the supply base. This phase will dramatically change the competitive landscape and perhaps global economic development. This phase is "c-commerce," or collaborative commerce, where virtual enterprises are formed that are hypercompetitive participants in both mature and emerging markets. Here we have the Agile Virtual Enterprise (AVE).

Agile Virtual Enterprise Model

The Agile Virtual Enterprise (AVE) is a hypercompetitive business organizational design. For complex manufactured products, think of AVE as a very lean shell company composed of highly talented people with integrated business development, project management, systems engineering, and information technology capabilities. They interface between the consumer and the supply base and transact business using the Internet and a business operation tool suite. Fundamentally, they create new commerce by using the excess capacity of existing companies in creating a virtual enterprise that rapidly forms to meet a market need for a product or service.

Various definitions of an AVE have been offered:

■ An AVE is a temporary yet structured alignment of independent companies linked by information technology to share skills, capacity, and innovation for mutual market success. Each company contributes only what it regards as its core competencies. The network has little hierarchy and focuses on functionality along the value chain.[1]

■ An AVE is a new organizational form represented by a temporary integration of geographically dispersed individuals, groups, or organization departments that are facilitated by electronic communication for carrying out their production processes to satisfy emerging market opportunities.[2]

■ The AVE is a dynamic alliance between companies that bring in complementary competencies, resources, and capacity scaling that are collectively available to each other, with the objective of delivering a product or service to the market as a community with mutual shared interests.[3]

The AVE has a strong ability to leverage its components' otherwise very specific knowledge and resources and can effectuate it in a nontraditional manner. Clearly, this innovative integration of individual companies' capabilities results in the amplification of competencies, skills, resources, and infrastructure and the extension of the reach of organizations, without extending their fixed overhead.[4]

AVEs recognize that technologies are changing so fast that nobody can do it all alone anymore; cooperation is clearly of the essence.[5] However, this is no regular cooperation; partners in an AVE bring in their critical core competencies, or in other words, the crème de la crème of their skills, capabilities, resources, and expertise. Thus, an AVE is ideally a combination of best-of-class core competencies,[6] applied dynamically and opportunistically to a market need, leading possibly, and hopefully, to best-of-everything organizations.[7]

Naturally, an AVE is not just a collection, gathering, or constellation of partners. It is a collaborative infrastructure, and this amplifies its apparent unbounded character. Cooperation ties and intertwines collaborators together to such an intimate extent that they are practically merged into one, though reconfigurable, organism. Since each constituent realizes only a special fraction of the value chain, together they have a clearly synergetic effect and possible formidable power. The whole situation is further amplified by the fact that AVE partners share their resources, infrastructure, personnel, research, information, knowledge, and know-how without relinquishing ownership.[8]

Partnerships and collaboration have yet another aspect to them. They render the virtual organization much larger in size and scope than it actually is. This brings yet another aspect of a lack of boundedness, or outright fuzziness, to the fore: The organization is perceived, treated, and reacted to by outsiders as if it were larger and more powerful than it actually is.[9] There is a clear incongruence between real boundary and perceptive boundary. Thus AVEs are "one plus one equals three" structures.[10]

AVEs not only hurl defiance at traditional enterprise boundaries, but also at those of industries, technologies, legislation, national borders, geographies, and time zones, all of which undeniably breeds fuzziness. They are predisposed toward it, thanks to bringing together the best-of-class complementary core competencies of the partners involved in the venture. Whereas no single enterprise can be equally at ease in different industries, its agile virtual challenger can overcome this problem bringing industries together and even cutting across other ones.[11]

The AVE is leveraged with technology, and the networked character of this technology makes it clearly boundaryless. The information technology of the AVE partners collectively makes up a system of virtual unity. Because the AVE partner companies are heavily dependent on the Internet for information exchange, they render the technology boundaryless in a global sense. Their strength is in integrating: They take responsibility for total results and provide complete solutions.[12] In summary, constructed out of a number of constantly modified, reshuffled, and intertwined constituents, AVEs form very agile networks cutting across nations, territories, and industry boundaries and blurring accepted boundaries of time, geographies, and language. They operate while transcending industries and markets in the public, private, and social sectors. Through boundaryless in many senses, they both propel and benefit from the downfall of traditional boundaries. In other words, they successfully leverage their lack of boundedness.[13] In such an environment it becomes more obvious why a mechanism is needed to provide some manner of instantiation for the legal, regulatory, financial, and risk management communities to participate in supporting the commerce being conducted by these entities.

AVEs are unlike organizations of the past in still one more respect that also breeds a lack of boundedness. Greatly simplified, traditional pyramid organizations are strongly based on command-and-control mechanisms, which lead to the formation of a distinct decisional center or headquarters. Hence an outsider knows more or less where the power is concentrated, and this gives the organization a clear shape and image. In stark contrast, AVEs are multicentered or even centerless.[14] They do not rely on mechanisms of command-and-control. Instead the constituents of the network (i.e., partners) are highly self-regulating through the self-control structures within the enabling framework.

In a similar vein, the cooperation of partners does not employ hierarchical coordination mechanisms and, as a consequence, is not formalized and institutionalized. On the other hand, AVE partners do not base their collaboration on one-off exchanges controlled by free market mechanisms.[15] They are somewhere in the middle—benefiting from both kinds of mechanisms. Furthermore, all of the elements of the AVE can be replaced and reconfigured and can also be apportioned, often naturally, elsewhere.[16]

AVEs operate in specific, though progressively common, circumstances. Their operating environment poses extremely high requirements on adaptability, flexibility, and reconfigurability. It is certainly not the environment where a particular structure can continue unchanged for a long time, and this is reflected in the nature of the AVE. The collaboration among the network partners is not only less formal than usual, but also less permanent; that is, it is very opportunistic and highly dynamic, much like the fast-changing opportunities AVEs pursue.[17] Hence, the AVE is not merely a network of complementary core competencies contributed by a number of partners collaborating thanks to leading-edge technology. Actually, the picture is more intricate: The AVE is at the same time a temporary structure that lasts as long as the opportunity is present and as long as it is necessary to attain the specific goals and objectives resulting from this opportunity.[18] After the business is done, the AVE disbands through a contractual closeout process. Moreover, participating in the cooperative arrangements is profit-driven or motivated by safe access to new markets and customers. Companies would tend to maintain their network association only as long as they achieve greater profitability or revenue growth than in their own enterprise or in another cooperative arrangement.[19]

It is true that AVEs are project- or task-driven; it is equally true that a particular project can be huge and last for many years. Therefore,

AVEs may continue for a long time yet change a great deal, too, over the course of time.[20] It appears, then, that what makes AVEs dissimilar from regular companies is not their temporary nature, but rather their strong reconfigurability and continuous reconstruction and design,[21] as well as element substitutability. At the same time, AVEs have a different life cycle from the companies we are used to. They actively pursue opportunities and undertake new projects. In the course of those activities, the AVE often modifies its partners, cooperative arrangements, and available resources. What's more, this process seems endless rather than a one-off occasion, like in the case of a project-driven setup.[22]

It should be noted that the AVE can also be looked at from three different perspectives. First, it can be entertained from an external perspective. In such an instance, it is a single entity and its boundarylessness consists in being unbounded or amalgamated within the AVE. Second, AVEs, considered from within, are constellations of a number of separate entities or partners that could potentially lose their identity. (Incidentally, this level of analysis is reflected in the majority of the definitions of the AVE.) Finally, AVEs can be viewed from the perspective of one of the nodes or one of the players in the cooperative game; any one of these players seeks complementary competencies or sells them. In that situation, individual-level fuzziness is about blending this particular entity with the rest of the network and the surroundings.[23] How companies view the AVE and their role in an AVE determines their state of readiness to participate in this organizational context.

The AVE is certainly one of the prominent structures for the future. The AVE thrives in the environment of dynamic economies that requires vivid interorganizational cooperation and a high level of flexibility. As we delve into an in-depth discussion of the critical dimensions of the AVE approach to collaborative commerce, we invite the reader to think about the movie industry and how it operates as an example of an industry where the application of these ideas is evident. While it is arguable that the movie industry operated prior to the emergence of academic interest in the AVE, there are important parallels to consider. The "opportunity" is the script. The networks are the studios that assess the script and create competitive proposals. Producers and casting directors are the "domain experts." Various combinations of actors, stage hands, settings, and directors are matched against budgets and schedule requirements. The financial backers pick the "winner." The AVE is the actual movie project. The competencies and capacities of all the people are brought together in a tightly linked union to serve the market opportunity.

Value

AVE and Business Process Reengineering

We first look at what the AVE must accomplish to achieve success in the spheres of new product development, quality enhancement, and administration. Through effective work tasks, AVEs help organizations faced with competition to generate value and reduce costs. This in turn helps them to achieve the following:

- Production of quality goods and services and dissemination of knowledge through successful conglomeration of geographically dispersed teams
- Easy and uniform access to invaluable information by cutting across geographical boundaries and diverse cultures
- Effective cost reduction through redundancy of travel-related expenditures
- Better project management through greater insight and reduced cycle times achieved with the help of immediacy in actions
- Constant upgrade of the knowledge base through a process of learning by doing

AVE and Best-of-Class Teams

The key to success in this electronic age is to penetrate cultural, time, and distance barriers and to take advantage of competencies, wherever they may be, by bringing them together. The benefits that accrue to organizations in the AVE setup are truly outstanding and include:

- Access to best-of-class competencies from all over the world in a cost-effective manner

- Effective solutions to present-day relevant issues such as inequitable distribution of valuable resources, costs associated with agility and adaptability, and indispensability of unique expertise with a knowledge bias

- Exploitation of the many characteristics of the electronic age, including easy and instantaneous access to a world of useful information and knowledge; the virtual workplace, where the need to physically travel is fast becoming a thing of the past; and the virtual learning process, where the learning curve is constantly advanced through electronic records and databases

AVE and Effective Communications

Communication is definitely the order of the modern business area. How the AVE helps to achieve this goal depends solely on how well its techniques and technologies are directed toward supporting effective communications. It is almost a foregone conclusion that a majority of failure in this new business world is attributable to lack of effective communication of relevant knowledge versus the transfer of irrelevant data and information. What we look at here is how AVE operations successfully lead to a cultural framework that helps participants be a part of this web of communication that is so essential for acquiring greater profitability and returns. The important elements of this framework are:

- Enabling continuous exchange of information and knowledge to better equip all participants with an understanding of current achievements and future goals
- Achieving simultaneity in tasks and processes through instantaneous global access to all personnel anywhere in the world
- Expanding the extent of know-how through a process of continuous learning
- Encouraging cooperation between culturally diverse participants leading to healthy relationships based on trust and communication

AVE and Cross-Organizational Training

To keep up with today's changing market demands, we need not only to develop and redevelop skills constantly, but also to revalidate the very system or methods that we adopt to achieve the same. Learning breeds learning, and the only known path to successful value creation is through the acquisition of better and more useful information and skills than competitors possess.

Therefore, the relevant question that needs to be addressed here is the nature of the model of learning that one needs to adopt in order to improve existing competencies and develop new ones. This is where AVEs would have the advantage of using virtual processes and technologies to conduct continuous and collaborative training procedures using the same network and information technology (IT) infrastructure. Thus they help in achieving:

- Appropriate specialization to satisfy ever-expanding and changing market demands
- Maintenance of existing core competencies and development of new ones
- Just-in-time solutions
- Methods of operation that transgress all organizational boundaries

The most essential reasons to consider transition to the AVE environment are centered in the following capabilities of AVEs:

- They leverage core competencies to be able to deliver a more focused, comprehensive, and competitive market solution.
- They enable organizations to acquire a proactive character in order to meet the increasing need to be "best in class" in all aspects of

business. To be able to capture new markets and market opportunities, the AVE setup helps organizations to make that most crucial trade-off between equity and world-class competence.

■ They pool together best-in-class competencies from around the globe. Because it is virtually impossible for a single firm to do everything and to do it in the best way possible, AVEs help to accelerate growth through a reduction in capital requirements, an increase in the speed of operations, the sharing of skills and resources, and an enhancement in profitability.

■ They lead to greater value addition for the customer through a more customer-centric strategy and simultaneous expansion in sales and profits.

Method

The main driving force behind the AVE model is responsiveness and the ability to better leverage assets across companies. Businesses have had to succumb to change and adjust to the prevailing market circumstances. Here, we briefly review the transition that has occurred in market requirements resulting in a new set of competitive criteria. Implementation of a strategy and agenda requires a proper understanding of the requirements of modern organizations. The issues discussed relate to management of core competence, customer satisfaction, prioritization, and synchronization in manufacturing.

Management of Core Competence

This has a two-level association with the workforce and product of 1) the individual and 2) the participating firm. The core competencies of individuals include their expertise, attitudes, knowledge, and skills.[24] It is possible to achieve a revision of the core competencies of individuals within the enterprise through appropriate training and education and to capture existing as well as potential market opportunities.

The creation of core competence, by no means an easy task, may commence at the learning process and work its way through the organization by means of integrated skills, technologies, cooperation, and value addition. Leadership in companies must do skillful scenario envisioning and use that to bridge the existing gap within the organization between current and potential capabilities. To achieve that goal, companies may resort to insourcing or mutual cooperation with competitors. It is precisely this compatibility between competition and cooperation that makes the AVE paradigm unique. It is this mutual cooperation that provides the platform for rapid response that is impossible for individual organizations acting alone to achieve.

For companies to achieve long-run benefits, they need to realize the strategic importance of core competence. However, this goal is achieved only when the following conditions are satisfied:

- There is provision for multiventures leading to diverse market access.
- There is satisfaction of widening customer choice and expectations.
- There are sufficient obstacles for competitors to indulge in emulation.

AVEs help to satisfy all of these conditions and go one step further: They allow geographically dispersed and organizationally segregated personnel to collaborate and meet new product requirements.[25]

Customer Satisfaction

Continuous change in market requirements and a shift in customer preferences have given birth to the quality crusade. Quality control has been the key focus owing primarily to increasing customer expectations as regards quality. This is further complemented by research on related concepts such as total quality management (TQM) and ways to simultaneously maintain competitive price. The changing market and shift in customer preferences in favor of quality have given birth to the quality crusade. This has led to aggressive and unprecedented focus on quality while maintaining competitive price.

Prioritization

The marketplace has seen the emergence of several criteria for competitiveness: responsiveness, product innovation, delivery, flexibility, quality, and environmental concern. All of these have turned the marketplace into an arena of competition.

Synchronization in Manufacturing

No amount of emphasis on speed seems adequate in this age of flexibility, be it in production or organization. Low costs, high quality, and decreasing lead-time are essential requirements for competitiveness. And what remains equally crucial is the competitive advantage in synergy.

■ ■ ■

The key to all of this is *integration*: both of a technical and social nature, in manufacturing, human resources management, and strategy formation. The competitive edge lies with those organizations able to use available resources leading us to the very core requirement behind the emergence of AVEs.

Responsiveness is a common theme running through the scenario depicted here. Successful organizations will be those able to foresee, adapt, and respond to change using tactical initiatives to achieve strategic objectives. Proficiency in creative adjustment will be a very helpful tool. Only those organizations that leverage their proficiency in change will survive and outperform their competitors—and this is precisely where AVEs have the competitive edge. The convergence of these forces now makes the implementation of AVEs feasible on a wide scale. Companies ready to implement AVEs are waiting for the surety systems to be put in place that allow the efficient and safe operation of the AVEs. G5 Technologies, working with various partners including several state governments, is now implementing these surety systems that provide assistance in digitizing trust, e.g., notarization.

A Matter of Trust

Trust as Responsiveness

Agile manufacturing, brought about by advances in multiple technologies, has led to a considerable shift away from the mass production system. The new system of agile production is based on certain related principles such as just-in-time and zero inventory as well as single lot sizes. These in turn lead to the integration of stages that are much more interdependent than ever before and take quality as a given prerequisite.

Thus, there is a distinct departure from compliance-based trust, as in a mass production system, and a transition to trust based on responsiveness: a situation where employees respond to problems as and when they arise and also respond to each other in order to move closer and closer to a defect-free production environment.[26]

Trust as Commitment

The word *virtual* in the acronym AVE means, among other things, fluid, temporary, immediate, and extensible and leads to an idealized mode of operation in a typical AVE setup. It is based on fluid and flexible teaming of various economic and social agents. Moreover, the setup refuses to acknowledge any geographical or administrative boundaries and transcends any traditional principal-agent distinctions. Hence, it is obvious that any kind of governance would necessarily have to be based on a system driven by market needs and would have to recognize mutual accommodation as an essential ingredient.

Trust, in such a system, needs to recognize the fluidity with which participants in such a setup can connect and disconnect. Thus, trust here hinges on commitment to quality and excellence in a boundless and continually changing environment. It implies commitment to the extent of meaningful restructuring of problems and solving them using best-of-class solutions.[27]

Taxonomy

In the literature search, twenty different characteristics emerged that could best be attributed to an AVE.[28] From these twenty characteristics, ten defining characteristics of Agile Virtual Enterprises are short-listed here:

1. *A Core Competencies Basis.* Participating firms only contribute to the AVE with their core competencies. They collectively decide on the necessary business processes, and the combination of core competencies leads to synergy and enables a flexible way of meeting market opportunities. Excellence is crucial: Since every participant contributes its core competence, it is possible to create a best-of-everything organization. Every function and process is world-class.

2. *One Identity.* Another foundation characteristic of an AVE is that it must have its own identity. Besides the identity of the AVE, the identity of the participating firms could also remain visible. Herein we could make a distinction between a soft AVE, in which the identity of participants is evident, and a hard AVE, which looks from the outside as one common organization.

3. *Small-Sized Partners: Small Companies and/or Parts of Large Companies.* As mentioned previously, firms participating in an AVE only bring in their core competencies, and this is often not the whole company. Furthermore, an ability to be flexible and fast moving are necessary for going after opportunities. Size is therefore redefined as the capacity of a defined set of competencies available to an AVE.

4. *Vague/Fluid Boundaries.* The AVE redefines the traditional boundaries of organizations. More cooperation among competitors, customers, suppliers, and designers, among others, makes it difficult to determine where one organization ends and another begins.

5. *Dependence on Opportunism.* Companies band together to meet a specific market opportunity and are most likely to fall apart once the need evaporates. The only reason to preserve the cooperation is the existence of a specific opportunity.

6. *Shared Risks.* AVEs respond to opportunities in the market. As market-based incentives become greater, the risk taking should increase. These risks have to be shared by every participant.

7. *Shared Ownership.* Every independent participant has its own interests in the AVE. So not only does the AVE as a whole have its

interests, but so do the participating firms. When the goal of a participant cannot be met, it should be able to step out of the AVE.

8. *Shared Leadership.* Every participant controls its own resources but not automatically the resources of the whole AVE.

9. *Dependence on Innovation.* AVEs require market-based incentives and corresponding responsiveness. To react in an adequate way, continuous innovation is necessary. This includes not only technical but also cultural innovation.

10. *Mission Overlap (Partial vs. Complete).* Some AVEs may have a partial mission overlap, and there are those with a complete mission overlap. Participating firms simultaneously involved in other AVEs and doing business outside the context of a specific AVE would have a partial mission overlap. On the other hand, with a complete mission overlap, all business would be done only within the organizational context of a specific AVE.

AVE Business Model

A depiction of the AVE business model (Figure 12-2) consists of companies and/or individuals who are organized and agree to form the resource pool of a business area community (BAC). This particular example has the capabilities to respond to a market described as "complex electromechanical systems." The companies can then make accessible, in a secure Internet environment, the essential aspects of their enterprise (e.g., core competencies, capabilities, and excess capacity) as represented in their "business certificates." A formal registration and certification process is used to assist companies in profiling their capabilities and capacity that subsequently form the constituent pieces of the virtual company.

A collaborative business network (CBN), which is an entity franchised and licensed by the enabling operational software, represents the BAC. CBNs provide marketing, business development, and project management leadership for the BAC. CBNs focus on select target markets and domains and form AVEs in response to new opportunities. Together the CBN, BAC, and operational software form an electronic business-to-business marketplace based on collaborative commerce that creates AVEs in response to market opportunities. The Virtual Corporation Management System™, developed by G5 Technologies, Inc., is the first enabling operational software to facilitate collaborative commerce in the Agile Virtual Enterprise model.

The Case of Agile Web

Roots of Collaborative Commerce

In 1992, efforts to protect the U.S. industrial manufacturing base and to promote national economic growth were commissioned through stud-

FIGURE 12-2
The AVE and VCMS™ Model

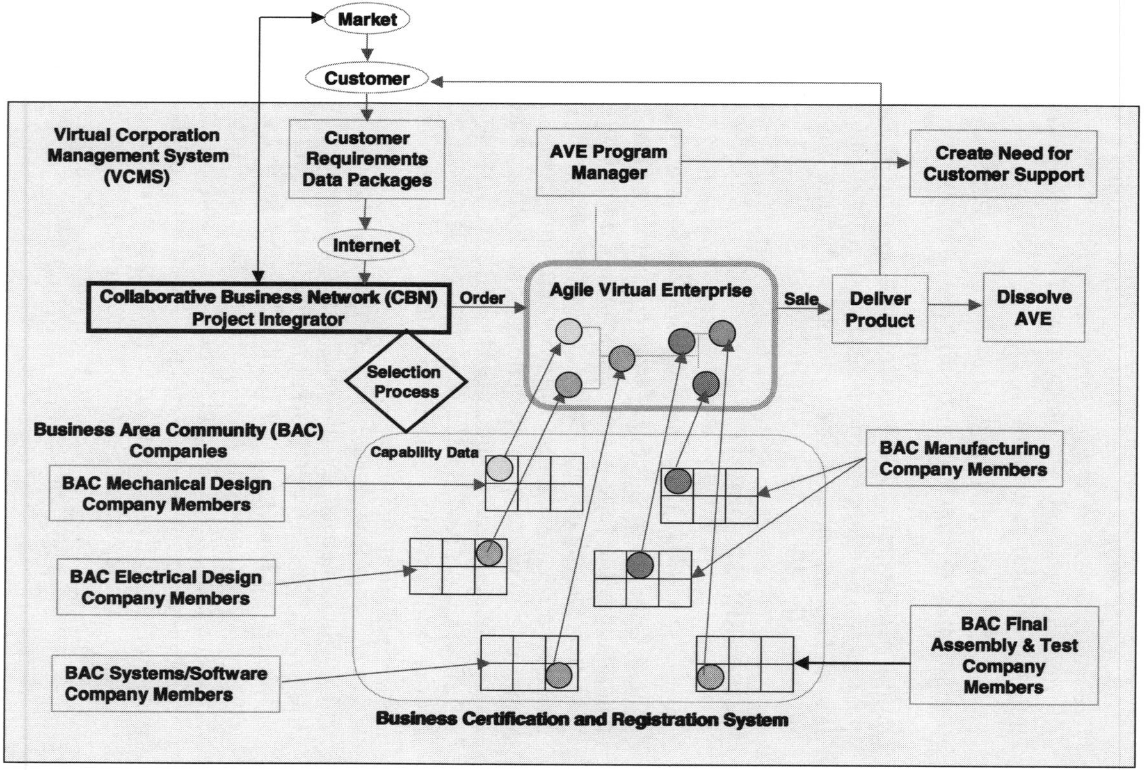

ies to explore the creation of competitive advantage techniques. Work at Lehigh University and the Iacocca Institute produced documents entitled *21st Century Manufacturing Enterprise Strategy*[29] and led to the creation of the Agile Web by the Ben Franklin Technology Center of Northeastern Pennsylvania, an integrated supplier chain made up of more than a dozen companies applying the techniques of agility in manufacturing.

A concurrent effort that drew heavily upon the Lehigh/Iacocca work was conducted in the southern tier of upstate New York. This region had suffered significant manufacturing job loss in the late 1980s and early 1990s due to dislocations in the defense and computer industries. A collaborative initiative among industry, government, and academia led to the creation of the Center for Commercial Competitiveness (C3).[30] C3 was initially a forum for accelerating processes that increase the competitiveness of local companies to win new business and to create jobs. In a short period, C3 became an early test bed for developing the framework for project-focused virtual companies. Twelve companies agreed to participate in the C3 collaborative business network, and the preliminary steps of profiling their core competencies and identifying project opportunities were executed. Then, however, the system stalled, and ultimately failed, due to lack of organizational processes, legal issues, and issues relating to trust.

The C3 forum had been designed to function as a teacher for these companies, developing and instructing them on the "ground rules" for achieving collaborative capabilities. The significance of C3 was that it was the first known government-industry-academic initiative that organized companies around their core competencies to pursue new market opportunities. A major barrier to emerge was the difficulty in facilitating collaboration among companies that were in different states of readiness to collaborate.

Another set of collaborative commerce lessons learned stemmed from the aerospace and defense industry. Aerospace companies understand complex systems and the need to pull together many suppliers to fulfill project needs over long periods of time. For example, in integrating the satellite products of more than 100 different suppliers from many different countries, collaboration became essential when system performance trade-offs required some suppliers to make major product changes to the specification and to still deliver on schedule and at the original prices. Presented with the prospect of reusing defense products in commercial markets, the ability of the aerospace and defense sector to produce complex products provided overwhelming benefits and possibilities for collaborative commerce through AVEs.

Establishment of the Agile Web

The history of the Agile Web can be traced back as far as 1991, when the Department of Defense, under ManTech sponsorship, tasked the

Iacocca Institute to develop an industry vision statement, the 21st Century Manufacturing Enterprise Strategy, that defined "agile manufacturing" at a conceptual level. In response, the government then sponsored a joint Defense Advanced Research Projects Agency (DARPA) and National Science Foundation (NSF) program entitled the Agile Manufacturing Initiative. This initiative, started in 1993, was comprised of three major research components and a set of pilot programs. The pilot programs were further divided into eight separate categories and funded over three years. Several of these pilots were funded under the federal government's Technology Reinvestment Program (TRP) and played a dual-use role falling under the "Agile" umbrella as well.

In 1993, the Ben Franklin Technology Center (BFTC) of northeastern Pennsylvania submitted a request for funding under TRP that proposed to "develop, demonstrate, and evaluate the dynamics of this new manufacturing system and practice, which we will call 'agile manufacturing.' " A carefully structured series of projects were to be executed through collaboration between a group of large manufacturers, small suppliers, and organizations that could provide business and technical assistance to these two constituencies. In late 1993, the BFTC was awarded $2 million under TRP to test the objectives of the "agile manufacturing" mantra over a three-year period. Furthermore, the project was supported by the Commonwealth of Pennsylvania with $1.5 million and $500,000 of in-kind support from participating companies. Wright Laboratories at Wright-Patterson Air Force Base in Dayton, Ohio managed the combined $4 million project.

After more than 700 companies were prescreened, twenty small and midsize manufacturers were pulled together as part of the project and represented a broad range of manufacturing capabilities and value-added services. They included electronics, castings, and metal parts manufacturers, as well as assemblymen and engineering designers. The composition of the firms within the supply web provided not only complementary services but competitive services as well.

After two years of conceptual work, Agile Web was incorporated in 1995 as a Pennsylvania for-profit corporation. The premise was to develop, experiment with, implement, and validate collaborative commerce concepts among a group of small and medium-size manufacturers. The objective of this technology demonstration project was that small firms, by teaming and working together in new ways, could become more competitive and productive, and provide a greater value-added service to their customers in an integrated sense than if they attempted to do so individually. The purpose of the creation of the separate corporation was to provide enough of a structure to facilitate and foster the creation of virtual enterprises from among the network members, while maximizing the flexibility and liability separation required for the Web to meet customers' constantly changing needs. Agile Web,

Inc. was created as a Pennsylvania corporation that uses standard corporate and contract law in creative ways to provide a balance of flexibility and instantiation. The creation of Agile Web, Inc. represented the first virtual corporation legally recognized in the world.

In 1996, as the TRP program was nearing completion, Bill Adams was hired as the president and CEO of Agile Web and was tasked to transform the corporation into a profit-making entity. Through 1996, Agile Web was still mainly a research project funded by the TRP program.

Development of the VCMS™ Solution

From 1996 to 1999, Adams implemented his own version of the AVE business model and systematically created a set of operating processes and procedures now known as the Virtual Corporation Management System™ solution. The VCMS™ solution is a protocol, a functional operating framework for the organization and management of CBNs and AVEs. It is a network of processes and procedures that rationalizes the myriad complexities associated with developing and managing virtual enterprises, including a broad range of areas from codifying capabilities of participating entities to dealing with a complex of potentially paralyzing responsibility and liability issues.

VCMS™ enables companies of all sizes to access and serve new markets and customers with their excess capacity and know-how. Companies can collaborate as individuals to form large enterprises that are specifically configured to serve customers without the need for joint ventures or mergers. This approach enables companies of all sizes in any geographic location to compete with larger, multinational corporations in accessing emerging markets.

The combination of the VCMS™ solution and the learning to date on the AVE business model allowed Agile Web not only to operate in a highly collaborative manner, but also created a new channel to market for many of the participating companies. Agile Web was transformed into a profitable operation with more than $50 million in potential contract backlog orders at the end of 1999.

Agile Web is currently the CBN for more than twenty small and medium-size manufacturing and service companies based primarily in eastern Pennsylvania. Through 1999, Agile Web successfully managed the operation of multiple-project AVEs, all of which were profitable and contributed revenues to the participating companies in new markets with new customers. Some of these AVE projects resulted in short-lived product development demonstrators (e.g., an automatic connector assembly system). Other AVEs resulted in sustained new product lines (e.g., a forklift control stick modeled from the F/A-18 fighter and a medical waste treatment system that sanitizes medical waste into municipal waste).

Agile Web was acquired by G5 Technologies (G5) in November 2000 and continues to operate as a CBN today, while continuing to push the limits of the AVE. G5 is currently leading a significant effort to develop the entire enabling legal infrastructure to optimize the functionality of these collaborative networks. Incorporated collaborative business networks are currently being created for new networks in powdered metal, complex metal structures, digital notarization, and media services. A large pipeline of new networks follows these early movers.

In October 1999, Governor Tom Ridge of Pennsylvania announced the formation of a program called Lightning Manufacturing (www. lightningmanufacturing.com). The establishment of this initiative signaled the birth of a compelling new form of business-to-business c-commerce and the coming of a new industry based on the Agile Virtual Enterprise. Contracted to identify and develop business plans of fifteen CBNs, G5 is currently developing six that will be operational by mid-2001: World Wide Powdered Metallurgy, Complex Metal Structures, Media Solutions, Industry/Academic Networks, and Medical/Pharmco, among others.

In summary, collaborative business processes established and proven through the Agile Web became the basis for development of the VCMS™ solution,[31] a process that provides the functional framework for developing and operating AVEs—collaborations to provide added value to customers in business-to-business c-commerce.

Race to the Future

Imagine assembling a dream team of the absolute best employees, equipment, and business processes that provide the required skills and capabilities to complete a unique task irrespective of location. Imagine pooling talent without being limited by geographical, time, or traveling constraints. In this newly emerging world of business, it is imperative for companies and their leadership to have an insightful understanding of the broad spectrum of issues affecting commercial uses of the AVE business model and the next-generation information infrastructure.

The AVE began as a vision of futurists, became a possibility for business theorists, and is now an economic necessity for corporate executives. All of this has occurred in a dramatically short period of time. This not only underscores the inevitability of this new business model but also hints at the accelerated sense of time that characterizes it.

For many firms the challenge of all of this change will prove too great. For some employees, the experience will be more traumatic than that of the changes demanded by past industrial transformations— though the threat this time may be unpredictability, lack of comfortable structure, and simply too much responsibility. Workers content to put in their hours, do their work, and go home may suddenly find themselves saddled with responsibility and control they never desired. Executive careers spent building power and influence may turn out to be superfluous, and companies content to maintain the status quo indefinitely may not only encounter change but also be forced to endure continuous transmutation.

To become a success, the AVE requires a different perspective, one that to our untrained eyes may even seem illogical at times. Without a doubt, this new business revolution requires new social contracts, ever-higher levels of specialized education, and a frightening degree of trust. But we have no choice. The AVE stands before us, offering us our best chance for revitalizing the global economy and guaranteeing meaningful value creation. If we do not walk through its doors, we may be left far behind in this race to the future. We feel that the adaptation of the AVE model can facilitate an explosion in growth and productivity heretofore unseen. We are very bullish on the future.

Endnotes

1 O. Arnold and M. Hartling, *Virtuelle Unternehmen: Begriffsbildung und diskussion*. Arbeitspapier der Reihe "Informations und Kommunikationssysteme als Gestaltungselement Virtueller Unternehmen" (Nr. 3/1995).

2 B. Travicia, "The Design of the Virtual Organization: A Research Model," in *Proceedings of the Americas Conference on Information Systems* (Indianapolis: AIS, August 15–17, 1997), pp. 417–419.

3 S. Ten Have, F. Van Lierop, and H. J. Kuhne, "Hoe virtueel moeten we eigenlijk zijn?" ("How Virtual Are We Actually Supposed to Be?") *Nijenrode Management Review* (Nr. 4, May/June 1997), pp. 85–93.

4 G. Moore, "The Virtual Corporation: Can We Ensure the Momentum?" *Open Comments* (Winter 1996). Available from http://www.opengroup.org/opencom ments/winter96/1text.htm (December 20, 2000).

5 John A. Byrne, R. Brandt, and O. Port, "The Virtual Corporation: The Company of the Future Will Be the Ultimate in Adaptability," *International Business Week* (February 8, 1993), pp. 36–40; and P. Sieber, "Virtual Organizations: Static and Dynamic Viewpoints," *Virtual-Organization.Net Newsletter,* Department of Information Management, University of Berne, Vol. 1, No. 2 (March 1, 1997).

6 F. Zimmerman, "Structural and Managerial Aspects of Virtual Enterprises," in *The Proceedings of the European Conference on Virtual Enterprises and Networked Solutions—New Perspectives on Management, Communication and Information Technology* (Paderborn, Germany April 7–10, 1997) (www.teco. uni-karlsruhe.de/IT-VISION/vu-e-teco.htm).

7 Byrne, et al., "The Virtual Corporation: The Company of the Future Will Be the Ultimate in Adaptability."

8 Tomasz M. Dembski, "Future Present: The Concept of Virtual Organization Revisited: The Nature of Boundedness of Virtual Organizations," *Virtual-Organization.Net Newsletter* Vol. 2, No. 2 (June 1, 1998).

9 Dembski, "Future Present."

10 C. Hardless, Virtual Corporations WWW site (wysiwyg://93/http://w3.adb.gu. se/~s96hardl/studying/virtual/virtual.htm), March 1997.

11 Dembski, op.cit.

12 D. Miller, "The Future Organization: A Chameleon in All Its Glory," *The Organization of the Future* (San Francisco: Jossey-Bass Publishers, 1997), pp.119–126.

13 Dembski, op.cit.

14 Ibid.

15 Sieber, "Virtual Organizations: Static and Dynamic Viewpoints."

16 Dembski, op. cit.

17 Ibid.

18 C. Kocian, "The Virtual Centre: A Networking Co-operation Model for Small Businesses," *Virtual-Organization.Net Newsletter* Vol. 1, No.2 (March 1, 1997); and C. Olander, "What Is the Virtual Corporation?"(www.sando.com/busart3. htm) and K. Shields, "Virtual Corporations Are Not New for Contractors," *Boston Business Journal* Vol. 14 (April 11, 1994).

19 C. Odendahl, P. Hirschmann, and A. Scheer, "Cooperation Exchanges as Media for the Initialization and Implementation of Virtual Enterprises," *Virtual-Organization.Net Newsletter* Vol.1, No. 3 (June 1, 1997).

20 Dembski, op. cit.

21 Odendahl et al., "Cooperation Exchanges as Media for the Initialization and Implementation of Virtual Enterprises."

22 Dembski, op.cit.

23 Ibid.

24 P. T. Kidd, *Agile Manufacturing: Forging New Frontiers* (Reading, MA: Addison-Wesley, 1994).

25 C. K. Prahalad and G. Hamel, "The Core Competence of the Corporation," *Harvard Business Review* (May–June, 1990), pp.79–91.

26 Raghu Garud, "Trust and Virtual Systems" (1997). Available from http://www. stern.nyu.edu/~rgarud/tele/tele6.htm (December 20, 2000).

27 Garud, "Trust and Virtual Systems."

28 Rene Bultje and J. van Wijk, "Taxonomy of Virtual Organizations, Based on Definitions, Characteristics, and Typology," KPN Research, The Netherlands.

29 R. Nagel, et al., *21st Century Manufacturing Enterprise Strategy* Vols. 1 and 2 (Bethlehem, PA: Lehigh University Iacocca Institute, 1992).

30 R. M. Wallace, *Making Change for Competitive Advantage.* Report for New York Department of Labor NYSST-C3-9210-001 (Albany: N.Y. Department of Labor, 1992).

31 Further information on the Virtual Corporation Management System solution is available from http://www.vcms.com/.

CHAPTER 13

E-Learning Solutions: Aligning Critical Development Factors

Shawn M. Clark, School of Information Sciences and Technology, The Pennsylvania State University

Cole Camplese, School of Information Sciences and Technology, The Pennsylvania State University

Kristin Z. Camplese, School of Information Sciences and Technology, The Pennsylvania State University

James B. Thomas, School of Information Sciences and Technology, The Pennsylvania State University

This chapter describes a model for e-learning solutions development involving the alignment of strategy, information technology (IT), process, organization, and content (i.e., the knowledge or subject material used for teaching purposes). We contend that aligning organizational structure as well as strategy and development factors is not only necessary for the successful design of online course delivery, but also critical for the effective e-learning experience needed for twenty-first-century education.[1] However, in the push to take advantage of IT, many organizations may neglect to pose, or answer, critical questions during the planning and development process. How do we link IT systems to a formal development process? How do we create a system that fosters flexibility in terms of content management? How do we create IT systems to foster interaction and creativity from development team members? What supporting architectures, applications, and communication capability do we need to make an e-learning strategy solution work? How do the skills and processes associated with developing and using IT for education and training relate to current skills and processes in our organization?

We suggest that leveraging IT means much more than converting the curriculum content developed for the traditional classroom and publishing it on the World Wide Web (WWW). While integrating curriculum content and web technology is necessary for creating value in education, it is not sufficient. Combining the technology, processes, human resources, skills, and input materials to match this integration is also critical for success. An alignment approach provides a logical framework for exploring these issues.[2] Thus, the objectives of this chapter are to:

- Identify the five key domains involved with e-learning solutions development.
- Illustrate how to effectively align the key domains of the solutions development process.
- Describe recent innovations associated with the e-learning solutions planning and development process.

Background

Information technology has emerged as a critical component of education and training in almost all organizations. Indeed, interest and investment in IT to support education and training have grown at an accelerated pace in the last few years. However, the application of IT for the purpose of education has left a gap in our understanding about what is effective and how technology should be applied. The risk, of course, is that many will rush to use technology and ignore the benefits of other more traditional teaching and learning approaches and techniques. Given this risk, it is not surprising that the need to effectively integrate IT into teaching and training using an integrated curriculum development approach is critical.

The issues, approaches, and innovations described in this chapter are primarily based on the experiences of The Pennsylvania State University's School of Information Sciences and Technology (IST) and its methodology for developing and delivering e-learning solutions. The IST e-learning solutions development methodology is designed to be a repeatable, reusable process for creating educationally sound courses in a financially responsible manner and to provide a system for the maintenance, customization, and enhancement of curriculum content.

One of the primary focuses of IST is instructional design and curriculum development. In collaboration with full-time faculty and others in the Penn State University system, IST is developing an entirely new online curriculum for both undergraduate and graduate programs. The mission of the school, and therefore of the development team, is to design courses that can be delivered via the Internet to the widest possible audience, including students, government administrators, company employees, and others. Penn State's undergraduate curriculum in IST is designed to provide students with the theoretical frameworks and skill sets necessary to compete and be productive in the information technology–intensive global context. Specifically, these courses are being developed to provide a learning experience that.builds an understanding of core information technologies and related areas of study; prepare students for the practical application of information technologies; and engage students in sharpening their abilities to think critically and to work in teams. All of this is being done with considerable interdisciplinary integration in order to expose students to the cognitive, social, institutional, and global environments of information technology.

As a first step, the school began with the design of Online IST 110, an introductory course for both IST's baccalaureate and associate degree programs, focusing on the fundamentals of information sciences and technology. As the school grows and matures, specialized courseware is being developed for industry and workforce development training certificates (credit and noncredit). For the purpose of describing the innovations and issues associated with e-learning solutions development, our experience designing and deploying Online IST 110 is referred to throughout this chapter. Online IST 110 presents learning material in a dynamic manner for an experience much richer than the mere reading of a textbook online. The focus of the course is on issues and case studies that managers and leaders in the information sciences deal with on a daily basis. This connection to the real world gives students not only more up-to-date content, but also a solid basis for solving problems that they will encounter when they ultimately enter the workforce. Working in teams, students in the course tackle several case studies developed by faculty members with corporate experience, as well as by IST's corporate partners. Electronic discussion forums, chat, e-mail, an online calendar, and dynamic interactions employing the latest technologies supplement the exercises they face.

The development of such a learning enterprise cannot be accomplished within a design silo. It must incorporate numerous, often disparate elements from both the learning and organizational contexts. Aligning these elements becomes a critical managerial challenge, comparable to the design challenge confronted in "traditional" online development organizations.

Five Domains of Alignment

In our view of strategic alignment, technology is just one of several key elements to consider when developing e-learning solutions. On the basis of our experience, those who will succeed in designing and developing e-learning solutions must:

1. Establish and communicate clear strategic direction for e-learning solutions development in terms of scope, governance, distinct competencies, and vision.
2. Implement a structured process management approach.
3. Establish practicable teams that incorporate the appropriate mix of skills and expertise.
4. Identify and manage curriculum content (e.g., text, graphics, multimedia) to meet student and instructor needs.
5. Identify, develop, and utilize appropriate information technology tools and systems.

Therefore, the effective application of technology really depends on a synthesis, integration, and alignment of technology, curriculum content, strategy, organization infrastructure, and the development process (see Figure 13-1). In summary, the success of e-learning solutions development depends on the integration and alignment of the appropriate set of elements and on the design and application of an effective, cross-disciplinary development approach.

FIGURE 13-1
Strategic Alignment Model

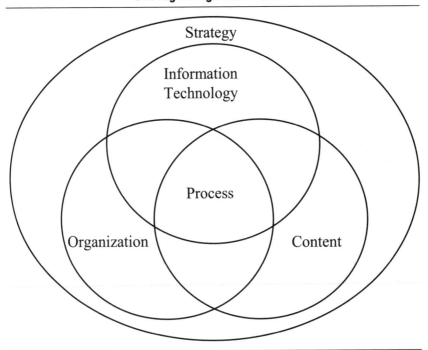

Strategy

Strategy is the keystone of the solutions development process. Overlooked by many, strategy provides a rationale for connecting, integrating, and aligning information technology, development, and delivery processes; organization; and curriculum content. A solution strategy consists of several interrelated elements including a description of where-to-educate, how-to-educate, and when-to-educate choices. It also defines how, what, and when to develop, and the audiences, markets, and customers that an individual, group, or organization intends to educate. The major variables, issues, and concerns within the strategy domain have been organized into four categories: scope, governance, distinctive competencies, and vision.

Scope

Central to decision making in the strategic domain are questions of scope: Will the solution be used to address needs in multiple market niches? How will the solution emphasize real-world problem solving and foster theoretical and conceptual thinking? How will the solution be used in multiple locations? Is the solution scalable enough to incorporate large pools of instructors, students, and/or teaching assistants? Will the solution be applied uniformly across multiple audiences and situations, or will it be tailored to different forums for learning?

Scope-related activities involve assessing, understanding, and identifying the target markets and key audiences to which e-learning solutions are directed, as well as understanding the competitive environment. For example, if a solution is intended for multiple audiences, then a development process and IT system should be developed that is flexible and efficient enough to cope with these demands. At IST, a computerized system has been developed to promote a high degree of flexibility in course design. Course content is modularized from the outset and stored in a database to facilitate reuse and customization. The system enables faculty and trainers to select appropriate lessons and chapters depending on their objectives and/or the needs of the audience.

In summary, strategic decisions related to scope take into account the positioning of a solution in the external environment and ultimately guide the arrangement and alignment of other key domains to form a process for executing the strategy.

Governance

Governance represents those decisions concerning how the development process is to be designed and managed, and key choices regarding the approach to development. Governance and process decisions are used to determine how content will be gathered, reviewed, stored, manipulated, and maintained. For instance, these types of decisions may dictate how modular to make the content so that it can be recombined into new courses later on. The governance strategy determines the sequencing of events, if and when quality checks will occur, and how and when to pilot test materials. Governance also involves decisions regarding collaborative mechanisms such as partnerships and strategic alliances. Do we develop our own content or do we develop an alliance with a publisher that has content? Can we develop online courses more effectively through a carefully designed network of corporate partners and alliances?

Governance also dictates the extent to which a formal methodology is used for development purposes. There are a variety of arguments both for and against designing a formal solutions development methodology and process. The advantages of a methodology are that it provides structure and guidelines for team members to follow. A formal process may also be used to ensure the integration of key domains involved in solutions development, and that attention is paid to important development issues such as pilot testing. Some may argue that formal methodologies are detrimental to creativity. Governance decisions determine if and to what extent a formal development process should be designed and implemented. A typical process map outlines the major steps and phases to follow in developing an e-learning solution and identifies the tools and techniques needed to perform the activities represented by these steps. A process-based methodology may include planning, analysis, design, implementation, testing, and knowledge management.

As the importance of online education and training continues to grow, organizations increasingly seek to formalize and improve the processes and methodologies used for solutions development. More formalized processes and methodologies are required to address the growing complexity of online course design and delivery. Online learning solutions must take into account database connectivity, graphic design, testing procedures, and the continuing need to bring together multiple sources of knowledge and experience to create valued products and services.

Another key element of governance and the solution strategy is the instructional design approach. The role of instructional design and instructional designers is to ensure that the final product is designed appropriately to promote learning and meet learning objectives. Furthermore, the role of instructional design is to ensure the selection and application of a sound instructional strategy. A variety of instructional strategies are available for a solutions development team including the case-study approach, problem-based learning, simulations, and others.

For example, at IST, a collaborative, problem-based learning approach was selected as a key feature of online course design. This strategic decision significantly affects course design, including website design. Instructional design decisions may also affect the scalability of the course in terms of how many students, instructors, and teaching assistants should be involved in course administration.

Distinctive Competencies

All decisions concerning solution scope, governance, and finally development and delivery can and should be viewed in terms of what the organization will excel at. What the organization excels at relative to competitors or other referents is defined as a distinctive competency. A competency is something an organization does especially well in comparison to others.[3] There are many possible types of competencies related to e-learning solutions development, including production excellence, low-cost production, exceptional quality control, speed of delivery, ability to customize products and services, innovativeness in course delivery, and strong understanding of customer needs. The importance of having distinctive competencies comes from the added capability it gives an organization to attract and meet the needs of customers in a particular market and the competitive edge it can yield. Therefore, strategic decisions related to development should foster the creation of distinctive competencies within the organization.

Vision Creation

An important starting point for understanding scope, governance, and distinctive competencies is vision creation. A well-articulated vision provides a crucial reference point for the development team. It helps motivate participants to action and serves as a starting point for goal identification. The vision provides the highest-level integrating mechanism for aligning other domains critical to success, such as process design, team formation, and content collection. At IST, the following tenets are used to define the vision for online and resident curricula:

- Build a program focused on educating leaders and problem solvers for the new digital economy.
- Educate students to understand the technology, but focus them on the application of technology as a solution and sensitize them to the people and policy issues they will confront.
- Educate them using real-world problems and engage them in the realities of information technology in the workplace.
- Put students into teams to deal with their exploration, and push them to build their oral and writing skills.

This vision is, in turn, leveraged by the development team to create e-learning solutions that achieve those objectives. The vision has become a specific reference point for determining the type of content, skills requirements, and instructional strategy for online teaching.

Process

The process of developing an e-learning solution raises many questions about organizational capabilities and how and when to perform important activities and tasks. A variety of key questions emerge when an organization engages in e-learning solutions development: What skills does the organization need? What tools and technologies should we use? What steps should we take first? How do we manage the development process? Many of these questions can or should be answered through the design and implementation of a sound development process. In general, processes are critical to individual and organizational performance, and they should be clearly defined and continually improved.

Organizational processes, whether they be manufacturing, administrative, or research and development–related, are typically defined as a series of ordered actions used to produce a valued output or meet a specific objective. Like most business processes, solutions development processes also tend to be repeatable, cross organizational boundaries, and have customers. In other words, a process is a set of procedures and rules that helps deliver, in a systematic and measurable way, a service or product to a customer, internal or external.[4] Steps in a process usually cut across traditional and departmental or functional lines and are performed by multiple individuals and groups. Finally, it is important to keep in mind that processes and process steps can, and often are, enabled by technologies and tools as well as other processes. For example, a database management system may be used to support steps in the online training process.

Defining e-learning solutions development as a formal process provides a basis for understanding many of the key issues, activities, technologies, and skills involved. A process orientation also forces an organization to think about its capabilities and distinctive competencies. Using a process perspective, many organizations have begun to look at how they are performing—what their capability is—in online course delivery, in the knowledge management area, and in meeting the needs of students and clients. Clearly, these development processes bridge several functional areas and require tight integration among them. In summary, a process perspective enables developers to:

■ Identify and clearly document the key elements involved in the development and delivery of e-learning solutions.

- Pinpoint issues, concerns, and opportunities for improvement.
- Align and integrate information technology with process activities and tools (e.g., manage content database).
- Fit team resources to steps in the process.
- Foster the communication and transfer of knowledge concerning processes, policies, and procedures.

IST has developed a repeatable process consisting of a series of multiple steps. Conceptual stages of a high-level solutions development process model are illustrated in Figure 13-2.

Typically, team resources, activity steps, and deliverables are clearly tied to steps or stages in a process. For example, when establishing project scope, the lead instructional designer, primary content developer, and project manager work together to establish the overall scope and major milestones associated with the effort. The major outcomes or deliverables from this step include a Memorandum of Understanding, content collection timeline, and content outline (including instructional goals and objectives). The scope of a solution is evaluated during this stage in order to determine the number of topics in the course, the number and type of exams, individual student activities and assignments, student team activities and assignments, ideal class size, and other important design points.

Designing and documenting a formal development process may have considerable value for some organizations. Many attack the development process informally, haphazardly, and inefficiently, and without the long-term perspective that takes flexibility and curriculum content maintenance into consideration. Determining and documenting the steps of a process bring structure and discipline to the work and provide the opportunity to transfer knowledge about the process to others more effectively. At IST, the solutions development process has been formally documented in a courseware production manual. This manual is used to train individual team members and to scale-up operations to bring new teams online as additional courses are developed.

In conclusion, the following four process management questions can be used to quickly assess how developed and/or structured your process perspective is:

1. Do you have a formally documented development process?
2. Is the process reviewed and improved on a regular basis?
3. Does the process support your strategy?
4. Is there a process owner assigned to oversee, manage, and improve the process?

Organization

Of the many kinds of organizational changes that can facilitate solutions development, one of the most powerful involves the formation of

FIGURE 13-2
Sample E-Learning Solution Development Process

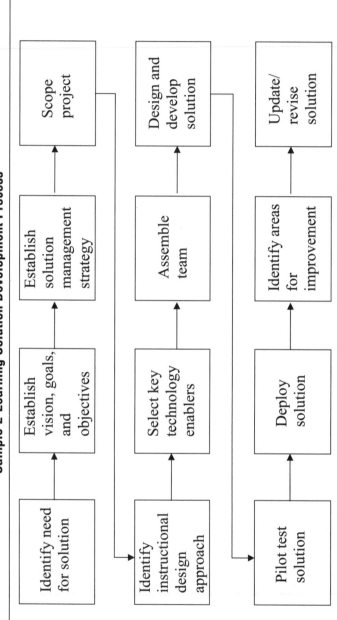

teams. Teams are frequently used to bring together cross-functional skills in a single work unit. Cross-functional teams facilitate the interface and alignment of multiple skills and perspectives and allow for parallel design activities. Another benefit of teams is that they include more opportunities for social interaction and creativity. A team-based approach also provides other advantages when it is properly aligned to a formalized, documented development process. In this case, an established team may be used to develop multiple projects, either sequentially or in parallel.

In many institutions of education, courses have traditionally been designed and delivered by individuals. For example, universities have traditionally relied on individual faculty members to develop, collect, and organize course content, and deliver it to students in a classroom. Recently, organizations have begun to recognize the importance of groups and teamwork for curriculum and other forms of solution development. One explanation for this is the impact IT and the WWW are having on instructional approaches and learning. Web-based teaching provides opportunities to apply a broad range of skills that a single individual is unlikely to possess. Compared to traditional in-class courses, cutting-edge online courses use many more communication and content elements including audio clips, video clips, rich media files, and text. For example, Online IST 110 consists of 700 screens of text, 153 images, 40 rich media files (e.g., flash animations, interactive exercises), 5 video clips, and 10 audio clips. Well-designed courses also integrate a wider range of techniques and tools for teaching and learning such as bulletin boards, instant messaging, e-mail, computer simulations, and chat rooms, as well as lectures, group exercises, and in-class discussions. To manage and/or use this set of methods and bring the appropriate skills to bear on solutions development, teams are needed.

An important innovation and trend in e-learning solutions development is the creation of appropriate solutions development teams to handle the development and integration of these teaching elements, tools, and techniques. While most faculty members are qualified content experts, many lack the skills and resources needed to develop and administer e-learning solutions effectively. Based on our experience at IST, the following skill categories have been identified as being relevant to successful solutions development:

- Instructional design
- Graphics design
- Project management
- Web development
- Team building

- Software programming
- Teaching
- Marketing
- Testing and assessment
- Knowledge management
- Database management
- Process management
- Strategic planning

Web-based training solutions development typically requires multiple individuals working together. This requirement strongly suggests the need to assign project managers and apply project management tools and techniques to the solutions development process. Almost all significant organizational actions, outcomes, and achievements are the result of projects and project planning. A project is defined as a temporary endeavor undertaken to create a unique product or service or to accomplish a major goal. Project management methodologies involve a unique set of tasks including identifying stakeholders, defining project scope, assembling the project team, creating a plan, estimating task duration, solving problems, tracking progress, conducting status meetings, and reviewing project outcomes. Project management provides the level of control needed to ensure success in bringing human resources, process, content, technology, and strategy together.

Content

Curriculum content is at the core of any course, whether it is an e-learning solution or a traditional face-to-face course. It consists of the intellectual property and core knowledge specific to a given solution. Before any development work begins, a successful e-learning solution designer should ask the following questions regarding curriculum content:

- What/who is the target audience?
- What/who is the content source?
- What type of content is it?

Target Audience

The level of learning should clearly be identified when undertaking e-learning solutions development. Is this an undergraduate college course? Is it an elementary school course? Is this a corporate training course? Or will multiple audiences use the end result? Asking these types of questions are some of the basic first steps in any instructional design process. The most fundamental underlying issue is, "Who is my audience?"

The answers to these questions will affect many other decisions regarding information technology, process, and strategy. For example, if a course will only be used by a training audience within one corporation, information technology decisions will be driven by the technology infrastructure of that corporation.

The current iteration of Online IST 110 was primarily designed for undergraduate audiences. However, the strategic vision involves reformulating some of the IST 110 content for training audiences, high school outreach programs, and, eventually, the graduate curriculum. By leveraging the content database, we can reduce our time-to-market for courseware, thus providing a richer, more current curriculum (and a financially leaner institution).

This "multiple levels of learning" vision means that the e-learning solutions designers need to ensure that content is flexible, modular, and appropriate for multiple audiences. In the case of Online IST 110, this means relying on a process that keeps raw course material in a database and "swapping" problems and case studies in and out to keep the content current and appropriate for each new audience.

Sources

Finding reliable subject matter experts and other sources of curriculum content is another important challenge. Content is pivotal to any e-learning solution. Even the best team of designers and developers can do little without a solid content baseline.

Who will provide content for a given e-learning solution? Will it be traditional faculty, researchers, graduate students, managers, consultants, or other subject matter experts? Obtaining quality content in a timely manner can be one of the most difficult challenges in any instructional design project. Thus, it is highly recommended that content providers be identified early and encouraged to stick to deadlines. Many e-learning solutions lose momentum or go over budget due to content provider issues and problems. For example, many research-oriented faculty members do not have their time-intensive, online course development efforts recognized in promotion and tenure criteria. As a solution to these types of content problems, IST hires nontraditional faculty members to write course content exclusively without the traditional pressures to research and publish. IST also uses a work-for-hire approach to acquire content. For a set fee, the university owns all rights to materials produced by a content provider for IST. In the business world, these problems are more easily resolved through contracts and financial rewards.

Another issue related to managing sources of content is intellectual property rights. Contractual templates should be developed that explicitly detail ownership of the material. Inevitably, a variety of contractual arrangements and templates should be developed to obtain the needed content.

Type

The type of content integrated into an e-learning solution is also an important consideration. To what extent is the content text-based? To what extent are diagrams and other visual representations used to communicate concepts? Content type is defined by the subject matter itself and tends to influence the instructional design approach. For example, HTML-based solutions involving statistics and mathematics require a unique approach and skill set. Currently, HTML does not support the necessary characters and symbols to portray equations on the WWW. As a result, each equation used in an online course must be produced and revised as a graphic. In this case, the development team must be structured to represent the increased need for graphic developers; in addition, timelines, process executions, and database storage practices must take the different content elements into account.

Information Technology

The IT domain is defined in terms of the hardware and software choices that must be made in order to implement an effective e-learning solutions development process and the positioning of the solutions and enabling technologies in the information technology marketplace. Just as developers must understand the positioning of their e-learning solutions in the larger marketplace for strategic planning purposes, they must also understand the dynamics of the IT marketplace for planning purposes.

IT choices center on the identification, evaluation, and perhaps adoption of an emerging technology. For example, choices may include understanding new wireless technologies or the use of a knowledge management system for content management. There are a number of technologies and technology combinations that may be leveraged to provide distinctive competencies for the overall solutions development process. Decisions to adopt technology standards, communication protocols, or application environments will directly affect the flexibility and availability of courses in education and training environments. The information technology domain also involves "make or buy" decisions. Do we build and maintain a system internally? Do we contract for all or some of our IT services? Do we establish alliances with other organizations to provide the e-learning services needed?

Information technology should be carefully aligned with other strategic domains including the development process. There are three key areas where information technology is positioned within an e-learning solutions development process. These areas are:

- Back-end technologies
- Intermediary technologies
- Front-end technologies

Back-End Technologies

Back-end technologies are the specific process enablers that facilitate team communication and knowledge and content management. Team communication is pivotal to a successful e-learning project and, for that matter, any project. Tools that provide e-mail, bulletin boards, and a common calendar for development team participants can be used to facilitate the project management effort. All communications should be documented with these tools to ensure that team members fully understand any changes to the project. Any formal process should document how and when communication tools should be used.

Back-end technologies also include the knowledge and content management tools that your organization chooses to use. Simple or even sophisticated database applications can be used to manage curriculum content, or what some organizations call "intellectual capital." This is imperative to any e-learning solution's development process. Keeping content separate from its eventual presentation medium allows for greater flexibility, increased modularity, and faster and more efficient revision cycles. These technologies are a necessary component of any instructional design process. Much like the publishing world, educational institutions must begin to store and reuse their intellectual capital systematically.

A specialized IT design system played an integral role in the development of Online IST 110. The system consists of an integrated set of design and development tools used for the efficient and consistent creation of content for online courses. The system also provides a powerful instructional asset management system specifically developed for the needs of the online learning community. All of the features of the system are supported by a team communication component that assists with content management, instructional design, and project management. The IST design system provides a powerful library structure that can be used for managing content at the overall curriculum level, as well as at the design level of a specific course. The benefits of such a system are that it:

- Provides all members of the development team full access to all course material
- Provides a communication tool to facilitate an efficient flow of information between and among team members
- Provides a searchable index of tasks for all team members involved in development

- Enables the reuse of course content quickly and efficiently
- Provides a method for reducing or eliminating HTML coding
- Warehouses references to copyrighted material
- Stores notes relevant to the inclusion of all content elements
- Incorporates relevant metadata for effectively indexing and re-trieving all course materials

Intermediary Technologies

Intermediary technologies are defined as the multimedia technologies used by both e-learning solutions developers and the eventual learners. For example, developers use tools such as Macromedia Flash, Macromedia Authorware, or Macromedia Director to create high-level interactive exercises or animations to enhance the textual content. In addition, software packages that assist in graphics creation are also considered intermediary technologies. The outputs from these technologies are enhanced multimedia elements. Individual learners do not interact with the specific software packages; however, they interact with the ultimate outcome—the multimedia element.

These technologies impact all areas of the e-learning solution strategy. For example, human resources needs are vastly different if the curriculum content design dictates the creation of interactions using tools such as Macromedia Flash or Authorware than if the design requires simple graphics or animations. The former will most certainly require a skilled professional.

Front-End Technologies

Front-end technologies are the delivery mechanisms for providing content to the learner. These can range from off-the-shelf tools such as WebCT or FirstClass, to traditional web browsers, to custom-made browsers for your course content. Many front-end technologies are also learning management systems capable of student tracking, assessment, and other forms of data collection and analysis. In the case of Online IST 110, a hybrid approach was selected that combines a custom course browser and WebCT to enhance communication capabilities and provide an effective forum for student and course evaluation. In general, any front-end technology (or combination of technologies) used must include an interface for content presentation, a common calendar for scheduling, private e-mail, bulletin boards for asynchronous discussion, chat for synchronous discussion, and quizzing or testing capabilities.

Other front-end technologies include supplementary CD-ROMs, videotapes, or other media that best suit the instructional and audience needs. Many solutions are targeted for the delivery of content via the WWW. However, the Web may have some deficiencies. Sometimes it is better to use a supplementary medium available to learners than it is to frustrate them with web-based technologies that are unreliable or slow. It is important to consider the curriculum content when making these decisions. For example, content that is heavily video-dependent may require supplementary CD-ROMs for delivery of that material.

Strategic Alignment: Issues and Examples

The key to e-learning solutions development is the acquisition and alignment of several key components. Clearly, exploiting the potential of IT involves much more than just putting lecture notes on a website. In this chapter, we argued that effectively linking IT and course content is just one of many linkages that must be taken into consideration. We have tried to conceptualize a more comprehensive view of alignment that takes into account all of the major elements of the solutions development process. More important, we have alluded to how each domain aligns to the others. In this section, we describe how alignment was manifested at IST and steps that should be taken to facilitate the alignment of key domains.

Aligning Instructional Strategy and Content Development

Strategic decisions guide the alignment and integration of process, information technology, curriculum content, and organization in a variety of ways. Strategy can and should be used as a reference point (see Figure 13-1). Each domain should be assessed to determine how well it supports the strategy. In almost all cases, the overall strategy development should be used as a lens for designing and making decisions about the other domains. For example, the content for Online IST 110 was organized into fifteen major topic areas. In a traditional classroom, each topic roughly equates with one week of instruction. To facilitate the alignment of content development with instructional strategy, the fifteen topics were grouped into complementary clusters appropriate for a problem-based learning approach. For each cluster, an overarching problem or case study was developed. To arrive at an appropriate solution, student teams are required to read and understand the established set of topics and tap into the external links provided in the material.

Aligning Organization Infrastructure and IT

The organization domain is becoming increasingly important to the success of development efforts that rely heavily on sophisticated IT systems for database and knowledge management. In these cases, the appropriate organizational infrastructure is needed to support selecting, creating, assessing, filtering, updating, and licensing the content information. It is impossible to develop IT systems that can determine what constitutes the right content for a given audience, or even when it is the right time to deliver a selection of content to the audience. E-learning solutions brokers will be needed to search for and select appropriate partners for solution development and facilitate the formation of effective development teams. IST has begun formalizing partnerships with corporations and faculty external to the school in order to acquire the subject matter expertise needed for curriculum development. Project managers are also needed to oversee the development and maintenance of IT systems used for solutions development and to lead the development of the solutions once a process is in place. Therefore, IST has begun developing and disseminating project management tools and techniques and initiated a mentoring program for project managers focused on online learning products and services.

Technology plays a central role in linking human resources and the skills sets of the development team members. One way to facilitate the alignment of organization infrastructure with other domains is to use technology to help collaborators quickly unite to exploit specific e-learning development opportunities. Once the opportunity is met, the participants may choose to disband. Using technology, teams of people from different organizations, locations, and disciplines work together concurrently and/or sequentially in real time. Professional editors, consultants, and other participants are brought on board, if only temporarily, to contribute to solution development. E-mail, a database management system, and other technologies enable this process.

One guideline for effectively aligning the organization and other strategic domains is to ensure that the right combination of individuals is selected and that participants are contributing their core competencies to the development team. It may be necessary to include individuals with competencies related to specific technologies, as well as strategic planning, content development, computer programming, process management, project management, and other domain-specific capabilities. If misalignment occurs during the development period based on shifts in technology requirements, strategy, or other factors, it might be necessary to change the team configuration. At IST, the assigned project manager is responsible for ensuring that the right combination of skills and knowledge is available throughout the project lifecycle.

Aligning Process and IT

Information technology is not only important in implementing new development processes; it also makes possible entirely new process designs. Therefore, IT should be considered for every stage of the process design. Solution developers should emphasize the question, "What could we do if we had [substitute specific technologies] in our process?"[5] After a process design has been implemented, the focus should shift to how IT can facilitate implementation of process outcomes through such activities as modeling and assessment.

For process designs that are aggressive or radical, substantial new IT capabilities may be required to support the new process with information. The application of new technologies to a development process is often feasible, but when combined they can add considerably to the cost and time requirements of changing a process in the future. Organizations also have to deal with issues of how their development and delivery processes relate to information systems that are available in the marketplace. Some organizations may be compelled to change their processes and outcomes in order to fit the way a package forces work to be done. This is the reverse of the traditional approach to automating a process wherein the nature of the process is determined first, and then the information system is built to support it.

Conclusion

There is widespread agreement that the WWW and other forms of IT should be used to promote and enhance learning. Furthermore, it has also become clear that exploiting the potential of IT involves much more than just moving content into web-based formats. We argue that the most effective way to develop online courses and other e-learning solutions is to link the five domains of strategy, process, organization, content, and IT. Few frameworks are available that depict how to effectively design courses integrating these components. The term *alignment* as used here implies the integration of these domains into a functional process, guided by a strategy. Conceptualization of how the domains interact and are fitted together has also been explored.

This alignment model also highlights a variety of challenges faced by solution developers and project managers. These challenges involve recognizing the opportunities and threats in the e-learning environment and attempting to manage the domains of solutions development to deal with these issues. The alignment perspective gives managers the opportunity to more effectively leverage the potential of IT while underscoring the importance of managing internal factors necessary for successful implementation. Accordingly, this model of development also implies that managers and leaders become familiar with each of these domains and the implications of aligning elements among them.

This alignment perspective demonstrates the need for leaders and developers to rise to the challenge of managing process, technology, and content as they would other domains they are more familiar with, such as strategy and organizational factors. In addition to recognizing the competitive potential of IT, managers must also provide leadership in implementing technology and aligning it with the other domains described previously.

Based on the alignment perspective, the strategic planning process should take into account the influence and importance of all of the critical domains so that key variables are not missed, ignored, or become under- or overemphasized. A strategic planning process that emphasizes one domain, or a small subset of domains, may inhibit the formation of comprehensive and valid assumptions concerning development, and ultimately undermine performance. Therefore, we propose that managers reconceptualize their planning processes to reflect all five domains of alignment. One of the first steps toward implementing this recommendation would, at a minimum, require assembling a team familiar or experienced with key elements in all five domains.

This planning and development approach is more complete in another way. Managers can learn how to exploit the potential of multiple domains and their interrelationships for competitive advantage. Through the use of a more holistic perspective, managers are more inclined to leverage a wider range of workable assessment, planning, and change management methodologies in order to make necessary improvements. For example, SWOT (strengths, weaknesses, opportunities, and threats) analysis, competitor analysis, and instructional design methodologies can be used for decision-making purposes in the strategic domain. Likewise, process reengineering techniques may be used to enhance overall process performance consistent with the interests of the process domain.

In summary, what the alignment model for development suggests is the importance of leveraging and integrating five key domains for planning and executing the e-learning development process. Organizations and managers must therefore recognize the need to adapt their planning approaches to achieve strategic alignment.

Endnotes

1 G. Labovitz and V. Rosansky, *The Power of Alignment: How Great Companies Stay Centered and Accomplish Extraordinary Things,* First Edition. New York: John Wiley and Sons, 1997.

2 J. C. Henderson and J. B. Thomas, "Aligning business and information technology domains: Strategic planning in hospitals," *Hospital & Health Services Administration* Vol. 37, No. 1 (Spring 1992).

3 A. A. Thompson, Jr. and A. J. Strickland, *Strategic Management: Concepts and Cases,* 10th ed. (Boston: McGraw-Hill, 1997).

4 W. L. Cats-Baril and R. L. Thompson, *Information Technology and Management* (Boston: Irwin, 1997).

5 T. Davenport, *Reengineering a Business Process* (Boston: Harvard Business School Publishing, 1995).

CHAPTER 14

E-Government: An Executive Road Map to the Digital Frontier

Frederick Loomis, School of Information Sciences and Technology,
The Pennsylvania State University
Charles Gerhards, Governors Office of Administration, Commonwealth of
Pennsylvania

The visions now being articulated by e-business leaders are also shared by many in the public sector. A shift toward a global e-business-enabled economy is driving dramatic changes in government operations. At the same time, governments at all levels are feeling pressure to "reinvent" themselves—empowered by web technologies that can transform the way they work, collaborate, and comply with the growing expectations of citizens and consumers. How will government move toward the digital frontier in the twenty-first century? Will the public sector lead or lag behind, and will government enable or inhibit innovation in the emerging e-world?

In many ways, governments function much the same as commercial enterprises—from ordering supplies and paying bills to providing products and services and collecting revenues. There are, however, important differences between business and government in the contextual forces and the operating environments. These forces need to be understood by government executives who must lead the transformation process and by business executives who are often critical suppliers and partners for government programs.

This chapter identifies several strategic issues facing executives who must lead or interact within the "e-government" environment. An executive road map for navigating and leading e-government initiatives is presented along with other resources and best practice models. Finally, the current state of practice of e-government is explored with an in-depth analysis of the Commonwealth of Pennsylvania case study.

E-Government Defined

Janet Caldow notes that while the term e-government has attained conversational status, a commonly used definition remains elusive.[1] Based on our review of current practice, we propose the following multidimensional definition to guide discussion here:

> E-government involves the use of strategies and technologies to transform government by improving the delivery of services and enhancing the quality of interaction between the citizen-consumer and all branches of government.

In our view, e-government is not a prepackaged set of procedures, checklists, and solution providers. More than anything else, e-government is about a focus on what we refer to as the *citizen-consumer—* individuals who expect and demand the same level of customer service and quality from government that they are currently enjoying in the commercial world. Governments will be successful in the digital frontier if they develop strategies that add significant value to the citizen-consumer relationship.

The digital frontier has the potential to affect all aspects of government operations and public discourse—from staffing to business practices, from agency services to digital democracy.

Figure 14-1 presents a model to help understand how e-government can be framed and discussed. The model uses a framework similar to the one discussed by David Partridge and Nirmal Pal in Chapter 5. The important addition here is the recognition of environmental influences and the policy within which leaders must operate in developing strategy for e-government.

The model is presented as a way of thinking about the elements that we think are important to effective e-government. As any executive can attest, it is difficult if not impossible to separate out these parts so neatly when one is trying to run any large, complex enterprise. Nonetheless, we believe that a heuristic framework such as this, with clearly defined terms, is important to develop when attempting to initiate an e-government enterprisewide initiative.

At the apex of our model is leadership that is focused on meeting the needs of the citizen-consumer in the context of the public policy environment. Issues such as privacy, security, and innovation, as well

FIGURE 14-1
E-Government Framework

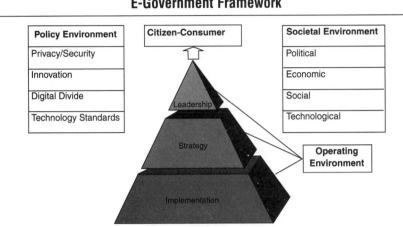

as environmental forces related to the political, economic, social, and technological context, all impact on the ability of government to move aggressively into the e-world. Within the e-government domain, strategy and implementation flow from the vision and values articulated by political leaders and public officials (e.g., elected officials, career executives, and chief information officers). It is also important to note that e-government functions within an operating environment that is often different from that found in the private sector. Leaders need to understand this difference in forging policy and strategy.

Key Strategic Issues for Executives

Using the e-government model as a point of departure, this chapter addresses the following questions that are important to the formation of e-government vision strategy:

■ What are the key environmental influences that government executives must pay attention to in the e-world?

■ How can we use technology to drive strategy development, innovation, and the "reinvention" of government?

■ What is the current state of practice in e-government? What can we learn from the early adopters?

■ How do changes in technology affect citizen expectations for government services and their interaction with elected officials?

■ What is the future of e-government and digital democracy? Can technology serve as a catalyst to improve services, access, involvement, and communication with all levels of government?

Environmental Forces and Policy Issues

We are living in a digital-based global economy. By this we mean the convergence of computing and communications technologies in the Internet and the resulting flow of information and technology that continues to stimulate vast societal change. During the last quarter century, digital information was found principally in back offices—in payroll records, typing pools, mailing databases, and the like. Today, it is everywhere, driving the global economy, attracting investment, reducing inflation, and increasing productivity.

The digital frontier also has the potential to change the fabric of democracy. A national survey commissioned by the Democracy Online Project at George Washington University (http://democracyonline.org) found that nearly 25 percent of the respondents had used the Internet to learn about candidates running for office. A state primary in Arizona has already been conducted online by Election.com (see Figure 14-2).

In addition, Minnesota Governor Jesse Ventura acknowledges that his election in 1998 would not have been possible without the Internet. With no campaign headquarters and only one full-time staff member, Ventura used his website and e-mail to mobilize his volunteers. In an ideal world of e-politics, money would become immaterial. Voters could bypass the media and tap into a wealth of candidate information online. The citizen-consumer would become more of an activist, instead of a passive receiver of information via television and mass media.[2]

The government is attempting to respond to the real or perceived demands of citizen-consumers for more online services. Studies indicate that spending on government Internet activities will increase from $1.5 billion in 2000 to $6.2 billion in 2005.[3] The number of U.S. households online has grown from 5.8 million (5 percent) in 1994 to 144 million (52 percent) in 2000, with projected growth to more than 50 percent by 2003.[4] By the year 2002, the Internet economy will employ more than 10 million workers in a variety of industries worldwide. The Information Technology Association of America estimates a current demand for roughly 1.6 million IT professional positions, with more than half of these positions going unfilled each year.[5] This human capital deficit places new pressures on government and education to produce the well-educated, highly skilled people that the public and private sector need to stay ahead.

In addition to the environmental forces, the following policy issues are at the forefront of the agenda for digital governments worldwide.

Privacy

Using the Internet, businesses have discovered an improved ability to target advertising to individual consumers, making it more cost-effective. This ability has also created an unprecedented market for personal information as an adjunct to e-commerce transactions, raising new concerns about privacy—a potential obstacle to wide acceptance of electronic commerce. Government must safeguard the integrity of online information and guard against external attacks to databases and systems. How can government build a defense against information warfare? What is the role of government in protecting the rights of individuals who do business online?

Innovation

Extraordinarily rapid technological and market innovation distinguishes the digital economy from other parts of the information economy—as well as from other fields of technology. Knowledge discovery and management is a key asset for organizations in the twenty-first century. What factors drive innovation? What is the role of government in encouraging innovation and knowledge discovery in the e-world? Within government, how can we best change old ways of doing business? More specifically, how can e-government capture the same kind of entrepreneurial spirit and dedication to excellence that is often found in the private sector?

Technology Standards

Most observers agree that open standards are an underlying technical and philosophical tenet of the expansion of electronic commerce. The widespread adoption of the Internet as a platform for business is due to its nonproprietary standards. Experience to date shows us that open standards do not have to be engineered by international committees, but can evolve within a large, digitally connected professional community. Standards for the adoption of new applications can greatly speed the development and interoperability of online transactions and services.

Digital Divide

The Internet has the potential to segregate nonusers from users. According to the U.S. Department of Commerce, whites are twice as likely to own a computer and have Internet access (41 percent) than are African Americans (19 percent) or Hispanics (19 percent). A study by Harvard's Center for International Development found that the information revolution could significantly improve the lives of 80 percent of the world's population living in developing countries. To do so will require an unprecedented collaboration between business and government to create the necessary infrastructure and conditions for entry into the networked community. Without such intervention, the use of technology will be limited to industrialized nations, and the digital divide will grow wider not only in the United States but worldwide.

The Operating Environment of Government

There are important differences between the public and private sector. Perhaps this is best understood by the United Kingdom's e-minister, Patricia Hewitt, when she stated: "If Jack Welch says that GE is going to become an e-business, it does, and pretty quickly. Government is different."[6] Politicians can be visionary, but government bureaucrats make things happen. Overcoming internal resistance to change is a significant challenge of public executives.

Figure 14-2 outlines the important differences between the public and private sectors. It is helpful if these differences are recognized by government executives who lead e-government initiatives and by business executives who are often critical suppliers and partners for government programs.

Public executives must navigate in an environment that is highly political, often constrained by a range of sometimes conflicting, ambiguous goals. Staffing flexibility can be limited by rules and union contracts, and government can be highly dependent on external technology providers. Internal and external stakeholders often contest decisions, many times in the press. In addition, resources in the public sector are scarce or require a high degree of accountability for expenditures.

A systems-contingency approach recognizes that not all elements of the environment are equally significant to public managers, who tend to focus on the most task-relevant influences.[7] As illustrated in Figure 14-1, both public and private sector executives should develop an understanding of the operating environments of government in the leadership, strategy, and implementation domains.

FIGURE 14-2
Comparison of Public and Private Sector Organizations

Attribute	Public Sector	Private Sector
Environment	Legal/Political	Market-Driven
Mission	Ambiguous Goals	Profit-Driven
Focal Point	Citizen-Consumer	Customer
Culture	Risk Averse	Entrepreneurial
Decision Making	More Political	More Rational
Staffing/Rewards	Civil Service/Union	Merit/Stock Options
Technology	Often Outsourced	Innovating
Resources	Tax/Free-Driven	Venture Capital/Profit

A Road Map for Executives: An Implementation Guide to E-Government

As a leader, the first and most important step is preparing your organization for success. This means building a clear and compelling vision, articulating your organization's mission, and developing strategy that will get your organization where it needs to be. Executives need to develop a personal "road map" or e-survival guide in order to lead effectively in this new environment. The key steps in the "road map" are depicted in Figure 14-3.

Leadership

Leaders stimulate followers to think strategically—to see the big picture, the broader purpose, and the public interest. They master the environmental context rather than surrender to it. They listen to citizens, consumers, and stakeholders. They pay attention to cultivating a strong culture within the organization, and they empower employees to be risk takers. The most effective leaders can articulate a clear and compelling vision—that is, "a realistic, credible and attractive future for the organization."[8] Quite simply, strong leaders make choices, including deciding what to do and what not to do.

The digital frontier needs leaders who have both vision and values. As Norman Schwarzkopf stated, "Leadership is a potent combination of strategy and character. But if you have to be without one, be without the strategy." Leaders lead by example. They evangelize, encourage, and empower those who follow them.[9]

Strategy

In our model, successful e-government executives achieve desired results if they:

- Define the levels of service that citizen-consumers expect.
- Identify appropriate benchmarks (including private sector organizations) providing similar services.
- Measure performance and communicate results widely.

These elements depend on the development of effective strategy. Michael Porter defines strategy as "the creation of a unique and valuable position, involving a different set of activities."[10] And Henry Mintzberg notes that strategies are "crafted" and often emerge in all kinds of strange ways and places.[11]

While some argue that public strategy is dependent on thoughtful dialogue, bargaining, and negotiation,[12] the time required to do this

FIGURE 14-3
Roadmap for Executives

Leadership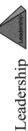

- Develop a clear and compelling vision for the initiative.
- Supplement the vision with guiding principles.
- Secure top leadership and stakeholder support.
- Ensure the vision is communicated by top leadership.
- Analyze environmental trends and policy issues.
- Identify citizen-consumers and determine needs.
- Define mission, roles, and core competencies.

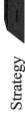

Strategy

- Develop an action plan, with process targets of opportunity and scorecard metrics for each e-government initiative.
- Develop partnerships with technology providers to address standards, infrastructure, and solutions (e.g. platform, network, security).
- Assign staff and project leaders who are change agents and will approach their assignments with a sense of urgency.
- Review critical processes and determine what to eliminate, improve, outsource, or transfer.

Implementation

- Develop three- to four-month business plans.
- Implement staffing and human resources in accordance with plan.
- Monitor progress on a monthly basis with e-government scorecard measures.
- Achieve objective and begin cycle again.
- Publicly recognize success of project team.

may not be available in today's e-world. More often than not, it is necessary to move ahead rapidly with process changes and prototypes. Nonetheless, public dialogue about proposed changes should continue during this phase of e-government innovation even with the recognition that there may not be complete agreement. Remember the adage, you can't please *all* the people *all* the time!

When developing strategy, it is also important for leaders and managers to be mindful of the need to integrate strategy formulation and implementation and align policy goals with information technology strategy and infrastructure.[13] Leaders must continue to ask the question of how technology applications are adding value to the citizen-consumer and whether stated policy goals are aligned with internal IT infrastructure needs.

Implementation

Leaders can modify strategy and address implementation issues by developing a scorecard to monitor key metrics. In addition to measuring investments of technology and human capital and monitoring project deliverables, leaders need to develop a balanced scorecard of measures. This can be a "strategic framework for action."[14] The scorecard should include key areas such as feedback from citizen-consumers, financial return on investment, product development, internal process improvements, and human resources development. The e-government scorecard provides feedback for learning, ongoing improvement, and the realignment of initiatives and targets. The scorecard should be communicated internally and shared with external stakeholders.

The Reinvention of Government Movement

Technology has not only changed the way we live, work, and learn, but also what we expect in terms of service delivery. Peter Drucker has noted that "all political theory, from Locke on through the Federalist Papers . . . deals with the process of government . . . with power, methods and organizations. [However], no one asks what results government should be held accountable for."[15] Drucker argues that instead of spending energy on ways to improve what we do, organizations need to step back and consider whether they should be doing these things at all. In developing strategy, organizations, both public and private, need to reconsider not only how they operate, but also what they do and whether it adds value to the citizen-consumer.

In their contribution to the reinvention movement, Osborne and Gaebler outlined ten principles for the foundation of entrepreneurial government:

1. Steer more than row.
2. Empower communities rather than simply supply services.

3. Encourage competition rather than monopoly.
4. Be driven by mission—not rules.
5. Fund outcomes rather than inputs.
6. Meet the needs of customers, not bureaucracy.
7. Concentrate on earning, not just spending.
8. Invest in prevention rather than cure.
9. Decentralize authority.
10. Solve problems by leveraging the marketplace, rather than simply creating public programs.[16]

These principles proved useful to the Clinton-Gore administration in 1993. Believing in the ideal that government does good and can do better, they embraced the reinvention movement and appointed the National Partnership for the Reinvention of Government, with leadership provided by the vice president. A central theme of the program is that government agencies must learn to meet the needs of their customers. However, few public agencies have used that term historically when thinking about their mission.

While we acknowledge the importance of being responsive to the needs of customers, we prefer here to use the term *citizen-consumer*. The use of the word *customer* tends to focus too much on the accumulation of narrowly defined interests and does not adequately represent ideals of democratic governance such as citizenship, engagement, and the public interest broadly defined.[17]

The reinvention initiative has lasted longer than any other government reform movement (e.g., Reagan's Grace Commission or Carter's Civil Service Reform) in part because of then–Vice President Gore's personal involvement and the Democratic Party principle that government is good and could be more responsive and effective. Since 1998, the reinvention movement, partly due to its focus on the "customer," has drawn more attention and energy to e-government applications and solutions.

A Global View

Demand for government Internet services is being fueled by the private sector, where citizen-consumers have grown accustomed to using the Internet from an ever-growing list of transactions. As a result, existing government websites are being transformed from encyclopedias to transaction processors. Government agencies are looking for ways to employ technology to improve services, streamline operations, and address citizen-consumer expectations. While every state and many local governments have websites, many governments have taken the next step in redesigning their web presence in a citizen-consumer–centric portal with e-commerce capabilities (instead of static web pages aligned vertically by agency).

In a study of governments worldwide, KPMG found that 80 percent of the respondents indicated that they provide information electronically through websites, and another 59 percent provide basic interactivity such as communicating with customers and suppliers via e-mail. Only 39 percent currently process simple online transactions such as order taking or online payments.[18] State and local government leaders reported a stronger commitment to technology investments and to performing functions electronically, in comparison to national leaders. The study attributed this to the difference in mission, with state and local governments focused on the delivery of services and interacting more directly with citizens, while national governments are typically more concerned with policy and national security issues.

Even if governments are successful in achieving a meaningful presence on the Internet, the question of uneven citizen access remains. Even in the United States, the proportion of people with an Internet connection in the home is just over 50 percent. In most of Europe, the penetration rate is about half that. It is important to remember that governments cannot choose their customers, and much of what they do involves serving the poor and elderly—the people least likely to be connected.[19]

Darrell West of Brown University studied the quality and effectiveness of e-government initiatives in an e-mail survey of government information officers and a content analysis of 1,813 federal, state, and local government websites. Researchers rated sites on whether they gave citizens clear information about contacting government offices, offered online services such as vehicle registration or searchable records, provided quality access for citizens with disabilities or limited English, and had policies to protect security and privacy. The survey found that 86 percent of CIOs said that e-government had improved service delivery, 83 percent said that it made government more efficient, and 64 percent indicated that it had reduced costs. The top-ranked states, according to the study, included Texas, Pennsylvania, Minnesota, and New York. The Brown University study found that state and federal governments are not taking full advantage of existing technology and recommended clearer standards for web content, design, structure, and security.[20]

E-Government in the Federal Sector

The federal government has more than 20,000 websites that use different formats and standards and have no single portal to tie them together. After two years of effort, on June 24, 2000, in the first-ever webcast to the nation, President Clinton unveiled new e-government initiatives, including a federal government portal—firstgov.gov—a search engine for government documents and one-stop access to grants and procurement opportunities. The President also called on citizens, students, researchers, and government employees to compete for a $50,000 award for the most innovative idea in advancing e-government. Under the direction of the National Partnership for Reinventing Government (NPRG), this initiative is designed to enable the availability of all government information, e-mail interaction, and online transactions by 2003. In addition, the initiative will expand training, identify best practices, and experiment with advanced technology applications.

President Clinton's 2000 e-government portal initiative began in September 1998, with an announcement that WebGov would be up and running in thirty days. The project was handed off to the General Services Administration, which took more than a year building prototypes but failed to deliver a solution. The team attributed its difficulty to its inability to coordinate activities across agencies that were to contribute to the effort. Eric Brewer, professor of computer sciences at the University of California–Berkeley, stepped in and offered to design a database and search engine for all government documents on the Internet. The result is FirstGov, and its goal is to put all online information published by the federal government in one place. The federal government projects that it will spend $3–5 million to bring the portal project online.[21]

It is fair to say that leadership and innovation on the e-government front is not present at the federal level. Leaders in this domain acknowledge this fact. In a July 12, 2000 keynote speech before the E-Gov 2000 Conference, Senator Joseph Lieberman noted that "progress of electronic government at the federal level has been inconsistent; some agencies are well ahead of the game, but many are lagging. The implementation of good ideas seems particularly difficult for e-government projects in which interagency or intergovernmental coordination is needed." Lieberman called for increased leadership, integrated service delivery, standards of interoperability, and new funding mechanisms to ensure effective collaboration.

State and Local Government

Several organizations have attempted to get a handle on the state of practice of e-government within state and local governments. In addition to the Brown University study noted previously, the Center for Digital Government has conducted a survey on the availability of online services and use of technologies for education and law enforcement, compiling state-by-state rankings. In September 2000, Civic.com recognized fifty state and local governments for "groundbreaking" information technology projects. Among those recognized for e-government service applications were the following:

Applications Online

New York State Online Permit   Provides users with access to

Database (www.nyspermits.org)	more than 1,000 permit types and can develop customized permit packages
ServiceArizona (www.servicearizona.com)	Enables citizens to complete vehicle registration renewal, change address, order license plates, and pay fees online
Illinois Campaign Disclosure (www.elections.state.il.us)	Offers electronic filing and publication of campaign information from Illinois candidates and political committees

Information Retrieval

Madison, Wisconsin Online Property Information (www.ci.madison.wi.us)	Enables residents and businesses to get property information online, including property assessments and tax payments
Kentucky Self-Service Geographic Information (www.ogis.state.ky.us)	Provides free website access to georeferenced photographs of the state
Access Washington (www.access.wa.gov)	Gives residents anytime, anywhere avenue for communications and transactions

Services

Pennsylvania Justice Network (www.oit.state.pa.us)	Links information from diverse systems under a common browser interface
Virginia Department of Motor Vehicles (www.dmv.state.va.us)	Has instituted a virtual service center open 24/7 online
Iowa Division of Health Facilities (www.dia-hfd. state.ia.us)	Publishes report cards of healthcare facilities available online
Morrow and Umatilla Counties, Oregon Work-Links (www.work-links.org)	Operates an online self-help tool for residents seeking employment opportunities as well as training and education, integrating

	fifteen public and private agency databases
Redmond Washington RideQuest.com (www.ridequest.com)	Offers commuters online ride-sharing information
MyVirginia (www.state.va.us)	Allows citizens to personalize their website with the information they want from state government

The ServiceArizona model in the above-mentioned list was the result of a unique public-private partnership. The website was built and is maintained by IBM Corp., which is paid 2 percent of the value of each transaction, or about $4 for each vehicle registration. Because online processing costs only $1.60 compared with $6.60 for a counter transaction, the state also saves money. With 15 percent of renewals now being processed by ServiceArizona, the state's motor vehicle department saves about $1.7 million a year.[22]

Many regard the City of Indianapolis as a leader in e-government. Its IndyGov site allows citizens to pay parking tickets, apply for permits, report problems, access geographic information system (GIS) services, and communicate with government officials. The site rivals commercial sites in terms of appearance and usability. The site earned recognition as the nation's best example of a service-based government website at the 1999 e-government conference.[23]

The National Association of State Information Resource Executives (NASIRE) completed a survey of state CIOs in May 2000 and identified statewide portals (i.e., umbrella sites focused on user interests) as the top e-government initiative. More than 70 percent of those surveyed had constructed a portal or planned to during the next year. The report proposed an action agenda for digital government that includes sharing best practices and reusable software modules, undertaking research on technology and security, developing educational materials, and highlighting case studies that would identify lessons learned and prescriptive steps for state executives.[24]

THE PENNSYLVANIA CASE STUDY

This section presents a case study of Pennsylvania's experience with information technology and e-government initiatives during the period 1995–2000.

Leadership and Vision

In 1995, Pennsylvania elected Congressman Tom Ridge as governor of Pennsylvania. Early in his administration, Ridge articulated a vision to make the Commonwealth "a leader among states and a competitor among nations." At the cornerstone of Pennsylvania's strategy was an aggressive enterprisewide information technology program designed to propel Pennsylvania to a leadership position as a "state of technology." With regard to e-government, the governor used the term "friction-free government."

Ridge defined this concept as speed to market—allowing private sector initiatives to move quickly in the new economy, reducing and removing regulatory barriers and government procedures that may inhibit technology innovation and new business start-ups. Friction-free also involves throwing out old, slow ways of providing services in favor of fast Internet-based applications. Ridge is widely recognized by his peers as being an active, visionary leader on technology issues, ranging from Y2K to e-government.

Pennsylvania's Strategy

IT guiding principles, coupled with three- to four-month rapid development project initiatives, replaced the previous practice of developing agency-specific, three- to five-year strategic plans. With regard to electronic government, the Pennsylvania State articulated a strategy to "provide efficient means of information and service delivery and e-business applications to the public, and among agencies through policies and process redesign that enable the use of Internet technology and electronic commerce activities" (see Figure 14-4).

The strategic guiding principles included:

FIGURE 14-4
Pennsylvania's E-Government Strategy

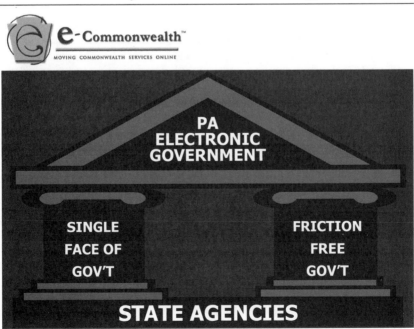

■ Begin technology transformation with top leadership commitment.
■ Invest in information technology that enables government to reengineer itself.
■ Ensure that investments result in processes that are more flexible and responsive.
■ Develop incentives for agency performance and results.
■ Centralize resources and invest in enterprisewide strategic solutions that include all state agencies, as well as local governments and communities.

The Commonwealth also articulated the following set of objectives, approved by the governor, to guide day-to-day operations:

■ **Break through barriers.** Streamline business processes and benchmark with the private sector to identify best practices.

■ **Enable electronic government**. By exploiting the advantages of the Internet, agencies can be more responsive to the needs of citizens and businesses.

■ **Leverage technology investments**. Share technology infrastructure resources and solutions so that all entities of government benefit.

■ **Safeguard commonwealth assets**. Protect resources from potential disasters (e.g., Y2K), ensuring that all entities of the Commonwealth have effective technology plans and contingency strategies.

Implementation
One of the Commonwealth's first technology initiatives focused on the Y2K computer challenge. This activity allowed state government, and many local governments, to learn much about their information technology operations. The Commonwealth of Pennsylvania was an early leader on the Y2K issue at the national and international levels. After developing a strategy for state government in early 1996, Governor Ridge called a national summit of chief information officers at the state and federal level in October 1997. The summit, which was the first meeting ever of federal and state CIOs, led to the development of guiding principles that were later adopted by the national Y2K council.

At the cornerstone of the state's Y2K strategy was executive leadership and clearly defined roles and responsibilities for Y2K compliance. Each state agency completed a detailed inventory of its computer hardware and software and focused highest priority on mission-critical business processes. The Commonwealth also took a holistic view of the Y2K problem, understanding that all organizations and communities had to achieve a level of readiness. As a result, in 1998, Pennsylvania entered into a partnership with the governments of Canada and Mexico to share information on solutions and best practices. The governor also launched a comprehensive statewide educational outreach program, in partnership with Penn State University and the AT&T foundation. During the ensuing two-year period, more than 2.5 million publications and educational kits were distributed in Pennsylvania, as well as other states across the country and in Canada and Mexico. In Pennsylvania, Y2K provided an unprecedented opportunity to forge partnerships between business, government, and education in communities across the state. These relationships will continue to assist the Commonwealth's future community and economic development.

While Y2K did not prove to be as catastrophic as once feared, the experience served to heighten awareness about the changing face of government and to demonstrate to communities and elected officials that embracing technology was a key to future success. By completing an inventory and assessing needs, governments were in a better position to make smart investments in new and emerging technologies. Government IT spending is projected to increase dramatically, with Y2K assessments providing the foundation for investments in e-government strategies. Government officials now better understand how to build public-private partnerships and the interpersonal and organizational aspects of technology implementation.

Culture Change

The Y2K program and other Ridge initiatives instilled confidence and a can-do attitude among the state's agency leaders and IT professionals. More than 85 percent of the state is unionized. There was a need for culture change when the Ridge administration took office. Many said things couldn't be done, and it was difficult at times to overcome the FUD (fear, uncertainty, and doubt) factor. The Commonwealth adopted a strategy of strong leadership, which encouraged cooperation over conflict, partnering with the private sector when necessary to break down cultural barriers to change.

Process Reengineering

As Pennsylvania listened to citizen-consumers and businesses, it became clear that enterprise-level services were needed. Citizen-consumers wanted a single point of contact, personalization, and a presentation of service offerings logically—not organizationally by silo. By developing enterprise strategies, the Commonwealth was able to challenge business process owners to eliminate, modify, or justify maintaining the status quo. The state's CIO coined the term "meandering stream" for agency processes that had gone far astray from the original intended course. One procurement process was documented to have more than twenty-five unnecessary steps, which were streamlined during the process review.

Project Management

The Commonwealth eliminated the submission of three- to five-year strategy plans and substituted vision and guiding principles. Agencies were asked to submit project proposals to the state's CIO, who was provided central funding by the governor. Projects were managed with a three-month "energy burst" cycle, using a strategy of rapid prototyping and continuous improvement (see Figure 14-5).

Technology Consolidation, Standardization, and Outsourcing

Pennsylvania took the initiative to outsource its seventeen agency data centers, the first and only state to do so. In addition, the Commonwealth entered into a strategic partnership with Microsoft Corp. to standardize the desktop, with forty-seven agencies receiving 40,000 seats of software. Also, Pennsylvania is imple-

FIGURE 14-5
Pennsylvania's "Energy Burst" IT Project Plan

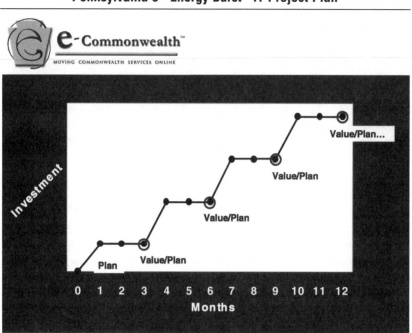

menting a wireless radio initiative (a 800 MHz network, with more than twenty-three agencies participating); it is the first state to use an IP-based radio system.

Most recently, the Commonwealth has adopted a "dynamic solutions framework" (DSF) a scalable, XML-enabled object library that integrates with existing databases, allowing for rapid application development across agencies. DSF modules have been developed for digital signatures, credit card transactions, calendars, custom web pages, and many other applications. Modules can be "plugged in," and IT professionals can develop and contribute to the state's DSF library of applications. This will allow agencies to accelerate their rollout of e-government applications while ensuring consistency throughout the enterprise.

The Commonwealth's E-Government Initiative

In 1995, Pennsylvania was one of only three states without a web presence. Within three years it received the award for the best state website from *Government Technology* magazine.[25]

In addition, the Taubman Center for Public Policy at Brown University ranked Pennsylvania number two in the United States for delivering public services via the Internet. In 2000, the Commonwealth allocated $20 million to its e-government initiative. More than fifteen agencies have been targeted to participate in the e-government project, which will include online license renewal and registration, permits, the filing of personal income taxes online, and online auctions for bids for goods and services. Other initiatives are targeted to expedite the process of starting new businesses in Pennsylvania.

In March 1999, an internal workgroup within the state's Office for Information Technology recommended that a state enterprise portal be established. In his address to the state legislature in January 2000, Governor Ridge stated that "the goal of the PA PowerPort is to ensure that businesses will no longer have to approach state government as an array of separate agencies, each concerned foremost with their own administrative needs. Rather, we will use the power of Internet technology to shift the focus back to where it belongs—on the customer."[26] Within the first three months of the initiative, Pennsylvania had two enterprise e-government applications: the PA PowerPort and PA Open for Business.

PA PowerPort

The portal PA PowerPort (see Figure 14-6) is intended to promote e-commerce, bring technology benefits to Pennsylvania schools and communities, and expand the Commonwealth's presence on the Internet. The Commonwealth chose Microsoft as its partner after considering a number of other vendors. The portal includes the following features:

- Links to statewide, online news services categorized by region
- Daily updates of the top state government news releases
- A new grouping of "Citizen Services" rather than organizational entities
- Helpful suggestions encouraging more Pennsylvanians to participate in the Internet by using e-mail

FIGURE 14-6
PA PowerPort Website

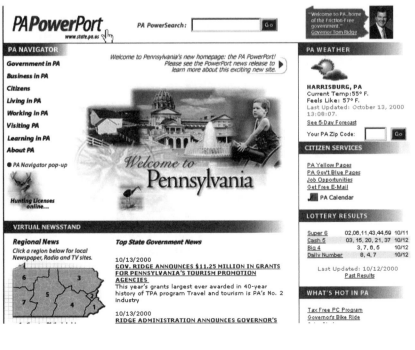

- An up-front listing of winning lottery numbers to make them more conveniently accessible
- A posting of the portal privacy policy
- A pilot of the state government calendar of events during the coming month
- Single point of contact, single data entry for individual data
- A powerful search engine to locate information quickly

PA Open for Business

This site (see Figure 14-7) provides entrepreneurs with quick access to the forms and other critical information needed to open a business in Pennsylvania. It gives entrepreneurs "one door" to access business information, financial options, and forms necessary to start and grow a business. Features include:

- An online interview that guides prospective entrepreneurs to business formation and filing requirements and gives useful information
- The ability to complete business filings from the Web for start-up businesses

FIGURE 14-7
PA Open for Business Website

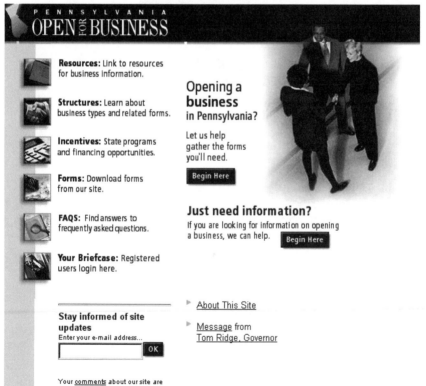

■ An online secure and private data folder for filing information that makes routine forms filing easy, requiring one data entry for numerous forms

The Commonwealth received the 2000 DELTA award for this site by the Pennsylvania Chamber of Business and Industry.

Governor Ridge has made technology a key component of Pennsylvania's economic development efforts by instituting measures such as:

■ Launching the nation's first-ever Tax-Free PC shopping week to encourage home computer use
■ Signing legislation to make Pennsylvania the first state to enact a uniform Electronic Transactions Act
■ Eliminating the 6 percent tax on computer services
■ Creating the research and development tax credit
■ Putting the state's web address on Pennsylvania's new license plates
■ Leading technology trade missions abroad to increase high-tech exports and high-tech jobs for Pennsylvania
■ Launching the Technology 21 initiative to catapult Pennsylvania into the top ten states for high-tech business
■ Creating the Made-in-PA database of Pennsylvania-made products
■ Expanding the net operating loss carry-forward provision to give technology start-ups a tax deduction

The Future of E-Government and Digital Democracy

Janet Caldow argues that no e-government vision is complete without attention to digital democracy.[27] She defines digital democracy as "any electronic exchange of value in the democratic process." This includes campaigns, elections, voter registration, voting, public opinion polling, electronic town meetings, wired legislative bodies, and other political processes. We're starting to see evidence of this trend, with campaign websites and the first online election in Arizona. This trend will continue and accelerate with the introduction of digital television and more ubiquitous high-speed access in the home.

In light of the 2000 presidential election, the mandate for e-government becomes even stronger. Clerks opening ballot envelopes and viewing stacks of partially punched cards is unnecessary in the information age. Electronic voting, if implemented properly, can be a secure, valid, and efficient way to tabulate votes. The technology exists to make voting more accessible and at the same time provide faster, more accurate election results. Pennsylvania, California, and other states are moving to empower more citizens to use electronic voting, including voting over the Internet. In all likelihood, the need to move to some form of online voting will be a consideration in every e-government plan adopted in the future. In a broader sense, the Internet has given government a renewed opportunity to reinvent the way it does business and the way the public interest is served. Like commercial enterprises, the public sector can now provide real-time data to the public and deliver services electronically, such as vehicle registration, permits, and health benefits. This self-service model is more efficient and can allow government to reduce costs. Online government allows citizen-consumers to access any information they want, anytime they want it.

From our review of the Pennsylvania case and national trends, it is clear that successful e-government involves leadership, vision, and transformational strategies. In our view, governments that focus on process change and technology applications that add value to the citizen-consumer will have a greater likelihood of success.

There is unlimited potential for e-government to help instill public confidence and lead to a more activist role in addressing problems. However, the barriers are equally significant: the need for active leadership, a complete understanding of process reengineering, and a strategy for overcoming resistance to change. Information technology, while a key ingredient to success, in all likelihood, is the least of our worries.

Endnotes

1 Janet Caldow, "The Quest for Electronic Government: A Defining Vision" (Armonk, NY: IBM Corporation, July 1999).

2 Rebecca Fairley Raney, "The Second Chance: The Potential of Politics Online," *Interactive Week* (July 3, 2000).

3 Gartner Group, Inc., 2000. Available from http://www.gartner.com.

4 Forrester Research, "The Forrester Report," August 2000. Available from http://www.forrester.com.

5 Information Technology Association of America, "Bridging the Gap: Information Technology Skills for a New Millennium" (Arlington, VA: ITAA, April 2000).

6 Matthew Symonds, "The Next Revolution," *The Economist* (June 24, 2000), p. 5.

7 John M. Stevens and Robert P. McGowan, *Information Systems and Public Management* (New York: Praeger Publishers, 1985), p. 35.

8 Burt Nanus, *Visionary Leadership* (San Francisco: Jossey-Bass, 1992).

9 Amir Hartman and John Sifonis, *Net-Ready* (New York: McGraw-Hill, 2000).

10 Michael E. Porter, "What Is Strategy?" *Harvard Business Review* (November–December 1996).

11 Henry Mintzberg, "Crafting Strategy," *Harvard Business Review* (July–August 1987).

12 John Bryson, *Strategic Planning for Public and Nonprofit Organizations* (San Francisco: Jossey-Bass, 1995).

13 John Henderson and James Thomas, "Aligning Business and Information Technology Domains: Strategic Planning in Hospitals," *Hospital and Health Services Administration* (Spring 1992).

14 Robert S. Kaplan and David P. Norton, *The Balanced Scorecard* (Boston: Harvard Business School Press, 1996).

15 Peter Drucker, *The Atlantic Monthly* (February 1995).

16 David Osborne and Ted Gaebler, *Reinventing Government* (Reading, MA: Addison-Wesley, 1992).

17 Linda deLeon and Robert B. Denhardt, "The Political Theory of Reinvention," *Public Administration Review* Vol. 60, No. 2 (March/April 2000).

18 KPMG, *Managing the Public Sector—Global Challenges* (May 2000).

19 Symonds, "The Next Revolution," op. cit.

20 Darrell M. West, "Assessing E-Government: The Internet, Democracy, and Service Delivery by State and Federal Governments," Taubman Center for Public Policy, Brown University, September 2000.

21 Doug Brown, "Feds Take Another Run at Governmentwide Portal," *Interactive Week* (July 3, 2000).

22 Symonds, op. cit.

23 Kelly Franklin and Tom Little, "e-Government Review," *SCT Report* (July 2000).

24 National Association of State Information Resource Executives (NASIRE, 2000).

25 Ted Karle, "Information Supernova," *Government Technology* (October 1999).

26 PhillyTech, July 2000.

27 Caldow, "The Quest for Electronic Government: A Defining Vision," op. cit.

About the Contributors

Nirmal Pal is executive director of the eBusiness Research Center at The Pennsylvania State University. Before joining Penn State in February 2000, Pal was director of IBM Global Services Consulting Group, White Plains, New York. As one of the leaders of IBM's e-business consulting activities, he was responsible for business development as well as development of supporting analytics, methods, tools, and other intellectual assets. Through IBM he was twice certified as a management consultant, was involved in many e-business strategy engagements with Fortune 500 clients, and gained significant personal insights into management and execution issues with e-business transformation. In his 38-year career at IBM he was based in India, England, Japan, and the United States and has consulted throughout the world, particularly in Asia-Pacific countries. He is a member of the Institute of Electrical and Electronic Engineers and remains actively connected to industry as a board member of several organizations. Pal received his bachelor of electrical engineering degree from Jadavpur University, Calcutta, India, and his master of science in computer science degree from Polytechnic University of New York.

Judith M. Ray is a senior research associate in the eBusiness Research Center, The Pennsylvania State University. In that role, Ray is responsible for developing and executing various e-business research and networking initiatives, including developing an e-business incubator laboratory, planning and organizing academic workshops and executive education and speakers' series, coordinating multidisciplinary research projects, and developing and implementing a web-based e-business benchmarking survey tool. Most recently, she was a senior instructional designer for Penn State's Smeal College of Business Administration, where she oversaw the development and implementation of electronic testing, multimedia case development, and web-based courses and other instructional material. Her prior experience includes fifteen years as a systems analyst in both large university and small business settings facilitating the transformation of these organizations from paper to electronic record keeping systems. She is a member of the Academy of Management and INFORMS (The Institute for Operations Research and the Management Sciences). Ray received an A.B. with honors in social relations from Harvard University. She is currently pursuing a Ph.D. degree in management and organization at Penn State.

William M. Adams is the founder and chief executive officer of G5 Technologies, Inc., a technology company specializing in the commercial development of an Internet-based system for building and managing collaborative business-to-business e-commerce networks. Before establishing G5, Adams was president and chief executive officer for Agile Web, Inc., a virtual corporation made up of twenty small to medium-size manufacturing companies in northeastern Pennsylvania. Before that, he held various engineering, manufacturing, and marketing positions with GE Aerospace and Lockheed Martin. Adams has degrees in electrical and mechanical engineering from New York Maritime College and is a graduate of GE's executive management training program.

Hemant Bhargava is on the faculty of The Pennsylvania State University's Smeal College of Business Administration as professor of management science and information systems. Before that, Bhargava was a visiting professor in The Heinz School of Public Policy and Management at Carnegie Mellon University and served on the faculty of the Naval Postgraduate School in Monterey. He serves on the board of directors of the INFORMS Computing Society and is an area editor covering computing and decision technology for the journal *Operations Research* and an associate editor for *Decision Support Systems*. Bhargava has a Ph.D. in decision sciences from The Wharton School, University of Pennsylvania. He has also received a bachelor's degree in mathematics at Hindu College, University of Delhi, and an MBA at the Indian Institute of Management, Bangalore.

Douglas S. Boothe is vice president and general manager, Xerox.com, for Xerox Corporation in Stamford, Connecticut. Since joining Xerox in 1994, Boothe has held a variety of managerial positions, including vice president, strategy operations for General Markets Operations; vice president, strategy and business development for the department business unit of the Office Document Products Group; and director, corporate business strategy. Previously, he held positions with Mars & Co., a strategy consultancy; General Electric; IBM; and Exxon Office Systems. Boothe received a B.S. in mechanical and aerospace engineering from Princeton University and an M.B.A. from The Wharton School, University of Pennsylvania.

John W. Boudreau is associate professor of human resource studies and director of the Center for Advanced Human Resource Studies (CAHRS) at Cornell University, which partners executives from America's top corporations with academic researchers to explore leading-edge HR issues. Boudreau's research addresses strategic human capital measurement, decision-based human resources, executive mobility, HR information systems, and organizational staffing and development. He has published more than forty books and articles, including the best-selling *Human Resource Management*. He serves on the executive committees of the Academy of Management and the Society for Industrial and Organizational Psychology. He consults and conducts executive development programs with companies worldwide and is a strong proponent of corporate/academic partnerships. Boudreau holds a master's degree in management and a Ph.D. in industrial relations from Purdue University's Krannert School of Management.

Michael E. Brown is a doctoral candidate in the Department of Management and Organization, the Smeal College of Business Administration at The Pennsylvania State University. Brown is a past recipient of the Kenneth E. Clark research award from the Center for Creative Leadership and the Edward and Susan Wilson Graduate Scholarship in Business at Penn State. Previously, he worked in the fund-raising and development field. He is a member of the Academy of Management, and his work has been published in *California Management Review* as well as in the Academy of Management *Best Paper Proceedings*. Brown holds a B.A. from Dartmouth College and an M.B.A. from the University of Texas at Austin.

Cole Camplese is the director of education and training solutions within the Information Sciences and Technology (IST) Solutions Institute at the School of Information Sciences and Technology of The Pennsylvania State University. In this role, Camplese directs all aspects of online courseware development, including process management and strategic relationships for both educational and training audiences. His research interests include process and project management for courseware development, as well as the information technology tools that enable both. He has extensive experience as a consultant, instructional designer, and multimedia developer. Camplese received an M.S. in instructional technology from Bloomsburg University and a B.S. in psychology from West Virginia University.

Kristin Z. Camplese is the manager of instructional design and research within the IST Solutions Institute at the School of Information Sciences and Technology at The Pennsylvania State University, where she oversees the instructional design process for all online IST courseware. She has a master's in education in instructional systems from Penn State, with a special focus on web-based and distance education, and a B.A. in international studies from West Virginia University. She is currently pursuing a Ph.D. in instructional systems at Penn State.

Shawn M. Clark is an assistant professor of information sciences and technology solutions in the School of Information Sciences and Technology at The Pennsylvania State University. Clark is also a member of the IST Solutions Institute at Penn State where his primary responsibilities include the development of online and distance education courses and corporate partnership management. Previously, he worked as a consultant in the Business Transformation Consulting Practices division of IBM's Insurance and Utilities and Energy Services groups. He has consulting experience in workstation deployment, business process improvement, change management, and strategic planning. He has published articles on strategic change, top management team information processing, and organizational identity in such notable journals as the *Academy of Management Journal* and *Organization Science*. Clark earned his Ph.D. in business administration at The Pennsylvania State University. He received a B.S. in zoology and a master's in organizational behavior from Brigham Young University.

Kevin G. Corley is a doctoral student studying organizational behavior in the Department of Management and Organization at the Smeal College of Business Administration, The Pennsylvania State University. He spent three years as a management consultant for Ernst & Young, helping organizations plan and implement strategic change initiatives. His research is published in the *Academy of Management Review, Academy of Management Journal, Corporate Reputation Review,* and the 2000 edition of *Trends in Organizational Behavior.* Corley earned a B.S. in business administration at Miami University of Ohio.

Rocki-Lee DeWitt is the associate dean for professional master's programs and associate professor of management in the Smeal College of Business Administration, The Pennsylvania State University. DeWitt has engaged in research, educational, and consulting activities with a number of public and private organizations. She is on the board of Intuitive Control Systems Inc. Before beginning her academic career, she served in a variety of sales management positions with International Harvester and Case-IH. Her writings have been published in *Administrative Science Quarterly, Academy of Management Journal, Journal of Applied Social Psychology, Journal of Experimental Social Psychology, Journal of Management, Organization Science,* and *Strategic Management Journal.* She received her Ph.D. and M.Phil. in strategic management from Columbia University, her M.S. in agricultural economics from Ohio State University, and her B.S. in marketing and management from New York University.

Mary P. Donato is vice president of the Global TeleWeb Channel for Xerox Corporation. She is responsible for one of the fastest growing channels within Xerox with over 800 employees in ten countries. In her twenty years with Xerox, Donato has held numerous positions, including VP of industry and marketplace transformation for Xerox's North American Solutions Group; VP of worldwide marketing for Xerox Business Services; director of integrated marketing for Xerox Canada; Minnesota district manager; and sales operations manager for the central region based in Chicago. She is a member of The Pennsylvania State University eBusiness Research Center Advisory Board and leads the marketing council of the American Management Association. Donato earned a B.A. degree in psychology with honors from Ohio State University with a minor in business communications.

Benjamin B. Dunford is a Ph.D. student in the New York State School of Industrial and Labor Relations at Cornell University. He has coauthored research articles in *Personnel Psychology* and *Small Group Research.* Dunford holds a B.S. in psychology from Brigham Young University and an M.S. in industrial and organizational psychology from Purdue University.

Liam Fahey is adjunct professor of strategic management at Babson College and visiting professor of strategic management at the Cranfield School of Management in the United Kingdom. Previously, Fahey taught at Northwestern University's J. L. Kellogg Graduate School of Management and at Boston University. His research, teaching, and consulting experience centers on linking strategy, scenarios, and knowledge. He has authored or edited eight books and more than forty articles or book chapters. His research has appeared in *Strategic Management Journal, Academy of Management Review, Academy of Management Executive, Journal of Marketing,* and *Harvard Business Review.* His most recent books are *The Portable MBA in Strategy* (2nd edition); *Learning from the Future: Competitive Foresight Scenarios;* and *Competitors: Outwitting, Outmaneuvering and Outperforming.* Fahey holds a

Ph.D. degree from the University of Pittsburgh and M.B.S. and B. Comm. degrees from University College Dublin, Ireland.

Stuart I. Feldman is director of the IBM Institute for Advanced Commerce and head of computer science for IBM Research in Hawthorne, New York. Before joining IBM in 1995, Feldman spent eleven years at Bellcore, where he held several research management positions in software engineering and computing systems. He was the technical leader of the Telecommunications Information Networking Architecture Consortium (TINA-C), an international research group. Before that, he spent ten years as a computer science researcher at Bell Labs, where he was a member of the original UNIX research team and is best known as the creator of the Make configuration management system and the author of the first Fortran-77 compiler. He is an ACM Fellow, an IEEE Fellow, and a member of the AAAS National Council on Science and Technology Education and the steering board of the joint ACM-IEEE Task Force on Software Engineering as a Profession. He has served on the board of the Computing Research Association and as chair of ACM SIGPLAN. Feldman has an A.B. in astrophysical sciences from Princeton University and a Ph.D. in applied mathematics from the Massachusetts Institute of Technology.

Charles Gerhards is deputy secretary for information technology in the Governor's Office of Administration, Commonwealth of Pennsylvania. Gerhards directs agencywide information and communication technology (ICT) policy and development and oversees the operations of the Commonwealth Technology Center (CTC). He is responsible for the establishment of policies, procedures, and guidelines governing the planning, management, acquisition, security, and use of ICT assets by all Commonwealth agencies and their nearly 80,000 state employees. Previously he was director of the CTC, where he also managed a number of Governor Tom Ridge's information technology initiatives that have gained national recognition for Pennsylvania as a leader in the innovative application of communications and computing technologies. Gerhards received his B.S. in accounting from The Pennsylvania State University and successfully completed the Governor's Executive Management Training Program.

Fariborz Ghadar is the William A. Schreyer Professor of Global Management and the director of the Center for Global Business Studies, the Smeal College of Business Administration, The Pennsylvania State University. Ghadar specializes in researching emerging multifunctional business issues that shape the global environment. A selective list of his publications includes "The Dubious Logic of Global Megamergers," with Pankaj Ghemawat, in the July–August 2000 issue of *Harvard Busi-*

ness Review; Financing Growth in Developing Economies; New Informa-tion Technology & Its Impact on Global Business Management; New Financial Instruments: Horizons for Risk Management; and *Global Busi-ness Management in the 1990s.* Ghadar earned a D.B.A. in international business and an M.B.A. from Harvard Business School. He holds an M.S. in mechanical engineering, a B.S. in biomedical engineering, and a B.S. in chemical engineering from the Massachusetts Institute of Tech-nology.

Dennis A. Gioia is professor of organizational behavior in the Depart-ment of Management and Organization, the Smeal College of Business Administration, The Pennsylvania State University. Gioia engages in both basic and applied research in organizations; he has investigated cognitive processes in organizational decision making and problem sol-ving; executive interpretation processes during strategic change efforts; the role of organizational identity, image, and emulation in managing change; negotiation processes in the siting of a hazardous waste plant; and leadership requirements of dot-com enterprises. His work has appeared in many journals, including the *Academy of Management Journal, Human Relations, Journal of Applied Behavioral Science, Orga-nization Science,* and *Sloan Management Review,* among others, and he coedited two books, *The Thinking Organization* and *Creative Action in Organizations.* Gioia served as project director for management devel-opment programs for the Florida State University Center for Applied Behavioral Science and is currently academic program director for De-veloping Managerial Effectiveness at Penn State. He worked as an engi-neer for Boeing Aerospace at Cape Kennedy during the Apollo lunar program and for Ford Motor Company as a problem analyst and recall coordinator. Gioia holds degrees in engineering science and in manage-ment from Florida State University.

Kathryn Rudie Harrigan is the Henry R. Kravis Professor of Business Leadership in the Graduate School of Business at Columbia University, New York. Her research interests include strategic alliances, internal venturing, industry restructuring, mature businesses, diversification, turnaround strategies, make-or-buy strategy, industry and competitor analysis, global strategies, and strategic planning. Her books include *Strategies for Joint Ventures; Strategic Flexibility: A Management Guide for Changing Times; Managing for Joint Venture Success;* and *Managing Maturing Businesses: Restructuring Declining Industries and Revitaliz-ing Troubled Operations.* Her articles have been published in the *Strate-gic Management Journal, the Academy of Management Journal,* and *Harvard Business Review.* She was elected to the Fellows of the Acad-emy of Management, has served on its board of governors, and was honored for her scholarly contributions to the Business Policy and Strategy Division. She received the Columbia Business School's Schoen-heimer Award for Research Excellence, an IBM Research Fellowship in Business Administration, and a Division of Research Fellowship from Harvard Business School. Harrigan holds a B.A. from Macalester Col-lege, an M.B.A. from University of Texas at Austin, and a D.B.A. from Harvard Business School.

Jun Lee is the director of eTechnology for eBusiness Services at Unisys Corporation in Blue Bell, Pennsylvania. He has managed and designed several enterprise-level e-business solutions as a chief architect and also served as the e-commerce solutions director. Currently he focuses on strategic work in overall e-business technologies. He is a member of the Thought Leadership Council at Unisys and the Unisys Architecture Committee. Lee has written several articles and research papers on ob-ject-oriented databases, data warehousing, parallel processing, and su-percomputing. He is pursuing a Ph.D. degree in computer science and received an M.B.A. from George Washington University. He holds a bachelor's degree in computer science from the State University of New York at Buffalo.

John K. Leonard is a veteran financial services executive with a record of successfully redirecting organizations to innovate and to achieve aggressive, competitively superior financial goals. Leonard recently re-tired from CIGNA Corporation, an international insurance and managed-care company, after working there for twenty-nine years. Most recently he served for nine years as president of CIGNA Group Insurance, which provides insurance and other financial services to more than 12 million consumers. He has a significant background in all aspects of commer-cial insurance, including strategic planning, marketing, acquisitions and divestitures, and financial management. He is also active in the leadership of a major nonprofit organization supporting Philadelphia public high school students, on the board of directors of an Internet business-to-business company, and in a national organization for the study of human resources management techniques. In October 2000, he joined Caregiver Media Group as its chairman. Leonard graduated from Colgate University.

Frederick Loomis serves as executive director of the IST Solutions Insti-tute in The Pennsylvania State University's School of Information Sci-ences and Technology. He oversees efforts to extend academic expertise to address workforce development, executive education, entrepreneur-ship, business incubation, faculty development, accelerated learning, and youth outreach. Loomis is also an associate professor of informa-tion sciences and technology. His areas of interest include e-govern-ment, e-learning, leadership, strategy, organizational development, and the management of information technology. He is a graduate of Penn State, with advanced degrees in higher education and public administration, and has been an administrator with Penn State since 1988. Previously, he worked for more than ten years with the U.S. Department of Education, Office for Civil Rights. In addition to leading Pennsylvania's educational outreach program on Y2K, Loomis developed the first Pennsylvania Governor's School for Information Technology, a summer residential outreach program for outstanding high school students.

Elliot Maxwell is special adviser to the U.S. Secretary of Commerce for the Digital Economy, where he coordinates Commerce Department activities regarding the Internet and its impact on other aspects of the economy. These activities include establishing a legal framework for e-commerce, privacy, consumer protection, access to bandwidth, and digital inclusion. He has participated in the government's Interagency Working Group on Electronic Commerce since its creation. Before joining the Department of Commerce, he worked for a number of years as a consultant and as assistant vice president for corporate strategy at Pacific Telesis Group, where he combined business, technology, and public policy planning. He previously served at the Federal Communications Commission as special assistant to the chairman, deputy chief of the Office of Plans and Policy, and deputy chief of the Office of Science and Technology, and as director of international technology policy at the Department of Commerce. He was also senior counsel to the U.S. Senate Select Committee on Intelligence Activities. Maxwell graduated from Brown University and Yale University Law School and has written and spoken widely on issues involving electronic commerce, telecommunications, and technology policy.

Judy Olian is dean and professor of management at the Smeal College of Business Administration, The Pennsylvania State University. Previously, she served as senior associate dean and professor of management and organization at the Robert H. Smith School of Business at the University of Maryland. She specializes in the design and evaluation of human resources management systems that are aligned with business strategy. Olian is the author of more than fifty articles and book chapters; her work has appeared in prominent books and journals including *Psychological Bulletin, Personnel Psychology, Administrative Science Quarterly, Strategic Management Journal,* and *Industrial Relations.* She has served on the board of editors of the *Academy of Management Review* and the *Journal of Quality Management.* She was also principal investigator of a multiyear DARPA project that culminated in a widely disseminated report entitled "Harnessing the Power of Net-centricity: The National Research Agenda." At the forefront of the development of technology-based learning and research environments, Olian speaks frequently to national and international business and professional audiences. She has an undergraduate degree in psychology from the Hebrew University, Jerusalem, and M.S. and Ph.D. degrees in industrial relations from the University of Wisconsin, Madison.

David Partridge is managing principal and director of the Intellectual Capital Development Group within IBM's e-Business Innovation Institute, responsible for developing industry-specific viewpoints on the evolution of e-business. Previously, Partridge had twenty-five years of experience as a manager within and consultant to the financial services industry. His expertise includes market opportunity definition, business vision, strategy formulation, and business process design. Prior to his current assignment, he led the strategy practice serving financial institutions within IBM Consulting's North America Banking, Finance, and Securities practice. He joined IBM in April 1997 from Towers Perrin, where he headed its Financial Institutions practice within the general management consulting division. Before that, he worked at Booz Allen and Arthur D. Little. He also served as chief operating officer for a major West Coast savings bank and cofounded and managed a start-up consumer financial services retailing business. He is a contributing author to *American Banker* and various industry trade publications and is a regular speaker at industry conferences. Partridge holds a B.S. in engineering from the U.S. Military Academy at West Point and an M.B.A. from Harvard Business School.

Peter M. Ramstad is executive vice president for strategy and finance at Personnel Decisions International (PDI). Over the past ten years, Ramstad has held various leadership positions within PDI and has worked firsthand with the core tools of business strategy, organizational effectiveness, and talent development. Before joining PDI, he was a partner with a major public accounting firm focusing on financial, operational, and systems consulting in high-tech and service environments. He has undergraduate degrees in mathematics and accounting and is a certified public accountant, certified management accountant, and a member of the AICPA. He has been a speaker at many professional and academic conferences. Ramstad has formed two research partnerships with faculty from major universities (Cornell and Texas A&M) to study how people create value and how that value can be measured. As a part of this research, he has worked with clients to understand and measure the financial implications of employee development and effective management. The models and tools he developed for this process are known as Return On People.

Charles R. Rieger is a principal for IBM Global Services, with responsibility for the development of approaches and practices within the IBM

Consulting Group. He specializes in helping senior managers determine and optimize the value that their corporations realize from their information technology investment. Currently, Rieger is responsible for external worldwide business research conducted by the e-Business Innovation Institute within IBM Global Services. Before joining IBM, he held a variety of staff and management positions with a nationwide retailer. He is a frequent speaker at industry conferences on strategic alignment, information technology, and networking. Most recently he published (in conjunction with the Economist Intelligence Unit) "Assessing the Strategic Value of Information Technology: Planning Perspectives for Senior Executives," and "E-business Transformations." Rieger obtained his M.B.A. from the Carlson School of Business, University of Minnesota. He earned a bachelor's degree in business management and marketing summa cum laude from Augsburg College in Minneapolis.

Arpan Sengupta is currently pursuing his Ph.D. studies in the College of Business and Economics at Lehigh University, Bethlehem, Pennsylvania. His research projects investigate the degree of diversification across debt-funding sources in corporate ownership structure; rules, discretion, and decision-making authority; agile virtual enterprise e-frastructure; and environmental degradation and its impact on the economy. He has also been entrepreneurially involved with the operations of a venture capital firm in India. Sengupta received his master's degree in economics with first-class distinction from Jawaharlal Nehru University, New Delhi, India, and his baccalaureate degree in economics from St. Xavier's College, Calcutta, India.

Venkatesh Shankar is Ralph J. Tyser Fellow and a professor of marketing at the Robert H. Smith School of Business, University of Maryland. Shankar's areas of specialization are e-business, competitive marketing strategy, international marketing, branding, pricing, advertising and promotion strategies, new product development, and bioinformatics. He has done extensive research on e-business issues in the auto, biotech, consumer goods, financial services, healthcare, high-tech, travel, paper, and utility industries. He has won several research awards, and his research has been published in leading academic journals and in business periodicals such as *The Wall Street Journal, Financial Times,* and *Executive Excellence.* He serves on the editorial boards of the *Journal of Retailing* and the *Journal of the Academy of Marketing Science* and is a member of CNN's international business expert panel. Shankar has consulting and executive training experience with numerous global organizations, including Mattel Toys and the Hong Kong and Shanghai Banking Corporation, and has delivered over seventy-five presentations throughout the world. He has worked in Canada, Hong Kong, India, and the United States. Shankar has a Ph.D. in marketing from the Kellogg Graduate School of Management, Northwestern University.

Rajendra Srivastava is senior associate dean and the Daniel J. Jordan Distinguished Professor of Marketing at the Goizueta Business School, Emory University, Atlanta. Srivastava also served on the faculty of the University of Texas at Austin (UT—Austin) as senior associate dean, where he held the George Kozmetsky Centennial Chair and Professor of Marketing position, and as a visiting faculty member at London Business School. His research on marketing and finance has been published in *Journal of Marketing, Journal of Marketing Research, Marketing Science,* and *Journal of Banking and Finance.* His current research focuses on the impact of e-business on corporate financial performance, particularly in the context of technology-intensive products and services. He was instrumental in the development of the Center for Customer Insight at UT-Austin to integrate research and teaching on e-marketing and e-CRM. He has developed executive programs on e-marketing and delivered invitational and keynote addresses in North America, Latin America, Europe, Australia, and Asia. He has extensive executive education and consulting experience and serves on advisory boards of several high-tech start-ups. Srivastava received his undergraduate degree from the Indian Institute of Technology, Kanpur, and he earned his doctorate at the University of Pittsburgh.

Thomas Summerlin is vice president of Unisys Corporation and the worldwide director of e-business strategy and marketing. Previously, he served Unisys as the product marketing manager for Europe, Africa, the Middle East, and Asia while based in London. Before joining Unisys, he was president for Provenance Systems, the first company to develop an electronic records management system He also served as VP of sales and marketing for USI, a Virginia-based services and product solutions company where he devised the e.State methodology, a consulting tool for the measurement of readiness for e-business and the development of a coherent road map for improvements; he also developed the e.Power brand as the framework for the delivery of end-to-end e-business and e-commerce solutions. Other senior-level positions he has held have included managing director of OMNI International and Washington Capital Markets and senior vice president for Mercantile Bank. He remains active in the venture capital and analyst communities, advising and assisting with company and product direction and investment decisions. Summerlin earned a master's degree in finance from Loyola College, an associate's degree in international studies from the University of Virginia, and a B.A. degree in Latin American studies and journalism from the University of North Carolina, Chapel Hill.

Richard Taylor holds the James R. and Barbara R. Palmer Chair in Tele-communications Studies and is co-director of the Institute for Information Policy, College of Communications, The Pennsylvania State University. He was formerly vice president, corporate counsel, and secretary of Warner Cable Communications Inc., responsible for the law department and all corporate legal and regulatory affairs. He was previously regional counsel for Group W Cable and Broadcasting. His scholarly work in the past five years has focused on information and economic development, especially in the Asia-Pacific area, and on electronic commerce. He has consulted with a number of companies and has spoken at professional meetings of telecommunications, cable television, broadcasting, and newspaper executives. He holds a B.A. from Manhattan College, an M.A. in mass communications from Fairfield University, an Ed.D. in mass communications from Columbia University Teachers College, and a J.D. from New York University School of Law.

James B. Thomas is dean and professor of information sciences, technology, and management in the School of Information Sciences and Technology, The Pennsylvania State University. Previously, Thomas served as senior associate dean of the Smeal College of Business Administration at Penn State. A specialist in strategic management, organizational analysis, and information technology, he is the author or coauthor of more than 100 articles, book chapters, reviews, and presentations. His work represents two major themes: cognition associated with top management team decision making and the relationships between corporate performance and the alignment of business and IT strategies. His work has appeared in *Administration Science Quarterly, Academy of Management Journal, Organization Science,* and *Organizational Behavior and Human Decision Processes,* among other top journals. He is involved extensively in executive education around the world through Penn State's executive programs and with individual Fortune 100 firms. A graduate of Penn State in pre-law, Thomas has a master's degree in government from Florida State University and his doctorate in strategic management from the University of Texas at Austin.

Albert A. Vicere is executive education professor of strategic leadership at the Smeal College of Business Administration at The Pennsylvania State University. Vicere holds bachelor's, master's, and doctoral degrees from Penn State and served for ten years as associate dean for executive education at Smeal College. He has held positions with the Pennsylvania Mirror Corporation and with Airco-Speer, Inc. In addition to his current duties at Penn State, he is president of Vicere Associates Inc., a consulting firm with global clients. Vicere was profiled as a "next wave guru" in leadership development in the journal *Business Horizons*. He is the author of several books and more than sixty articles for journals such as *Planning Review, Human Resource Planning,* and *Employment Relations Today,* among others. His latest book, *Leadership by Design,* coauthored with Robert M. Fulmer, was published by Harvard Business School Press (and outside North America by Capstone Publishing Ltd. as *Crafting Competitiveness*). Vicere is a member of the Executive Committee of the International Consortium for Executive Development Research and serves on the editorial boards of Human Resource Planning (U.S.) and Career Development International (U.K.). He is an equity partner in The Learning Partnership and a member of the Financial Times Knowledge Leader Dialogue.

Raymond M. Wallace is chief operating officer of G5 Technologies, Inc., and an adjunct professor of the College of Business and Economics, Lehigh University. In his role as COO, Wallace is responsible for all operational aspects of G5, a start-up management consulting firm and provider of Internet-enabled collaborative commerce business-to-business solutions. Previously, he held senior executive positions in a number of firms. He was vice president of business development for Allied Signal Defense & Space Systems; vice president of business development for Lockheed Martin Telecommunications Systems; and senior vice president for Grimes Aerospace. At General Electric Aerospace he served as program general manager for both the Intelsat VIII Satellite and the Engine and Flight Controls divisions. He began his career with Pratt & Whitney Aircraft and United Technologies Research Center. He is a member of the board of directors of the Government Electronics Industry Association. Wallace earned a B.A. in economics as well as an M.S. and B.S. in materials science (dean's list with honors) from Brown University.

Index